invertonomics

invertonomics

8 ideas to transform India

Goonmeet Singh Chauhan

HarperCollins *Publishers* India

First published in India in 2020 by
HarperCollins *Publishers*

HarperCollins *Publishers* India, Cyber City, Building 10-A, Gurugram,
Haryana – 122002, India

www.harpercollins.co.in

2 4 6 8 10 9 7 5 3 1

P-ISBN: 978-93-5357-735-3
E-ISBN: 978-93-5357-736-0

Printed and bound at
Repro India Ltd.

*

HarperCollins *Publishers*, Macken House, 39/40 Mayor Street Upper,
Dublin 1, D01 C9W8, Ireland

To all my teachers, especially Dr J.S. Neki ji, and
my beloved parents, Satpal and Lilly Chauhan, for giving me
the courage to dream and the confidence to pursue my passion
for problem-solving and transformation

Contents

Foreword

Navin B. Chawla
Former Chief Election Commissioner of India,
Founder Trustee of the Darshan Trust
and The Lepra India Trust

I first met Goonmeet Singh Chauhan when I requested him to design a building for my NGO, The Lepra India Trust, in Delhi. I found in him not just a fine architect but also a fellow traveller in my concern to design a low-cost building to create a happy and bright atmosphere while simultaneously incorporating all safety standards. It was to be a school for underprivileged and disabled children, where the need was to keep maintenance costs as low as possible, so that every rupee thus saved could be used for the children. The building Goonmeet designed achieved all these aims.

From the start, I had sensed that he was (and is) not just an architect but also a humanist with a philosophical bent of mind. This came through in the many discussions we had on making our cities and towns cleaner, more efficient, safer and altogether citizen-friendly. These ideas would need to be translated into policies which could in turn be channelled into implementable schemes. Goonmeet realized from the start that if these ideas were to be successfully put into practice, they would also need to pay their own way, whether it was at a governmental level, or in the private sector or even at the level of the individual.

Foreword

There is now vastly enhanced global awareness for cleaner and safer cities, encompassing air pollution, traffic management, waste disposal and access by all to public toilets. The models presented here are not only self-sustaining but can generate funds for the public exchequer.

We might well argue that the quantum of profits analysed in each chapter is not realistic and that there may be impediments along the way, including the ugliness of corruption. Perhaps. But all of us who now live in cities in India – 25% of the population – struggle with our daily share of woes. Witness the endemic and severe flooding in our cities that constantly leaves families destroyed in their wake. Witness, too, the daily traffic logjams that render us helpless on even our six-lane national highways, where we might be stuck for even 2 hours at a stretch.

The solutions that are offered in this book are those that can be catalysed by our administrators and planners across the country. For instance, why should there not be easy access to clean toilets for all our citizens at a convenient distance. Does air pollution know any barriers?

Cutting across income brackets, our young and our elderly in particular have become increasingly vulnerable to disease. Surely, clean air is a fundamental right.

With 40 years' experience as an administrator behind me, I feel that this book offers solutions that are practical and, far from depleting public funds, actually augment them. The underlying theme is equally dominant: it makes for people becoming stakeholders of their own lives.

Preface

'Invertonomics' is a new way of looking at problem-solving.

Quite literally, this is a breakthrough methodology that inverts problems into economic opportunities. It brings all stakeholders together and binds them into physical and financial ecosystems wherein individuals' actions begin to align with collective good. This collective action sets in motion great spirals of positive transformation at the level of communities, cities and eventually as a nation.

Invertonomics promises to change the pace of change. It is going to ensure that India's tryst with greatness happens in our lifetimes. To accomplish this, a dream for a great India is proposed, which creates an apt context for the application of this methodology. You shall find here a refreshing new approach to dreaming and realizing dreams.

A meaningful proposition to transform a nation must embody some basic values. In my view, these are:

- **Inclusion**
- **Idealism**
- **Pragmatism**

Inclusion: The dreams and solutions presented must transcend social, economic and geographical boundaries and foster a greater sense of connectedness, celebrating pluralism and yet emboldening the fabric that unites us and inspires each of the many Indians that animate our nation to move forward on the transformation curve, irrespective of whichever point they might find themselves on today.

Idealism: The only value that can demolish the limitations imposed by 'timing' and 'inertia' is idealism. Possibilities soaked in idealism, combined with inspired leadership and action, help to create inspired citizenship, unleashing a sea of energy that is key to any meaningful transformation.

Idealism is the only vehicle that allows top-down and bottom-up transformational energies to resonate, and their ethos is inclusive and non-violent and encourages enterprise and accountability. The resultant is a sustainable transformation. It results in the creation of what we call a great nation.

Pragmatism: While intellectuals have the liberty of engaging in conversation on nations without the pressure of being judged on the basis of their actual impact on ground, leaders must temper their sense of idealism with pragmatism and present an action-oriented approach that can create longstanding and fruitful partnerships with all stakeholders. Dreams need to be implemented using strategies that are based on ground realities, whether they are physical, financial or social, strategies that are judged purely on the binary scale of 'this will work' versus 'this will not work'.

A dream is also being put forth through this book which envisions a great India with a high index of inclusivity, an inspired ethical and empowered India that is effectively able to surmount its challenges. New institutions and detailed solution models that would fulfil the objectives are captured in a chapter-wise manner. They could also be read in skip sequence.

While the topics are serious, the narration of the solutions is peppered with subtle humour and supported with interesting infographics. Simpler problems like honking and air pollution are solved in the first few chapters to easily explain how Invertonomics shall solve problems with certainty and generate close to Rs 1 lakh crore annually! The book then suggests solutions for universal access to sanitation, universal access to education, smart garbage management, safer cities where women can express themselves and can move around unhindered, where pedestrian safety and convenience become the new reality and, eventually, solutions for reviving our decadent rural economy. These simple yet seminal solutions would empower Bharat and our farmers and help our nation regain the title of '*sone ki chidiya*'.

Preface

Impacting the development indices and social behaviour is one of the most critical challenges faced by all governments that seek to transform the quality of life of their people.

This explains why most governments pursue a development-oriented governance model where project implementation through agencies such as the National Highways Authority of India, Airports Authority of India, NBCC, Delhi Metro Rail Corporation and Indian Space Research Organisation becomes a key tool in showcasing physically verifiable signs of progress.

Another key development tool that is often employed is that of 'doles' or 'subsidies' or 'reservations' which, though necessary and sometimes helpful, often comes in the way of meritocracy and fair play. It also furthers the fragmentation of the social fabric. After 70 years of Independence, this has become a tool of vote-bank politics, rather than a tool for social transformation.

This book focuses on creating models that engage with the citizens to solve problems. To accomplish this engagement with society, where individual actions start aligning with collective good, I propose a three-pronged approach based on:

Measurement of existing status of an issue on a contextually appropriate scale.

Transparency wherein the scores are published on an accredited e-platform (like TripAdvisor) that allows you to gauge performance on pre-stated parameters.

Connectedness where all the stakeholders can work together to impact the present score towards a brighter, measurable future target.

Uber is a fine example of how real-time connectedness can revolutionize the method of collaborations, its pace and efficiency. It is also a fine example of top-down and bottom-up resonance wherein a possibility is simultaneously delightful, useful and allows a limitless scale of transactivity to transform an entire industry. It has created a new ecosystem of taxiing which has disrupted the old, added convenience and efficiency, and brought down costs. It is revolutionary ecosystem-based models such as these that are being proposed in this book.

These ideas and the methodology can also be used to solve similar problems globally, especially in emerging economies. Some of these ideas have been shared with municipalities and have met with an optimistic response.

I am hopeful this book reaches all Indians with optimism for our nation and mild enthusiasm for reading. It hopes to inspire the youth and the elderly alike and incite meaningful transformations through collective action. It hopes to seed the path towards making India a great nation with an exalted index of inspired citizenship, equality and inclusivity!

Acknowledgements

The journey of writing this book has taken six long years and it would not have been possible without the patient and affirmative support of my wife, Dr Ritu Singh Chauhan, and my children, Simar and Seerat, who were often the first people to hear the idea and mostly in its raw form and at odd hours! My most willing sounding boards have been my morning-walk partners, Mr O.S. Pasricha, Pradeep Narayan and Sachin Taneja, who were always eager to listen and offer meaningful critique. In fact, Sachin introduced me to Ms Aditi Anand, who became my guru and co-author on this quasi-literary journey. Aditi's team at WordPress has done a thoroughly professional job of researching every piece of data and helped in stitching together a cogent argument in each of the four solution chapters that the team worked upon. Many thanks to Ms Bigsna Gill for tirelessly transcribing all the audio recordings. Immense gratitude to Ms Achala Upendran for meticulously editing the final draft of the book. I would also like to acknowledge Mr Pierre Mario Fitter, one of the most professional people I have worked with, for co-authoring two critical chapters, one on rural rejuvenation, called 'Office of Bharat', and another on city waste management, called 'Currency of Garbage'.

The book relies heavily on graphic communication and the effort was led separately by Ms Jaskeerat Bedi, an exceptionally gifted design professional; Mr Paramvir Virdee, who produced crisp graphics for a few chapters; and Ms Mariyam from Epistle Communications. Mr Himanshu Thakur and Ms Noor Us Saba, faculty at College of Art, Delhi, have also contributed to the graphic illustrations. Immensely grateful!

What can one do without friend–mentors? Perhaps none of this would have been possible without the support and guidance of Amarjeet S. Chandioke, Siddharth Mishra, Reena Mishra, Harmeet S. Chauhan, Tanya Khanna, Yograj Arora, Anand Sharma, Anoj Tevatia and Amandeep Singh, whose unquestioned love for me and this project remained my key anchors.

There were many occasions of self-doubt during the journey and my close friends with whom I shared these ideas always provided encouragement, critique and affirmation: Mrinal Dasgupta, Devraj Mishra, Ashish Jaiswal, Amit Kharbanda, Amit Saxena, Pravin Lal, Abhijit Satsanghi, Madhu Bajwa, A.S. Pasricha, Pankaj Bhushan, Abe Dubash, Mona Baswani, Sandeep Satija, D.N. Saigal, Prakash Khemani, Pranay Sinha, Prashant Solomon, Savita Punde,

Vikas Gore, Amar Cheema, Yamini Girotra, Anupam Kathuria, Rehan Khan, Siddharth Verma, Amandeep Narula, Manoj Nagpal, Abhijit Chatterjee, Arijit and Amrita Sanyal, Harish Bahl, Hardeep Bhalla, S. B. Singh, Vinay Kr Singh, Yogeshwar Sharma, Monica Khanna Gulati, and Manmeet Marwaha. Thanks for all the meaningful advice.

Some of my teachers left an indelible impression of honest purpose and selflessness that has always inspired me. It would be impossible to sufficiently express gratitude and I guess this isn't an autobiography, but one instance is unforgettable.

I remember my mathematics teacher in grade 5 was so keen to teach me that she would coach me at her home in the evening along with her own children, and once my mother offered to pay tuition fee but she refused to accept it. She taught purely for the love of teaching. This memory is etched deeply and since then I have come to rever my teachers immensely. My educational journey at my alma mater, IIT Kharagpur, further reinforced this belief and the multidisciplinary traits of the solutions proposed here are entirely attributable to the teachings at IIT. Some individuals, however, inspire not only through guidance and teachings but also through their actions – here I would like to deeply acknowledge the mentorship of Shri Navin Chawla, whose commitment to selfless service, apolitical leanings, high integrity and administrative insightfulness were critical to examining the practicability of the ideas proposed in the book.

Most crucially, I would like to thank you, the reader, for picking up this book and finding time to read it. Nothing is more redemptive for an author than the knowledge that the book is being read and the ideas heard! Your contribution to getting this message through to the appropriate offices is key and I would invite you and urge you to visit the website www.invertonomics.org and sign the petitions to our respected prime minister and all chief ministers to help implement these breakthrough solutions, and help us live the great Indian dream!

Jai Hind!

Chapter 1

TOWARDS A HONK-FREE INDIA

On a majority of roads in cities such as Bangalore, Mumbai, and Delhi, noise pollution can measure nearly 80 to 90 decibels during peak hours.

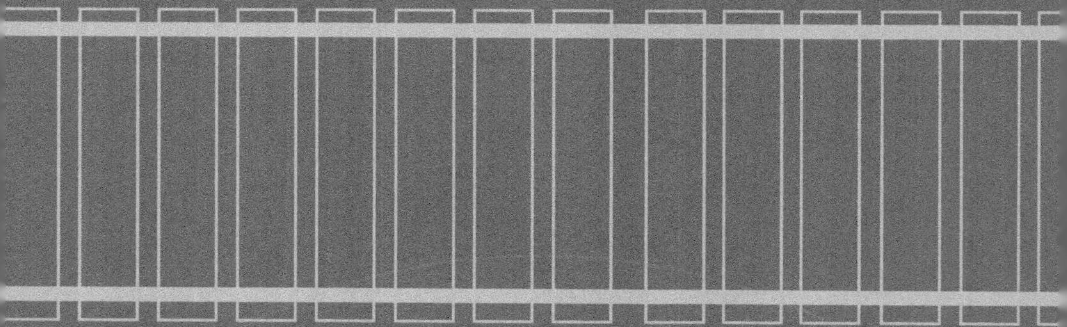

That's roughly the equivalent of standing

15 feet from a passing freight train.

Introduction

In ancient Indian and Chinese texts, writers noted that the ultimate form of torture involved subjecting captives to loud and horrible noises. It is an interesting paradox that we now live in the modern world as free citizens and all we need to do is stroll down the street to be exposed to noise loud enough to make us physically ill – elevating our blood pressure to unhealthy levels, interfering with our sleeping patterns and causing a whole host of stress-related disorders.

Although the Indian government has prescribed a standard noise limit for residential, commercial and industrial areas, with restrictions being 55, 65 and 75 decibels, respectively, for anyone who walks down the street, it really shouldn't be all that surprising that these limits are violated regularly during the course of the day.

The Problem

The Honk-Happy Indian Driver

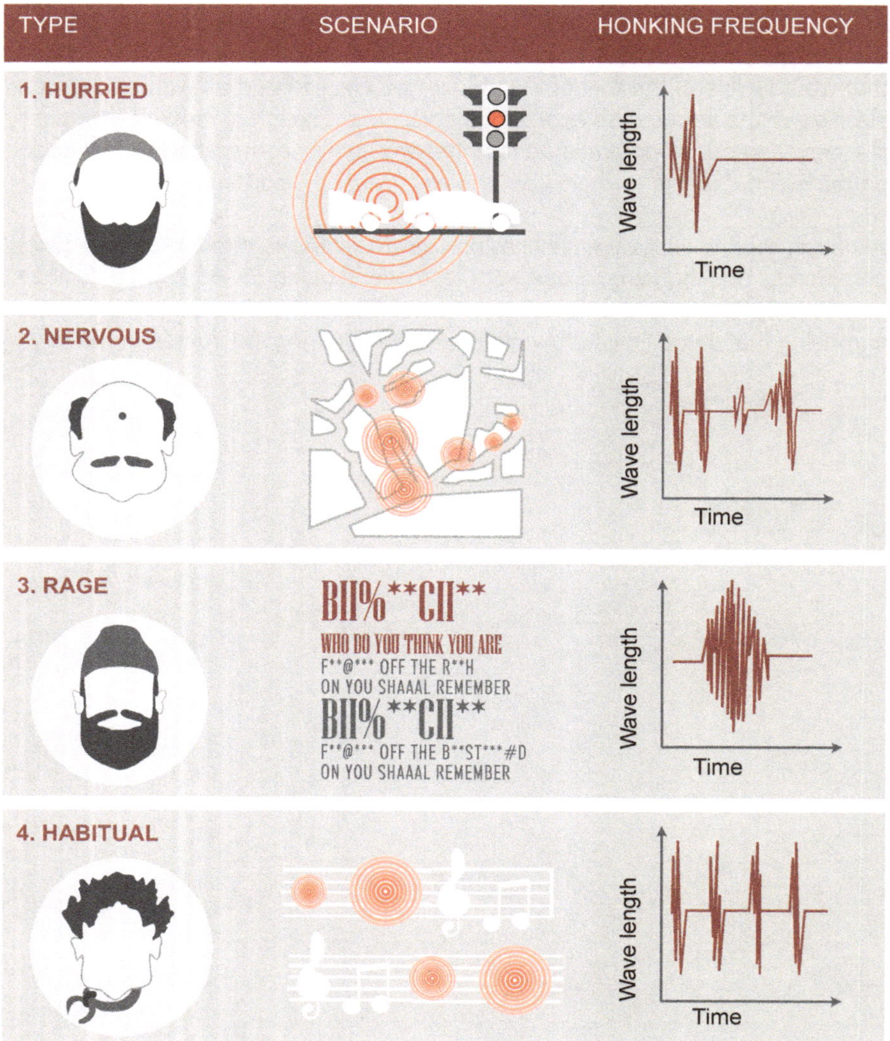

Note: All figures in this book are author's own unless specified otherwise.

Honk If You Know Why You Are Honking

India is the honking capital of the world. Drivers here tend to honk for all sorts of reasons or for no reason at all, adding significantly to the urban soundtrack. Pradeep Kakkar, founder and managing partner of the social concern group PUBLIC (People United for Better Living in Calcutta) classifies the 'honk happy' Indian driver into four different categories.[1] 'For some, honking is a way of communication – one driver's way of establishing social contact with another,' he explains. 'Others honk out of nervousness, since drivers here don't observe traffic rules such as lane driving and there is overwhelming uncertainty about what the next car may do or what may shoot out of the next intersection. Some drivers honk out of sheer rage,' when buses and taxis stop or change lanes without warning and pedestrians wander across the street. 'Finally, for some, honking is simply fun. You are feeling happy, so you honk, almost as if you are a kid playing with a noise-making toy.'

Taxi driver Ratan Shaw presses the horn every 30 seconds regardless of whether there is a vehicle before him or not. It is an involuntary action that he shares with others of his kind. Executive Anindya Ghosh honks instinctively at traffic signals. He spells out the reasons why. 'If it [the traffic light] is green, then the intent is to urge the motorist ahead to speed up so that the light doesn't turn red when I reach the signal,' he says. 'And when it turns from red to green, motorists honk in unison as though those ahead have no clue that the signal has changed.'

The first thing Pritam Singh did when he purchased an Ambassador taxi was to get a new, louder horn installed. And when Rajesh Chauhan went to buy a car, the thing he was most particular about was the horn. He rejected two cars because the horns weren't loud enough. 'To drive in Kolkata, a loud horn is absolutely essential. With a horn not so loud, you can't wade through the traffic', he reasons.

When the late Karl Slym took over as president and managing director of General Motors India, one of his first lessons was on the horn. He discovered that while the horn is the customers' last consideration elsewhere, it was absolutely vital in India. 'In most countries, a horn is used only in extreme emergency or panic. Hence, the sound is muted. But in India, the device is almost an extension of the driver. It is in his psyche to sound it now and again,' he said.[2]

The etiquette of not honking unless necessary is virtually absent on Indian roads. Drivers here honk excessively with little consideration for others, contributing significantly to ambient noise and nuisance on the street. Even where honking is unlawful, such as in designated silence zones around major hospitals and schools, drivers turn a blind eye to No Honking signs, knowing it is difficult for police to spot offenders in dense traffic. Drivers will even honk threateningly at pedestrians trying to cross the road at zebra crossings. Anywhere else in the world, the offenders would get hauled up. But here, they get away scot-free.

What Are We Doing About the Problem?

No Horns Please

According to the recent diktats of the Karnataka State Pollution Control Board, all motorists should go easy on honking while driving on Bengaluru roads. This is to lower the levels of noise pollution in the city (the seventh noisiest in the country). Noble thought, but in India, the indiscretion of honking has more to do with people not realizing the nuisance they cause, than anything else. Although citizens are becoming increasingly aware of the problem and many civic organizations are attempting to educate the public, thus far, awareness campaigns have made little difference.

On 7 April 2008, commuters in Mumbai were asked to observe a citywide 'No Honking Day' in an attempt to educate the city's 15,00,000 drivers to be more considerate.

A total of 800 policemen and 2,000 community workers were deployed to enforce the initiative and over 1,00,000 stickers were distributed to build awareness on sound pollution. It was the first time a campaign like this had been held in India and although organizers said that they would punish indiscriminate honking, commuters were disappointed, as honking levels were not exactly noticeably reduced.[3]

In December 2009, the NGO Earth Saviors Foundation, in collaboration with the concessionaire of the Delhi-Gurgaon expressway, launched a similar anti-honking drive at the congested Gurgaon toll plaza. Volunteers urged motorists not to blow their horns, removed Horn Please signs from commercial vehicles and displayed eye-catching anti-honking slogans to build awareness against honking.[4] Though no measurable results could be established, it did bring the spotlight onto this issue.

More recently, *Times of India* had spearheaded a no-honking drive from 15 August to 22 August 2016 to create awareness backed with well-researched data on honking behaviour across cities and vehicles. It is a step in the right direction. We would however need to use invertonomics if we wish to see the transformation within this decade!

Mission Peace, another citizens' group in Bangalore, holds regular anti-honking rallies on the 10th of every month and interacts on social networking sites, such as Twitter and Facebook, to address and discuss issues relating to noise pollution.[5] These campaigns, though laudable, have done little to change honking behaviour across Indian cities.

The Solution

Taking India by the Horns

In India, the bandwidth of the citizen set is so wide that to expect to cause a paradigm shift in behaviour through education and awareness campaigns is novel yet naive. And even if as a responsible citizen you were to choose to 'honk with care', you would soon run out of steam simply because the number of 'smart citizens' (like you) would be too small to make an appreciable difference to the problem.

The LPG Cylinder Case Study

There is, instead, another powerfully effective way to transform the way people think about honking and that is by making them pay for using the horn. The principle of this is that the moment you begin charging for something, people tend to become sensitized to its use. Now, to charge for something, you must first be able to measure it – that is fundamental. Take the case of the humble LPG cylinder. Not a particularly expensive consumable but every Indian household, however wealthy, is aware of how many cylinders it uses every month. This is simply because LPG is measurable and not free of charge, unlike water, which is cheap, difficult to measure and consequently lends itself easily to waste and misuse.

Based on the same principle, if we can find a way to measure the incidence of honking and consequently charge for it, citizen sensitivity to the use of the horn is likely to increase exponentially.

So,

What if we were charged Re 1 for every honk?!

Is there a scalable model to implement this? Read on...

Technology That 'Measures' Honking

The Smart Citizen Card Model

Modern telecom technology offers an optimal and efficient way of measuring and charging for individual honking behaviour by making it possible to provide continuous real-time data on the number of times the horn is used by each vehicle on the road.

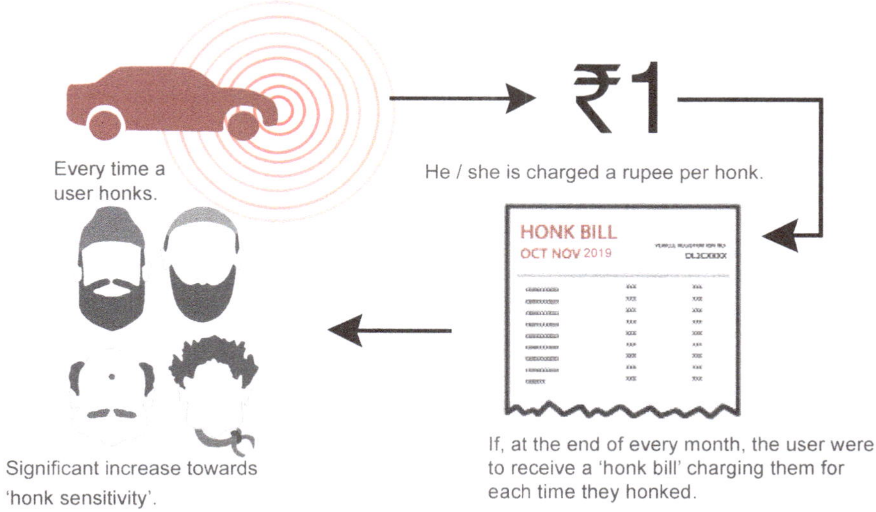

The technology model consists of a single GPS-enabled SIM card (Smart Citizen Card), much like those we use in mobile phones, to be installed in all vehicles. This would have the ability to monitor or record the number of honks and transmit the information to receiving towers managed by operators, who are authorized to charge for honks in the form of periodic Honk Bills delivered directly to citizens.

CONSIDER THIS

The average 'honk happy' driver is accustomed to using the horn at every opportunity, unaware of the nuisance and sound pollution he causes. If, at the end of the month, he were to receive a honk bill charging him for every time he used the horn (at the rate of Re 1 a honk, the bill could be as much as Rs 3,000), he would be likely to become much more 'honk efficient'.

1. INSTALL

GPS-enabled SIM device fitted in vehicle.

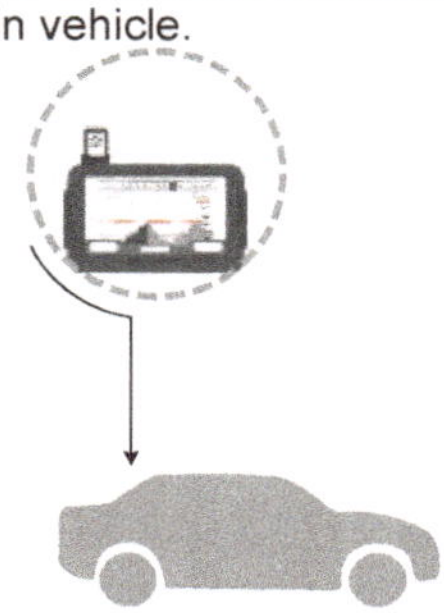

2. MONITOR / RECORD

GPS-enabled device monitors and records the number of honks pressed per vehicle.

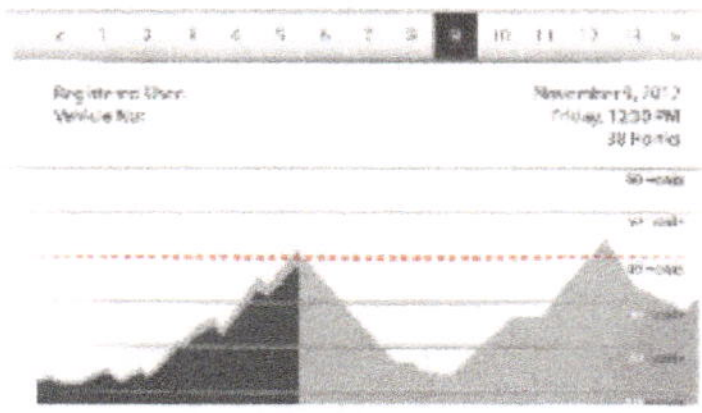

3.TRANSMIT

GPS-enabled SIM device transmits the collected information to receiving towers managed by operators.

4. OPERATOR

The operator is authorized to charge for excessive honks in the form of periodic bills.

5. HONK BILL

These bills are sent to registered users via email / post along with cellphone bills.

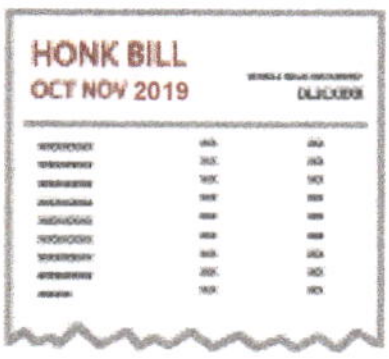

6. ENLIGHTENED USER

Inverting the Problem into an Opportunity

Harnessing the Energy of Honking and Converting It to Money

While the Smart Citizen Card Model provides an effective way of measuring and charging for individual honking behaviour, its viability rests on the creation of an operationally efficient and enduring 'mechanism of measurement', to facilitate and support the solution.

History has shown that in India, most mechanisms, whether managed by the government or the private sector, tend to fall into disuse due to the lack of an appropriate system of checks and balances. In the case of the synchronized bomb blasts in Mumbai, for instance, CCTV cameras that could have been a valuable source of information were found to be faulty and producing blurred and unclear footage.[6] Similarly, footage from CCTVs on the highly sensitive Bandra-Worli Sea Link in Mumbai was of little help to police officers investigating the suicide of businessman Lalit Sheth, as three of the six cameras were not functional when the incident took place.[7]

In fact, unless there is a profit or loss riding on the operational goodness of a system, it becomes dysfunctional very quickly. It is only if there is an agency that invests in the system, operates it for profit and then uses a portion of its revenue to maintain the system that a natural structure of checks and balances is created that ensures the system will work.

The solution then becomes to give the system a live existence and introduce it in a manner such that its operation becomes positively remunerative to some party, creating an incentive to run it efficiently.

The underlying idea of the Smart Citizen Card Model, therefore, is to control the problem by monetizing it and inverting it into an opportunity for profit (money), enabling private enterprise to manage the solution and drive it for revenue, creating an enduring, operationally efficient system geared towards reducing the incidence of honking.

Revenue Model

With 55,00,000 registered vehicles, Delhi has the largest vehicular population in India. At an average of 30 honks per day, per vehicle (a spectrum of 0 to 60 honks), the total number of honks per day amounts to a staggering 16.5 crore. Even at a negligible charge of Re 1 per honk, that many honks would convert to a revenue of Rs 495 crore per month for Delhi alone. For ten cities, it would add up to a staggering Rs 60,000 crore annually, or a fraction of it, which would still be a huge amount. This sum would be more than sufficient for an operator to set up the necessary infrastructure, provide for its maintenance and earn a substantial revenue from the model even after sharing a portion of the proceeds with the government, if required to do so.

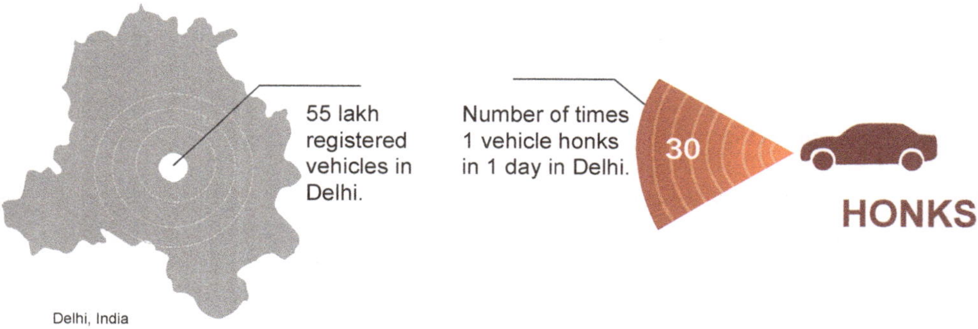

Delhi, India
Latitude: 28.38N; Longitude: 77.12E

No. of horns emitted by cars
55 lakh cars = 165,000,000 honks

Revenue from honks

1 Honk	=₹1
16.5 cr Honks	=₹165,000,000 / day
1 Month	=₹4,950,000,000

'If one city can generate ₹500 crore, 10 major cities in India can lead to ₹5,000 crore per month or ₹60,000 crore annually.'[8]

The Car Horn Is *Beeping* Uselessly[9]

In theory, the horn is a safety device; it might rightly be called the world's first 'collision-avoidance system'. But exactly how many collisions it serves to avoid has never been clear.

From its earliest days, some observers wondered whether the horn wasn't actually facilitating certain road mishaps by shifting the burden of evasion from the honker to the honkee. A Londoner argued this case in a 1912 letter to the *Times*: 'Drivers have escaped punishment because they hooted loudly just before killing an aged and deaf colonel or an elderly woman, deaf, and blind of one eye or capsizing another car and injuring three or four persons... Ordinary care and precaution would have prevented each of such accidents. Hooting, however, is counted a sufficient set-off against the lack of such care and precaution.'[10]

By the 1930s, this theory was gaining ground. First Paris and then London outlawed honking at night and in Berlin, the Nazis put yellow spots on the cars of people who honked unnecessarily. In 1935, New York Mayor Fiorello La Guardia kicked off a night-time honking ban stating that automobile accidents, fatalities and injuries had been reduced to an appreciable extent merely because the campaign against horns in those cities had caused drivers to drive more carefully.

Jeff Muttart, a traffic accident re-constructionist, has pored over hundreds of surveillance videos of real-life car crashes and near-crashes. In 2005, he concluded that emergency horn use is not associated with decreased accident involvement. He found that drivers never steered and honked at the same time, and usually, they didn't honk at all. About half of emergency honks were meant to chastise and came only after the danger was past. The other half were just preludes to a crash. 'It really didn't serve any purpose at all. It was just "Hey, by the way, I'm going to hit you."'

A 2001 survey for the U.K. Institute of Traffic Accident Investigators shows that most people take two-to-three times as long to honk as they do to brake or steer. Muttart explains this honking deficiency by the fact that many people view the horn as a tool for scolding rather than safety. So when we want to avoid a crash, we don't think of using it (you don't look for a phone when you need a fire extinguisher).

The Way Forward

LEGISLATION

LAW FOR NEW VEHICLES
Mandatory for all vehicles to be sold pre-fitted with GPS-Enabled SIM Card Technology

LAW FOR OLD VEHICLES
all existing vehicles to be similarly retrofitted by a certain cut-off date to be specified by the relevant authorities

AUCTIONING OPERATIONAL LICENSES

1. Telecom companies
2. Invite competitive bids and auction operational licences
3. Consortiums

LEAD OPERATOR

PRE-PAID HONK CARDS

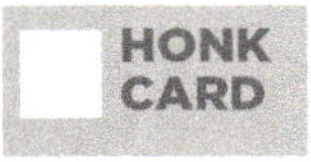

COLLECTING HONK INFORMATION

Charge users for excessive honk usage

VALUE ADDED SERVICES

FM channels and advertisement space

Legislation

The implementation of the Smart Citizen Card Model requires that the government passes appropriate laws and legislations making it mandatory for all new vehicles to be pre-fitted with the Smart Citizen Card Technology and for all existing vehicles to be similarly retrofitted by a specified cut-off date. Mr Nitin Gadkari, presently the Minister of Road Transport and Highways of India, has expressed his support to the *Times of India* 'No Honking Drive' and has already moved amendments to the Motor Vehicles Act to deal with the increasing noise pollution. It would be appropriate to build in the Smart Citizen Card Model into the new legislation in terms of including the necessary legalese that could enable its implementation.

Auctioning Operational Licenses

The next step is for the government to invite competitive bids and auction operational licenses to telecom companies or consortiums, authorizing them to issue Smart Citizen Cards, collect honk information and charge for honks on behalf of the government.

Some Might Argue

As in any model for social change, there is always the challenge of political vested interests and corruption derailing the licensing process. To this we submit that while there may be no way to control or eliminate the corruption inherent in all politico-government processes, the Smart Citizen Card Model makes it possible to remove the average citizen from the ambit of the corrupt transaction by eliminating opportunities for human interface between the citizen and the agent of enforcement (operator), since the measurement of incidence of honking shall be implemented automatically. The transmission of the honk bill and collection of honk charge shall also be executed as part of the mobile phone bill.

Creating Competitive Markets

The Smart Citizen Card Model operates by aligning public interest with the business interests of the telecom sector. It provides telecom companies with an attractive potential market, supported by the sector's pre-existing infrastructure and the opportunity to earn significant revenues without the need for further capital expenditure.

Key to this process is the adoption of policies and the introduction of appropriate institutions and regulations required to create a robust, competitive market including, most significantly, the allotment of multiple licenses (to at least one government player and two or more private operators) to promote transparency, efficiency and equity.

Some Might Argue

1. Allowing private operators to manage the model would bring in privacy issues and a conflict of interest between the operator and the citizen since the former would be geared towards profit and not solving the problem. Our take on this is that of the services that have been revolutionized in India, most cases are those where an appropriate market has been created in which multiple parties (private and government) compete on the basis of value and efficiency. The telecom industry is a good example of this model's success. This is supported by a near universal consensus that open markets and private investment are the key to economic growth and development. In fact, the successful transformation of the Passport Office by Tata Consultancy Services (TCS), which was appointed as the service provider in May 2008 for the implementation of the Passport Seva project by the Ministry of External Affairs, is a fine example of public--private partnership in sensitive governance projects.

2. Since honk charges are likely to be stipulated by legislation and will remain fixed across operators, there will be no basis for competition between them. To this we submit that the addition of certain value added services to the Smart Citizen Card Model, apart from creating a fresh revenue stream, can and will provide a powerful basis for competition.

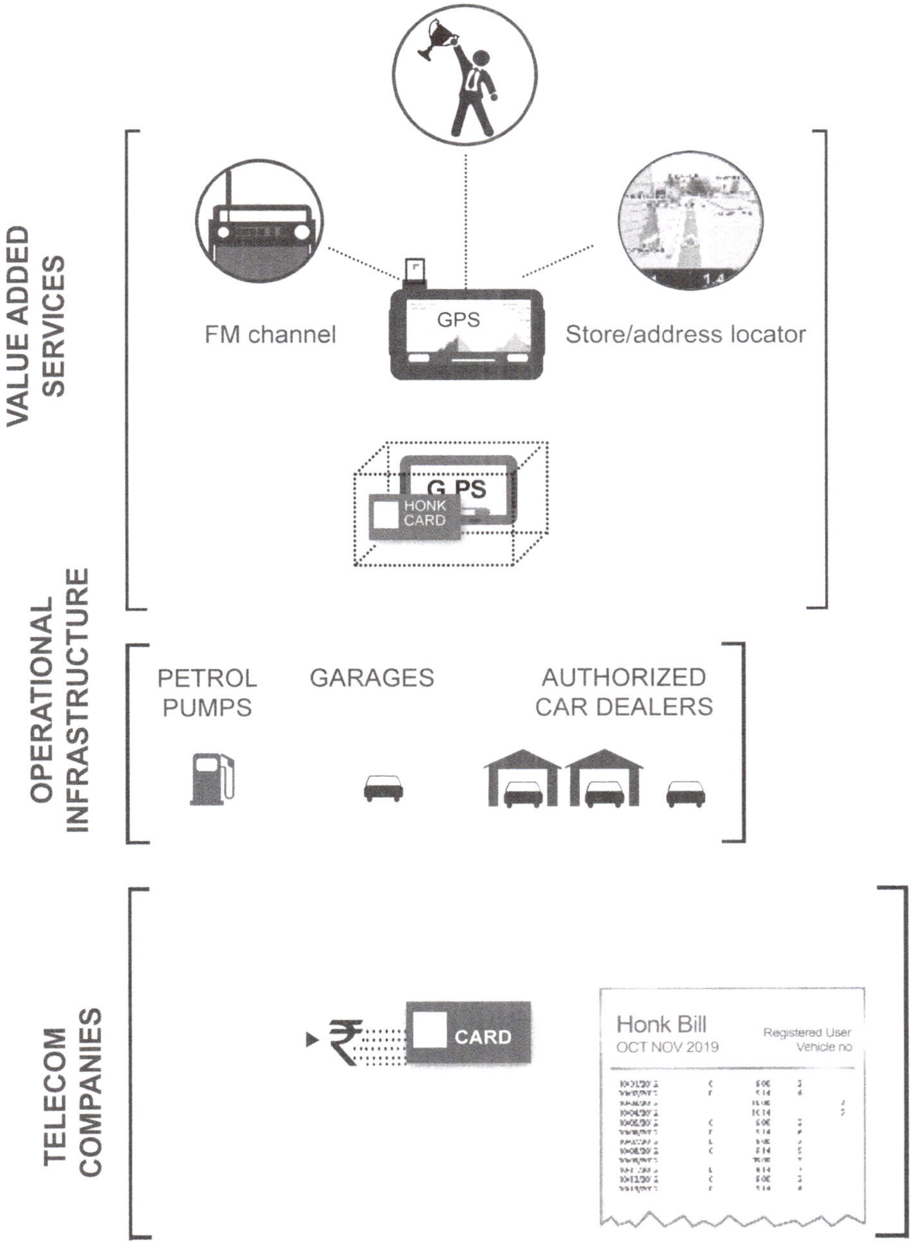
VALUE ADDED SERVICES
FM channel
GPS
Store/address locator
GPS
HONK CARD
OPERATIONAL INFRASTRUCTURE
PETROL PUMPS
GARAGES
AUTHORIZED CAR DEALERS
TELECOM COMPANIES
₹
CARD
Honk Bill
OCT NOV 2019
Registered User
Vehicle no

Value Added Services

An inherent institutional conflict exists between the key stakeholders of the honk-regulation ecosystem with the operator seeking to maximize the number of honks (revenue) and the citizen seeking to reduce the number of honks (liability). A means to dilute and rationalize this conflict in a constructive manner is to include an array of value-adds to the Smart Citizen Card Model in the form of infotainment services, such as music on demand, restaurant locators, best-route analysers, diversion alerts and reimbursement statements, strengthening the revenue model by reducing dependence on charges for honks and creating a fresh source of profit for operators.

The Smart Citizen Card Model will make it possible to provide drivers with a variety of location (GPS)-based services, such as finding a particular address, identifying the shortest and quickest route to the destination or simply locating the nearest restaurant, hotel or hospital. It will also allow drivers to create a customized playlist and stream music from a vast database organized by song, album, artist, or genre or for the older and more technologically challenged citizen, to simply make a phone call, connect to an operator and order the service they require.[11]

Setting Up Operational Infrastructure

Finally, the government must permit an initial holding period of 6–8 months to allow operators to set up the operational infrastructure required to manage the Smart Citizen Card Model and to give citizens sufficient notice to install the technology in their vehicles and purchase pre-paid Smart Citizen Card Kits, to be made conveniently available across petrol pumps, garages and authorized car dealers. The model will require citizens to maintain a minimum balance on their Smart Citizen Cards so that honk bills can be automatically deducted from the balance. Any failure to maintain a minimum balance or pay a honk bill would attract a penal interest of 18% per annum payable by the citizen to the operator.

The Stakeholders

Current Ecosystem

Central to the current traffic ecosystem is the citizen–driver who is both cause agent and suffering stakeholder. Powerless and frustrated by excessive honking and noise pollution and correspondingly prone to using the horn more frequently, the citizen–driver remains locked in a vicious downward spiral even as the government looks on, indifferent and immobile. The third stakeholder is the traffic policeman in the role of a silent spectator, aware of the problem but unable to intervene due to lack of appropriate legislations and regulation structures.

New Ecosystem

The Smart Citizen Card Model seeks to bring about a substantial transformation in the current dysfunctional system with the introduction of a new, key stakeholder – private enterprise.

In the new scenario, the government as the policymaker or change agent must institute appropriate laws to facilitate the role of private enterprise as the enabler and entrepreneur and the citizen as the empowered agent of social change, establishing a vibrant, participatory network between the primary stakeholders, promoting awareness and ownership of the solution and encouraging stakeholder participation in achieving its objectives.

Later in the book, we shall also demonstrate how monies collected shall be also earmarked for upgradation of the road-safety infrastructure and the welfare of traffic policemen, who are key stakeholders in this domain.

Bringing Social Change

Creating Etiquette towards the Common Good

In India, we suffer from a lack of connectedness as a society, with no sense of what is important for the collective good. Although citizens follow and obey punitive laws, other unwritten rules that govern conduct in public spaces or intercourse between citizens are disregarded since there is no consensus on what constitutes 'good behaviour' and thus no way to measure or punish those actions that infringe upon it. Therefore, before we can think of restoring order or regulating the public space, it becomes imperative to create a standard set of rules (etiquette) for situations not governed by the law, in this case, honking behaviour.

As Indians, we are averse to standardization, reveling instead in the cacophony of interests, opinions and voices that exist in the public space. Take McDonald's, for instance, arguably the best-known fast-food chain in the world. Founded in California, by brothers Richard and Maurice McDonald in 1940, the company was transformed eight years later by a production-line system that rolled out burgers in a quick-service style similar to the one we know today. Since then, McDonald's has sold well over 200 billion hamburgers worldwide.[12] In India, while we may aspire to make a million paranthas a day, every household will use a different recipe – in effect, we are each making our own parantha! It is a challenge to bring everyone within the fold and enforce participation in an activity that is essentially for the common well-being of society as a whole. But for those who are keen on participating, the Smart Citizen Card Model creates a standard set of rules (etiquette) providing citizens with a sense of direction, a way forward and a means of contributing in a meaningful and effective manner.

Obfuscation of Laws

In Western countries, even the average man on the street knows the laws applicable to him in terms of taxes or expected behaviour. He knows them because they are simple rules of prescription that are easy to understand and obey, much like the rules children must follow in school. For instance, a school may require each student to carry a school bag with four notebooks covered in brown paper and a zippered pencil box with two sharpened pencils, an eraser and a scale. Since the rules are simple, children can understand and obey them easily and feel satisfied with the idea that they are positive citizens.

In India, laws tend to be so complex that it becomes difficult for the common man to understand them. Poor understanding leads to low compliance rates, thus setting up a vicious cycle wherein the citizen is often caught on the wrong end of the law and compelled to seek the exit route most easily available to him – that of seeking favours from officials through bribery. Thus it becomes okay to do what you want and if you get caught, to simply pay your way out of it.

This obfuscation of the law has led to an incremental lowering of the median of moral integrity in our country with future generations learning by example and acquiring a sort of flexible morality when it comes to the public domain.

Etiquette

Life as an individual

Convenient but without regard for aesthetic sensibility and experiential goodness for others

DO NOT SPIT ON THE WALL

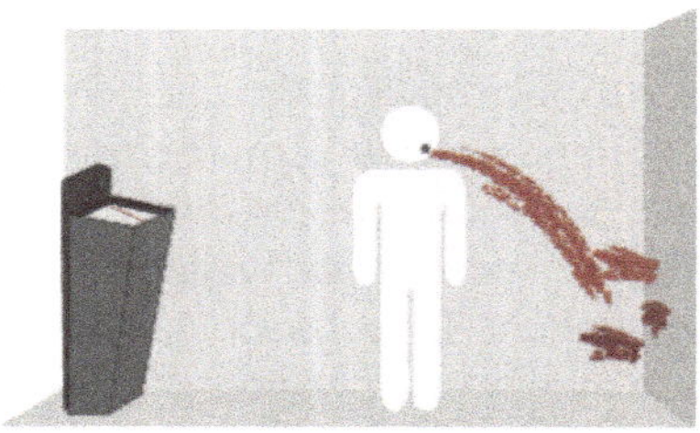

AFTER DINNER

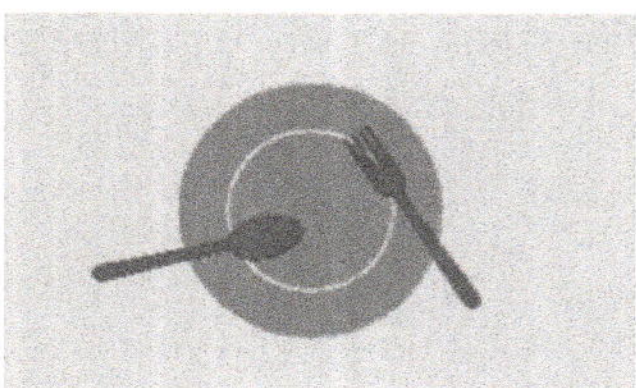

TRAVELLING IN PUBLIC TRANSPORT

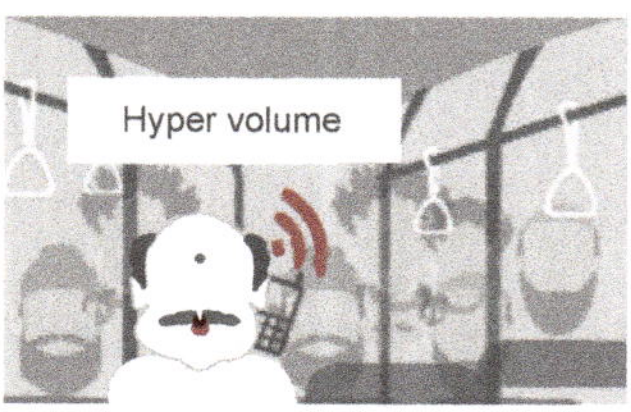

Life in a community

Structured around informal mannerism that offers a more aesthetic, synergistic and experientially sound existence as a Community

DO NOT SPIT ON THE WALL

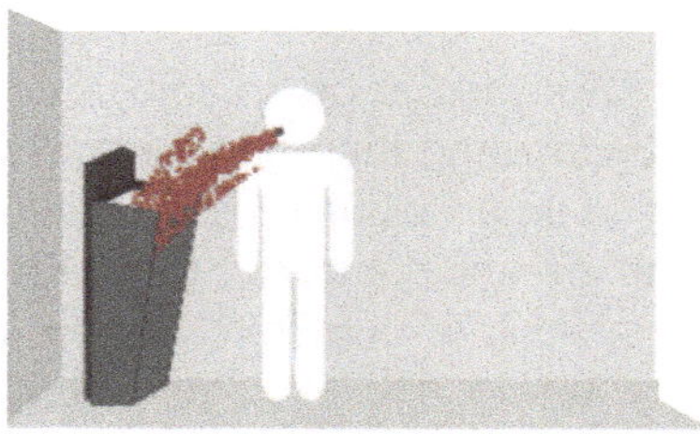

AFTER DINNER

TRAVELLING IN PUBLIC TRANSPORT

Paradigm Shift in Citizen Participation for the Common Good

While long-term solutions such as sensitizing the public through education and awareness campaigns or by imposing penalties on honking are desirable and may appear to be the only way to address the issue, there is a need for a faster, more efficient means of modifying citizen behaviour.

The Smart Citizen Card Model provides an immediate solution to controlling honking by using money – the life force of any vibrant society – to bring about a shift in citizen behaviour in a non-invasive, neutral manner. The model seeks to sensitize the citizen to the use of the public auditory space as a sort of limited bandwidth to be shared and used sparingly only for purposes of safety. It represents that certain actions belong to the collective space and since that space or resource is limited and must be shared equally by all citizens, one must be prepared to pay in order to utilize it. The extent of charge could also be calibrated, to say, 10 fold in silent zones around hospitals and schools.

Here we have a novel approach to controlling honking through a process of positive reinforcement by projecting it as a privilege that is charged rather than a violation attracting a penalty.

Some Might Argue

There is likely to be great resistance on part of the public to the implementation of the Honking Model and the subsequent charges that would be imposed. To this we submit that while the charges envisaged by the model are insignificant when compared to money spent by drivers on petrol, maintenance and other incidentals of car ownership, the potential for change is so huge that the moment citizens begin to see a visible shift in compliance levels, resistance to the new model is likely to disappear.

Perhaps the pilot implementation could be done through a government-owned PSU, and started in a calibrated manner, beginning with cars of 2,000 cc and above, and then applying to 1500 cc and above, and eventually to all cars and two / three wheelers.

'Seed for Change' – Legislation

In India, we are in a negative cycle as far as citizen participation for common good is concerned since the experience of interacting with each other and the environment in public spaces is often an adverse one. There is therefore a need to transform the narrative of citizen participation from negative to positive and ideally this shift should come about as a result of education. However, in a country as diverse as ours, where everyone is at a different point on the etiquette curve, education through a strong and stable process is simply not powerful enough to catalyse the change. This shift can only come from policy change and legislation aimed towards the creation of definitive goals that act as the lowest common denominators of social good so as to minimize conflict and bring about an alignment in citizen thought and action.

Citizen–Law Enforcement Bhagidari

By creating simple, well-defined rules geared towards the common good, the Smart Citizen Card Model helps to generate a positive experience of transactional citizen behaviour. The model also brings about a critical level of transparency (an itemized honk bill details how many times each person has honked), substantially altering citizen behaviour, shifting the onus of compliance from the government to the citizen and ushering in a new era of 'citizen–government–private enterprise bhagidari'.

The model envisages the creation of a compulsively enabling environment where non-compliance attracts a charge and the 'nuisance' of being barred from using certain elements of traffic infrastructure such as toll roads, petrol pumps and public parking facilities, while compliance is rewarded with free parking, discount coupons, paid holidays and other incentives from socially responsible corporations.

The goal is to achieve voluntary compliance with honk regulations using minimally punitive measures and an innovative combination of charge and reward, shifting the onus of compliance to the citizen and strengthening the citizen–law enforcement partnership.

We shall examine how the same Smart Card Model can be used to solve key problems of 'air pollution', 'traffic compliance' and 'lane driving' in subsequent chapters.

We saw how 'Honking' was INVERTED from being a problem to an ECONOMIC OPPORTUNITY. A simple Re 1 charge could generate Rs 60,000 crore annually and reduce honking.

We saw how an ecosystem-based model could cause a shift in individual behaviour from self gain to 'collective good'.

The Smart Citizen Card shall now solve many more serious problems using invertonomics.

Read on for more such solutions...

Chapter 2

TOWARDS CLEANER AIR

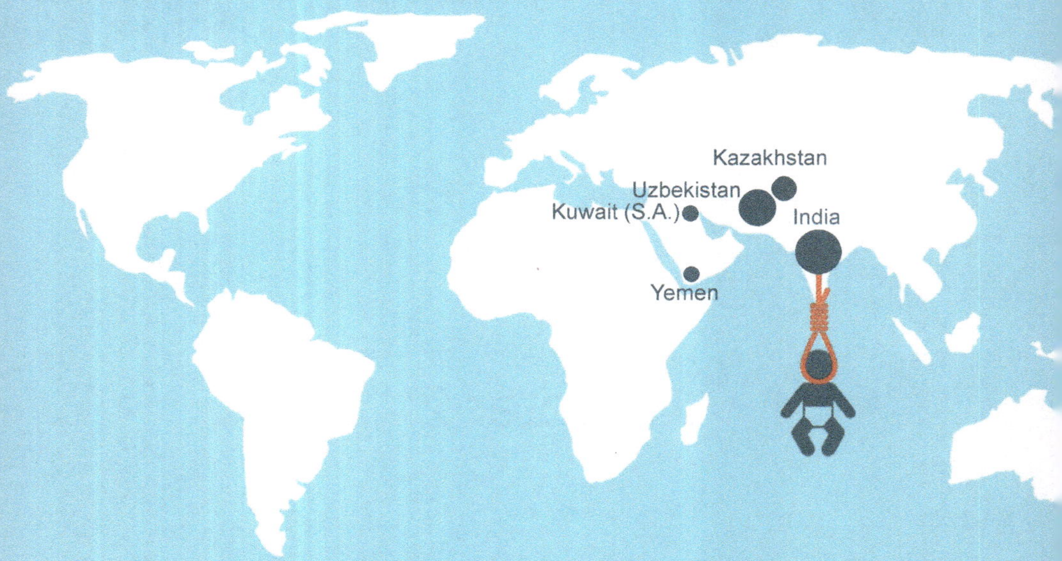

Graphical representation of the level of air pollution in different countries

India's air pollution level ranked:

174 / 178

according to Environmental Performance Index at World Economic Forum, Davos, 2014

Acute respiratory infections

kill 13% of India's children (under 5 years)

Delhi is the world's most populated city

(150 to 200 micrograms per cubic metric)

Air pollution level 2 to 3 times higher than national safe standards

(Safe limit is 60 according to National Ambient Air Quality Standard for India)

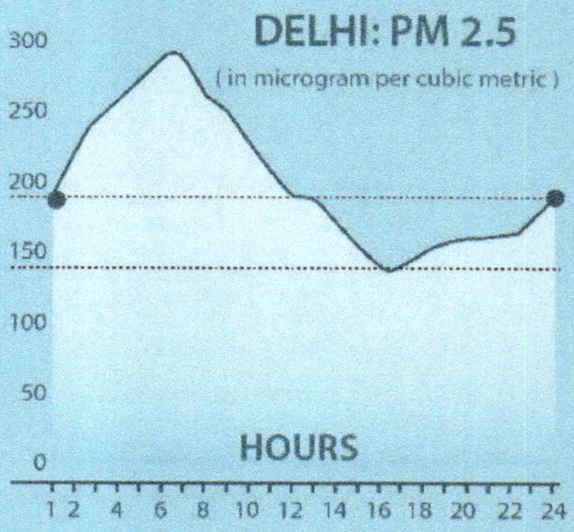

Introduction

The World's Unhealthiest Air

According to the Environmental Performance Index, India's air quality is among the worst in the world. The results of the 2014 Index, released during the World Economic Forum in Davos, show that of the 178 countries surveyed, India ranked 174th in the 'Air' rating.[14] Findings indicate that India now ties with China in terms of the proportion of population exposed to average air pollution levels exceeding World Health Organization (WHO) thresholds.[15] Despite Beijing's reputation of having the most polluted air of any major city in the world, an examination of daily pollution figures collected from both suggests that on average, Delhi's air contains greater concentration of dangerous particulate matter than Beijing's.

Most recent data from the Central Pollution Control Board has shown that in Indian cities, levels of respirable particulate matter are nearly six times the threshold at which they become unsafe for human beings. In Delhi, the concentration is 13 times higher than what WHO safety guidelines permit.[16] Various studies suggest that high levels of particulate matter are the leading cause of acute lower respiratory infections and cancer and the WHO has found that in India, acute respiratory infections are one of the most common causes of death in children under 5 and contribute to 13% of all in-patient deaths in paediatric wards across the country.[17]

The main culprit behind this is the growing number of vehicles on Indian roads. Rapid urbanization and lack of mass transportation facilities have resulted in a tremendous increase in the number of private vehicles across cities. This increase in mobility comes at a steep price. Motor vehicles are estimated to account for 72% of the total air pollution load in major metropolitan cities, of which two-thirds is contributed by two wheelers alone.[18] And while the country still has far fewer vehicles per capita than developed nations, India's cars are some of the most polluting in the world.

According to Anumita Roychowdhury, executive director of India's Centre for Science and Environment, Indian emission standards are still nearly a decade behind their European counterparts and are not legally enforceable, unlike in countries such as the United States, which has the Clean Air Act. 'We need to take big steps or the problem will overwhelm us,' she says.[19]

Responding to the gravity of the problem, the Indian government has attempted to develop a number of mitigation strategies to improve urban air quality and to make our cities cleaner and greener. These include an increase in the use of cleaner fuels, the introduction of vehicles with advanced emission control devices, an attempt to raise awareness on the possible economic and health impacts of air pollution and the formulation of necessary legislations for the enforcement of vehicle emission standards. Compliance with pollution control norms, however, remains dangerously low, contributing to the meteoric increase in air pollution levels across the country.

The Problem

In Indian cities, compliance with pollution control laws is dismal at best, with little or no infrastructure geared to handle the horrific scale of the problem. Although the law makes it mandatory for all vehicles to obtain periodic emission check certificates between two and four times a year, in the current system, the enforcement model depends on random physical checking, leading to poor implementation of emission norms and low compliance rates.[20]

Another problem is that pollution-control initiatives tend to target private vehicles though large commercial vehicles, including those belonging to the government that are often the most culpable when it comes to contributing to air pollution. In India, not only is there a complete absence of an appropriate system of inspection and maintenance – the first and most important step towards emission control for large commercial vehicles – there is no enforcement of the ban on old or outdated vehicles or the registration of new vehicles not using compressed natural gas (CNG) or any other clean fuel. Many taxis and autorickshaws run on cheaper adulterated fuel blends that emit increased amounts of pollutants, while outdated government vehicles continue to ply on the roads since the police is uncertain of their jurisdiction to stop and book them for traffic and pollution offences. The result is that the roads are full of trucks, buses and taxis of uncertain vintage spewing oily smoke, oblivious and uncaring of the damage they cause to the environment.

The Delhi government has taken up the problem of vehicle pollution quite seriously and in a pathbreaking manner, engaged with citizens (vehicle owners) and made them part of the solution in the odd-even scheme. In this scheme, the number of vehicles plying on road were rationed on the basis of the last digit on their registration plates. While the efficacy of the short trial is debatable, the scheme clearly succeeded in engaging the citizens to act individually for the collective good. The courage demonstrated by the government was also laudable. The same scheme, however, suffered on account of implementation challenges. This is where this new idea will succeed.

The Typical Pollution-Happy Indian Citizen

Here are a few characters, citizens who do not help, and indeed, actively hinder attempts to check the rampant air pollution in India.

Mr Y. Do I Care has a busy schedule and a limited budget. He drives a car that is cheap, fuel efficient and low on maintenance. As long as it continues to run smoothly and gives him the mileage he wants, he has neither time nor inclination to have his car pollution-checked or serviced. Why should he care about pollution, he says – it is the government's problem to ensure the air is clean.

Mrs Who Checks drives her little red Wagon R through the by-lanes of Lajpat Nagar, expertly avoiding all the police check posts in her area. She will tell you with pride that in ten years of driving, she has never been stopped by a traffic policeman. Confident that no one will ever ask to check her Pollution Under Control (PUC) Certificate, Mrs Who Checks has her car checked on an average of once every two years, only when the government declares a special drive to enforce pollution-control norms.

Mr I. M. Government, a mid-level bureaucrat, is extraordinarily proud of his lal batti ambassador which he believes gives him the license to break traffic and pollution laws with impunity. Mr I. M. Government thinks he is above regulations; he drives around Delhi like the king of the road and if any policeman dares to check him, he gets away with the simple expedient of flashing his central government identity card, which he keeps in his pocket for the express purpose of intimidating traffic cops and minor functionaries.

Mr Cocktail Cab's only religion is cheap fuel. He cuts costs by running his autorickshaw or taxi on a noxious mix of kerosene and diesel, openly flouting pollution-control norms to make a quick buck. Unaware and indifferent, Mr Cocktail Cab is oblivious to his toxic tailpipe emissions and of its effect on public health and well-being.

Regulating Vehicular Pollution

What the Government Is Doing about the Problem

Mandated Fuel Regulation for Public Vehicles

In 2001, the Supreme Court ruled that all buses, taxis and autorickshaws in Delhi must run on CNG. Under the Court's directive, similar regulatory initiatives were set in motion in several other large- and medium-sized cities. Environmental impact studies from Delhi have shown that as a result of the switch from petroleum-based fuels to natural gas, there was a significant reduction in the atmospheric concentration of harmful gases and respire-able particulate matter.[21] However, ten years on, the CNG advantage appears to have been lost with Delhi's air once again, turning into a deadly cocktail of pollutants.

The official transport research body, Indian Foundation of Transport Research and Training (IFTRT) claims that this increase in pollution is due to the government's failure to implement loading and air pollution norms for heavy and commercial vehicles specified under the Central Motor Vehicles Act, 1988. It is interesting to note that only buses owned or operated under local Delhi permits are required to be fitted with CNG engines. An additional 1,000 buses that link Delhi with neighbouring states still run on diesel and are allowed to enter Delhi for a maximum distance of 16 km every day. Transport vehicles that are 3.5 to 7.5 tons with local permits were to convert to CNG by July 2005; the deadline was later extended to 2009. 'Only to escape this and continue running on diesel, operators chose to have national permits, even though they operate within Delhi,' says S.P. Singh, coordinator of IFTRT. The result is that about 25,000 to 30,000 diesel trucks pass through Delhi each day while another 75,000 goods carriers and trucks operate within the city on local routes, Even if they are running on CNG, they release massive emissions when overloaded.[22]

In December 2015, the Supreme Court ruled that no new registrations of diesel SUVs and high-end vehicles above 2,000 cc shall be permitted in Delhi. Later, the Supreme Court lifted the ban. A more stringent directive followed, limiting the lifespan of use of all diesel vehicles to 10 years and petrol vehicles to 15 years. The vehicle registration shall be valid only till those many years.

Stringent Vehicle Emission Norms

India adopted first-stage emission norms for petrol and diesel vehicles in 1991–92. In April 1995, the fitting of catalytic converters in new petrol passenger cars sold in the four metros of Delhi, Kolkata, Mumbai and Chennai was made mandatory and the supply of Unleaded Petrol (ULP) was affected in these cities. Subsequently, the availability of ULP was further extended to 42 major cities and now it is available throughout the country. In 2000, passenger cars and commercial vehicles were required to meet Euro I–equivalent India 2000 norms, while Euro II–equivalent Bharat Stage (BS) II norms came into force from 2001 in the four metros of Delhi, Kolkata, Mumbai and Chennai.[23]

Cleaner Fuel Quality

In keeping with the strict emission norms, the Bureau of Indian Standards (BIS) has laid down fuel quality specifications for gasoline and diesel for the period 2000–05 and beyond 2005 for the country as a whole. Given its increasing consumption, the sulphur content of diesel was reduced to 50 ppm (parts per million) under Bharat IV standards. For gasoline, lead was phased out in the entire country with effect from 1 February 2000.[24]

However, since India only embarked on a formal emission-control regime in 1991, fuel quality and vehicle emission standards lag behind international leaders by more than a decade. India is at risk of falling behind other developing countries as well. China, Brazil, Mexico, Thailand, and South Africa have plans to reduce fuel sulphur content and tighten emission standards beyond those India has in place.

Indian policy on air quality and vehicle efficiency is also undermined by its reliance on two parallel standards, BS IV for a handful of cities and BS III for the rest of the nation. This creates confusion and treats consumers and businesses outside major cities inequitably. Further, it weakens the logic of the policy overall, since all heavy-duty trucks meet only BS III standards and nothing prevents BS IV vehicles that require low-sulphur fuels from refueling in high-sulphur fuel areas.[25]

The conclusion is that while stricter fuel-quality and vehicle-emission standards nationwide are needed to reduce pollution in the long term, in-use vehicle-emission control measures can have a more immediate impact. Indian policy must, therefore, ensure that vehicles already on the road are operating to their design specifications and not emitting excess pollutants.

The government is currently considering plans to leapfrog to stricter emission norms of BS VI fuel specifications and bypassing the BS V norms. The target date is April 2020. A new automobile scrapping policy is also under consideration.

Outdoor Air-Purifiers

In early 2010, the Delhi government implemented a pioneering pilot project towards reduction of citywide pollution. Italian firm SystemLife installed a massive outdoor air filtration system at Palika Bazaar in the heart of Connaught Place. This heavy equipment was used to suck pollutants from Delhi's smog-choked air. According to SystemLife, the unit purifies 360,000 cubic metres of air each day. That's enough to provide fresh air to 18,000 residents for a day. The unit is effective within a radius of half a kilometre. SystemLife felt that seven machines could significantly reduce air pollution levels for the entire Connaught Place. We shall explore a bit further in this chapter how this concept can be used to combat citywide pollution.

The Problem of Scale

In India, the problem of enforcing compliance with vehicular pollution laws is fundamentally one of scale. In a city like Delhi, for instance, with roughly 55,00,000 registered vehicles, to expect the police to physically check each and every car is virtually impossible.[26]

Let us assume that the government deploys 500 policemen divided into 250 teams to check vehicles in Delhi for valid PUC certificates. On an average, it would take each team at least 15 minutes to diligently check a single car, making it possible to check four cars per hour and approximately 20 cars a day – based on 60% efficiency during an average 8-hour work day. This would mean 5,000 cars checked in a single day (by 250 teams) and a maximum of 1,50,000 cars checked every month, which is less than 3% of the total vehicular population of Delhi. At this rate, it would take the 500 policemen more than 36 months to physically check every car on the road, not taking into account the associated difficulties of re-checking the vehicles or the fact that all vehicles (whether previously checked or not) would require their certificates to be checked every three months.

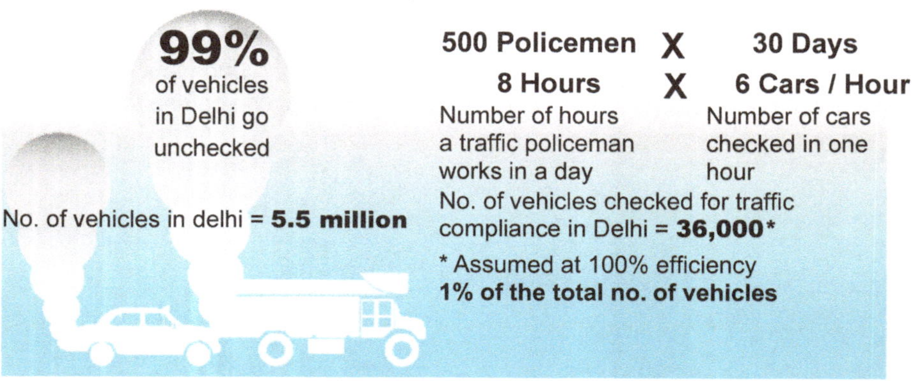

Number of vehicles checked is less than 1% of the total number of vehicles

Looking at the numbers, it becomes clear that the current methodology of enforcing compliance with pollution-control norms is grossly inadequate and there is no way that the government can ensure a high degree of the same in an environment where the citizen is callous and fails to see himself as a stakeholder.

The only solution, therefore, is to adopt a model of enforcement capable of managing scale and which shifts the onus of compliance from the government to the vehicle owner.

NON-COMPLIANT
CAR OWNER

SMART CITIZEN CARD

PUC checking fee not paid
Pollution fine = ₹ 5,000

COMPLIANT
CAR OWNER

SMART CITIZEN CARD

PUC checking fee paid ₹500 / quarter
Pollution fine = ₹0

'We assume your vehicle is non-compliant because we have not received your compliance certificate for the quarter. Your pollution fine will be added to your mobile bill or deducted from your pre-paid smart citizen card.'

'Three corporations wish to extend discount to you as part of corporate social responsibility programme. To avail the reward for being a complaint citizen, please SMS SCC_AWARD 121'

SHIFT IN Responsibilty

GOVERNMENT

The onus of compliance is shifted solely and completely on the vehicle owner.

VEHICLE OWNER

Vehicle owner must ensure compliance certificate is uploaded on his Smart Citizen Card on a quarterly basis by visiting a pollution control centre for a reasonable fee of Rs 500 per quarter, failing which a non-compliance fine of Rs 5,000 will be levi

The Solution

Shifting the Onus of Compliance from the Government to the Vehicle Owner

The idea is to monetize the mandatory pollution-check regime. If the average vehicle owner can spend Rs 5,000 to Rs 10,000 per month on petrol, he can certainly afford to pay Rs 500 to get his pollution checked every quarter. For the owners of two wheelers, the fee could be a function of vehicle size – so a 100 cc bike would pay a much lower fee than a 2000 cc car. In fact the fee could easily become part of the normal cost of maintaining a vehicle in the city. What this will do is spawn a whole host of pollution-checking agencies including petrol pumps, garages and other independent pollution-control centres along roads or next to taxi stands which will be looking to make Rs 500 for every car they check – the revenue from which could be shared between the agency and the government.

What the model requires, in the first instance, is legislation that makes it mandatory for all vehicle owners to maintain a minimum balance of Rs 5,000 on their Smart Citizen Cards as part of their compliance with pollution-control norms and further, to pay Rs 500 to get their cars pollution-checked every quarter by an authorized agency. If the owner fails to get his vehicle checked, a default penalty of Rs 5,000 is automatically deducted from the vehicle's Smart Citizen Card. For the compliant vehicle owner, therefore, who has his car checked every quarter, the cost of compliance is a mere Rs 500 per quarter. But for the non-compliant vehicle owner who neglects to get his car checked, whether intentionally or unintentionally, the cost of non-compliance is the penalty of Rs 5,000 along with the denial of many other privileges that the Smart Citizen Card has to offer.

In this case, the Smart Citizen Card functions as a sort of pre-paid Pollution Super Cop, pushing the vehicle owner to get his car checked and shifting the onus of compliance from the policing agency to the citizen who becomes negatively incentivized to ignore pollution-control laws.

Smart Citizen Card Model

The Pre-paid Pollution Super Cop

The Smart Citizen Card Model or the Pre-paid Pollution Super Cop enables a 100% pollution-check regime by making it possible to hold drivers accountable for every incidence of non-compliance with vehicular pollution norms. The model also envisages a series of incremental penalties for serial defaulters along with incentives for those who conform in the form of credits to Smart Citizen Cards, corporate discounts and other awards and schemes. This combination of charge and reward could be a critical game changer, increasing compliance rates from the existing 2% to 90%, and reducing pollution in Indian cities to a quarter of existing levels.

Consider This

The errant driver of a battered old truck spews clouds of smoke, oblivious to the pollution he causes. He is unconcerned because he knows that the chances of his being caught are low and even if a cop does haul him up, all he has to do is either pay a small bribe or show his national permit, which makes him immune to the jurisdiction of the city policeman. Suddenly, the driver finds the owner of the truck (his boss) insisting that he get the vehicle pollution-checked every 3 months. The owner, newly sensitized to pollution laws after a hefty charge was deducted from his Smart Citizen Card, puts pressure on the driver to get the check done, threatening to deduct the fine from his salary if he doesn't.

Invertonomics

Inverting the Problem into an Opportunity

The Pre-paid Pollution Super Cop offers the opportunity to create an integrated approach to the restoration of air quality in Indian cities. While, on the one hand, it helps to monitor the pollution levels of every vehicle on the road, on the other, it makes it possible to generate substantial revenue that can be used towards the mitigation of the ill-effects of vehicular pollution on the environment.

Revenue Model

Let us assume that of the 55,00,000 car owners in Delhi, 80% are non-compliant with the pollution-check regime in the first year. The level of non-compliance is likely to be very high in the first year and therefore, the number of citizens paying the penalty of Rs 5,000 will be much higher than those paying the Rs 500 fee. The operator of the Pre-paid Pollution Super Cop Model thus collects fines from Delhi's 44,00,000 non-compliant vehicle owners – a sum that amounts to Rs 8,800 crore. The pollution check agencies in turn generate an additional revenue of Rs 220 crore from pollution checks conducted on the remaining 11,00,000 compliant vehicles, bringing the total to a sum of Rs 9,020 crore per year for the city of Delhi alone. Across all major cities of India, this figure could be as high as 10 or 20 times the amount, resulting in a turnover of Rs 90,200 crore to Rs 1,80,400 crore. This could be used for forestation at a phenomenal scale and for other active interventions intended to mitigate the ill effects of vehicular pollution in India cities.[27] This could include the establishment of an innovative city-wide air purification infrastructure consisting of a series of air purification pillars installed along all major highways and roads.

The Money Trail

YEAR 1

Consider quarterly cost from non-compliant users

No. of Vehicles	Quartely Amount	% of Non-compliance
5.5 million	**5,000 pollution fines per quarter** SMART CITIZEN CARD	**80% Non-compliance**

X **4** (yearly) X **10** (nationally)

Total cost incurred from defaulters = **₹88,000 crore** **A**

YEAR 1

Consider quarterly cost from compliant users

No. of Vehicles	Quartely Amount	% of Non-compliance
5.5 million	**500 pollution fines per quarter** SMART CITIZEN CARD	**20% Compliance**

X **4** (yearly) X **10** (nationally)

Total cost incurred from Smart Card Users = **₹2,200 crore** **B**

THE REVENUE POTENTIAL

YEAR 2

Consider quarterly cost from non-compliant users

No. of Vehicles	Quartely Amount	% of Non-compliance
5.5 million	**5000 pollution fines per quarter** SMART CITIZEN CARD	**10% Non-compliance**

X **4** (yearly) X **10** (nationally)

Total cost incurred from defaulters= **₹11,000 crores** (C)

YEAR 2

Consider quarterly cost from compliant users

No. of Vehicles	Quartely Amount	% of Non-compliance
5.5 million	**500 pollution fines per quarter** SMART CITIZEN CARD	**90% Compliance**

X **4** (yearly) X **10** (nationally)

Total cost incurred from Smart Card Users= **₹9,900 crores** (D)

A + B YEAR 1

₹90,200 crore

C + D YEAR 2

₹90,200 crore

The Modern Day Tree

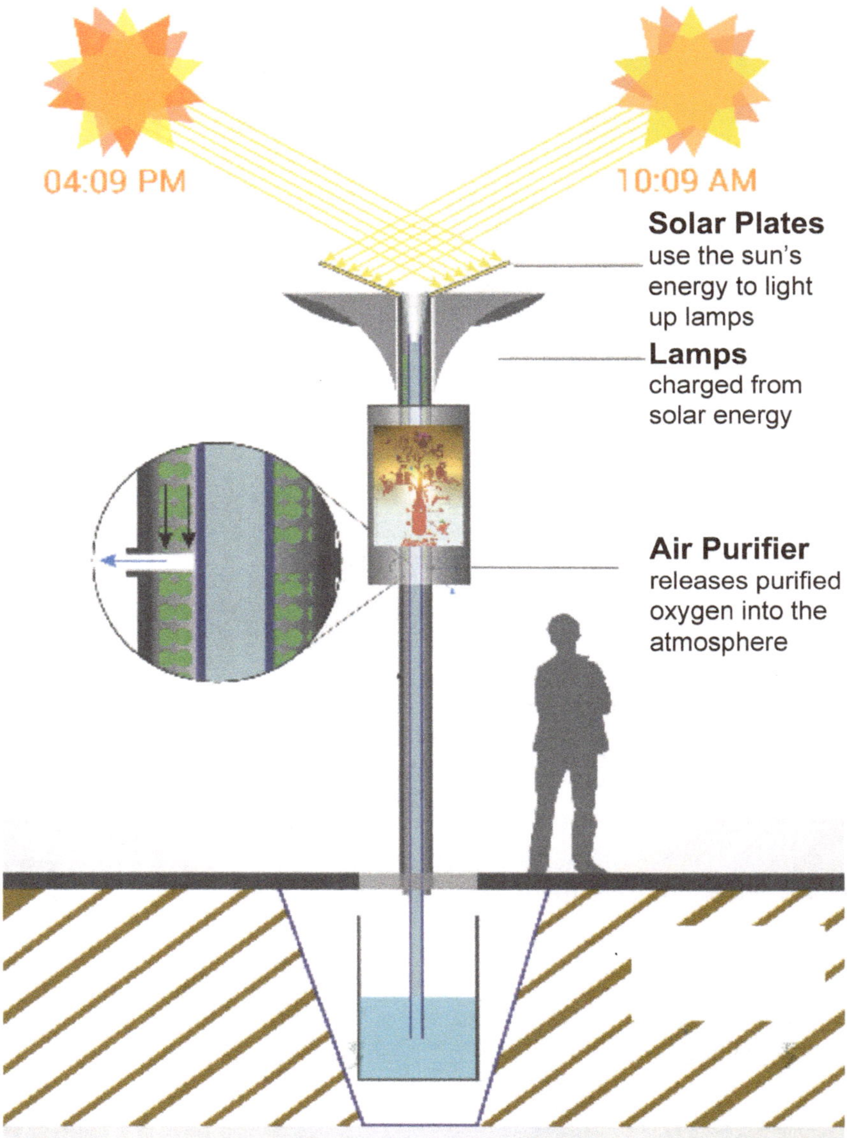

The Air Purification Pillar

The air purification pillar is a unique multi-functional device. It consists of an external air suction assembly (a fan motor with a rotating shaft) installed on a pole with a stainless steel tank at its base. The suction assembly uses a solar battery to draw in polluted air and pipe it to the steel tank at its base. In the tank, a pump circulates the air through water, charcoal or another filtering medium to rid it of impurities and then pumps it back out into the atmosphere through a perforated outlet at the top of the pole. To save street space and allow for the free movement of pedestrians on pavements, the pillar also functions as a solar-powered streetlight with a dustbin and spittoon at its base and a large advertisement panel in between. The latter is intended for the display of print advertisements, the revenue from which can be potentially used to fund the device.

Think of it as a modern-day tree – taking in polluted air and pumping back clean pure air in – a sort of mechanical photosynthesis. Now the air purification pillar becomes a supplement to forestation and the Forest Department may prescribe the following measure: every time you cut down a tree to make way for a new road or building, not only will you have to plant ten new trees to replace it, you will also have to pay for the installation of two air purification pillars in the same location.

The government could choose to fund and manage this air-purification infrastructure with the money trail generated by the Smart Citizen Card Model, from directly selling advertising space on pillars to consumers or from revenues generated by an excess mileage cess levied on vehicles travelling long distances (to encourage the use of public transport). However, based on the argument articulated in the case of the Honking Model, it would be far more pragmatic to weave a separate economic opportunity around the infrastructure to ensure its sustenance and operational efficiency.[28] Here again, a model is created that allows for a public–private partnership with the government auctioning and issuing licenses to private enterprise to install, manage and maintain air purification pillars in particular geographic areas and to profit from selling or renting advertising space on each pillar. Delhi, for instance, could be divided into three 'Air Zones' and licenses issued separately for each one, enabling the creation of a certain competitive environment in terms of pricing, efficiency and equity.

Stakeholders

In conclusion, therefore, the government as primary stakeholder plays the role of legislator and cause agent, bringing in private enterprise to ensure the enforcement of vehicular pollution laws in place of the police. The result is that instead of the police wasting their time checking cars for pollution, they are freed up to enforce the law and secure the average citizen of the city. The pollution-checking centre as third-party agency becomes an additional stakeholder who audits as well as maintains all vehicular pollution records and provides other aids and technologies that can be deployed to mitigate vehicular pollution. Pollution-checking centres would now become profit centres.

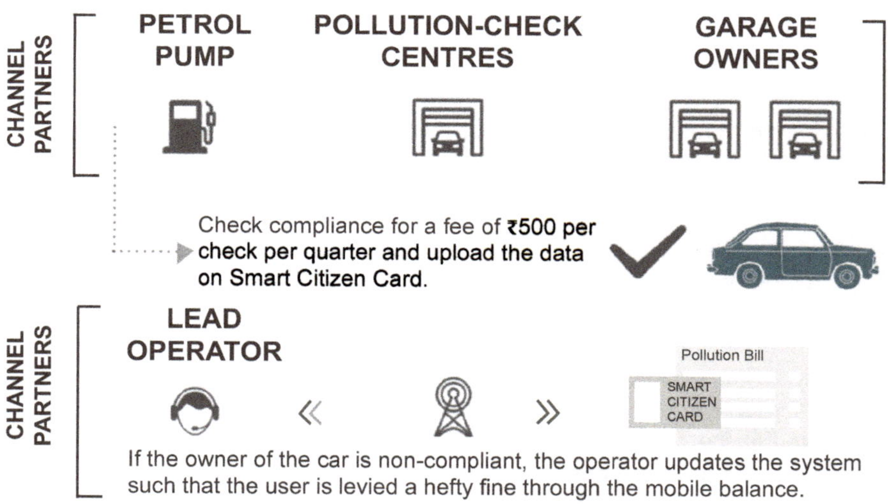

The fourth and final stakeholder is the citizen, who becomes actively engaged and finally sees himself as a dynamic participant in the vehicular pollution ecosystem resulting in a paradigm shift in the relationship that he has with the damage he is causing to the environment.

The problem of vehicle-based air pollution is inverted into an economic opportunity and using invertonomics, the new ecosystem shall be able to handle the mammoth scale of the problem, potentially reduce non-compliance to under 10% and generate ₹20,000 crore anuually for the government.

The Smart Citizen Card again helps in surmounting the challenge of mammoth scale.

Read on to see how we propose to solve the problem of traffic compliance.

Chapter 3

TRAFFIC COMPLIANCE

12,56,600

people killed in 2009
due to road accidents

Introduction

Defensive Driving

In India, drivers make their own rules. Vehicles veer recklessly between lanes, jump red lights, disregard speed limits and stop without warning, often in the middle of the road. Traffic is chaotic, with buses and cars packed bumper-to-bumper and side-to-side with two- and three-wheelers wedged into every possible space in between.

Overtaking is aggressive and threatening, vehicles zip past from every conceivable direction and it is not unusual to see cars climb onto and drive along the pavement or stop abruptly so the driver can open his door and spit in the middle of the road. The idea is to get to your destination as quickly as possible with little regard for life, limb or law – not really driving but simply aiming the car in the right direction.

The Problem

The Severity of Non-compliance – The Price We Pay

In Indian cities, compliance with traffic rules is alarmingly low, resulting in the highest rate of traffic casualties in the world. More than 7 million Indians are victims of traffic accidents every year, suffering from simple or grievous injuries to death due to poor infrastructure and dangerous driving habits. More disturbingly, most of those who suffer are from the most vulnerable group of road users – pedestrians, cyclists and motorcyclists.[29]

Apart from the obvious considerations for safety, poor compliance with traffic rules (specifically the absence of lane driving) adversely affects capacity and performance of the road network. Capacity, defined as the rate at which vehicles can be reasonably expected to traverse a specific section of a road at a given time, under prevailing traffic conditions, is highly influenced by driver behaviour. In India, where traffic is indisciplined and compliance with traffic rules is low, capacity of the road network is considerably lowered leading to congested roads, unreliable travel times and a loss of valuable man-hours.

As more and more people find themselves in a hurry to reach their destination, unreliability of the road network becomes a substantial source of anger and frustration for road users. Add to this the increasing number of vehicles jostling for limited space on congested roads, prolonged periods spent driving in chaotic traffic and drivers taking far too many liberties with traffic. The result is rising anger levels and abnormally aggressive driver behaviour set amidst pressure-cooker-like traffic conditions, setting the stage for untoward incidents, violence and road rage.

What Is Causing the Problem?

I. The deliberately delinquent driver, who is casual about following legally prohibited or socially accepted codes of traffic behaviour, and thus puts both himself and others on the road in danger because he knows that the likelihood of being caught is low.

II. The ill-informed driver, who is unaware of even simple traffic rules due to poor training, corrupt license-issuing authorities and easily manipulated entry-level testing. In India, the preparedness of the average driver to be roadworthy is poor. Driving schools teach only basic maneuvering skills while on-road rules and the nuances and technical aspects of vehicles and driving are completely omitted from the curriculum. In fact, most schools openly flout the law, operating without proper facilities, classrooms or even a trained faculty. There is also almost no formal training for drivers of motorized two-wheelers based on the misconception that since they have graduated from bicycles, they do not require instructions, and very few driving schools exist for the heavy motor vehicle segment, often the most grievous offenders on the road. Unlike Western countries, where testing is very stringent and you can fail a driving test for something as simple as not parking within a line, in India, the license to drive is equivalent to the driver's ability to move the car backwards and forwards at a certain speed. Poor testing procedures are easily circumvented and fail to take the operating environment into account, making no distinction between the ability to drive in a field and a congested city, leaving drivers fundamentally unprepared to deal with the volume and scale of traffic on city roads.

III. In the absence of traffic engineering, the road infrastructure is often unprepared for the scale and volume of traffic, creating an operating environment that is not conducive to traffic compliance. The lack of lay-bys for bus stops, for instance, often constricts or stops traffic in the slow lane and causes confusion when drivers are forced to abruptly switch lanes to avoid getting caught behind buses at stops.

The lack of traffic engineering also means that the road network is not designed to accommodate the needs of all those who use it. Roadway modifications that include widening streets, adding lanes and other traffic solutions to increase vehicular efficiency are often not properly considered and fail to take pedestrian safety into account.

What Is the Police Doing about the Problem?

In an attempt to streamline traffic in Indian cities, the police have launched sporadic 'Zero Tolerance' campaigns with the objective of strictly enforcing traffic regulations.[30] As part of the campaign, the police have typically focused on the enforcement of simple rules such as traffic signal compliance, mobile phone usage, speeding and parking on zebra crossings by deploying the use of extra force to keep a tab on road users and send a strong message to violators. However, these measures are inclined to run out of steam given the limitations of physical policing and its inability to deal with the scale of traffic in Indian cities.

The state is also trying to bring about change by laying stress on road-user awareness through traffic schools, regular advertisements, interactions on social media and other education-based intervention measures aimed at reducing the incidence of recurring violations. As part of one such intercession measure, traffic violators in Gurgaon are required to attend a 90-minute class on traffic rules and safe driving to be let off the hook. The police say that this has helped reduce repeat traffic offences in the area.

Vikas, a resident of Gurgaon, believes, however, that such measures are counter productive and will result in a lesser number of challans being issued, as offenders choose to avoid the inconvenience of the procedure and pay a bribe to get away with the offence. On his refusing to pay cash after jumping a red light, Vikas was slapped with an additional challan for dangerous driving and asked to report to the Road Safety Knowledge Centre in Gurgaon. Vikas says he had to go to the centre three times before he could see the safety movie and pay the challan. 'Most people being made to watch the movie were asleep,' he says. 'Do you think I will opt for a challan again if I get in the same situation?'[31]

In an effort to tighten the noose around habitual traffic offenders, the government has approved a five-fold increase in fines under the Motor Vehicles Act and a substantial hike in compensation to accident victims.[32] These changes have been incorporated in the Motor Vehicles Act through an amendment.

While the police say that the increase in fines will act as a deterrent to traffic violators, people fear that higher fines will translate into heftier bribes for the police. 'It is good that the government is coming up with harsher punishments for traffic offenders. But, at the same time, corruption and misuse of power by traffic police should be checked,' says Ratika Dang, a Delhi-based interior designer.

The cabinet approval for hike in traffic fines has come at a time when Delhi is gearing up for two major technological advancements in traffic management – the e-challan system and the installation of night-vision cameras across the national capital.[33] While cops say enforcement of the hike will be made easier, thanks to the two technological changes, the failure of the Intelligent Traffic System (ITS) installed by the Pune Municipal Organization indicates otherwise. The system with 120 closed circuit television (CCTV) cameras positioned all over the city is beset by connectivity issues due to lack of proper maintenance. Authorities are able to monitor the footage of only five of the cameras, the only ones which remain operational.[34]

In a recent development, the Rajya Sabha has given its assent for Motor Vehicles (Amendment) Bill 2019. The amendment aims to impact road safety by laying much higher fines. In a significant way, it proposes that in case of offenses committed by juveniles, the guardian / owner shall be deemed guilty. Juveniles shall be tried under the Juvenile Justice Act and registration of motor vehicle will be cancelled.

Moving towards a Solution

Rules of the Operating Environment

Every operating environment must have a set of rules, which all entities within that environment comply with in order to have a coherent synergistic coexistence.

Consider the operating environment for commercial aviation. The industry keeps more than 3 million aircraft in the air, with each airline administering policies and procedures necessary to preserve passenger and plane safety; maintain inspection and repair capabilities and provide flight operations, sales, marketing and customer services, including pricing, scheduling, advertising, ticket and cargo sales, reservations and food. The reason this complex system of processes works efficiently is that the actions of all personnel involved directly or indirectly in producing or selling an airline's services – the mechanics who maintain the planes; the pilots who fly them; the flight attendants who serve passengers; reservation clerks, airport check-in and gate personnel; ramp-service agents and security guards – are aligned with the rules of the industry's operating environment. Even travellers are obliged to follow the rules of airline and airport safety by arriving two hours ahead of flights, restricting hand baggage and complying with security procedures, though it may cause them some inconvenience.

It can be said of everything Indian that we choose not to state, or define clearly, the rules of the operating environment. Consider something as simple as holidays. There is such great difference of opinion on the number of public holidays and when they fall that it is impossible for any intelligent person to remember them. And even if they do, the pundits of the community ensure that there is confusion till the eleventh hour as to when the holiday actually falls.

The Indian traffic ecosystem, with its multitude modes of transport (Delhi has over 30 different kinds of vehicles on the road) and lack of standardized traffic control, represents the typical paradigm of a chaotic operating environment.

Any operating environment consists essentially of three elements – the physical infrastructure, the people participating in that operating environment and the processes that actually link them together. If we were to look at the operating environment in the context of traffic, these would translate into an ambiguity in, or a poor understanding of, traffic rules, and hence a fundamental unpreparedness for the driving environment and a below-par road infrastructure which is itself designed on the assumption of a low level of compliance. The result is compromised safety resulting in the highest rate of traffic casualties in the world, congestion leading to reduced capacity and inconvenience in the form of poor predictability of travel times, loss of valuable man-hours and increased driver aggression .

The first step towards restoring order is, therefore, to identify and address the different elements of the Indian traffic operating environment and align them towards a synchronized goal to achieve the three desirable parameters of the goodness of traffic – safety, capacity and convenience.

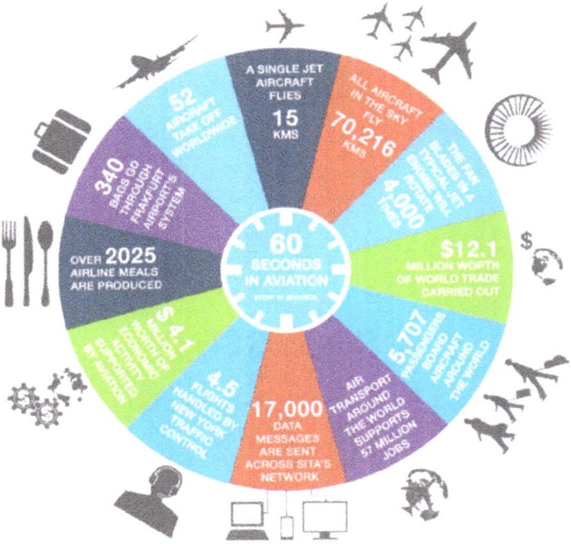

THE OPERATING ENVIRONMENT OF AIR TRAVEL

The Operating Environment of Traffic

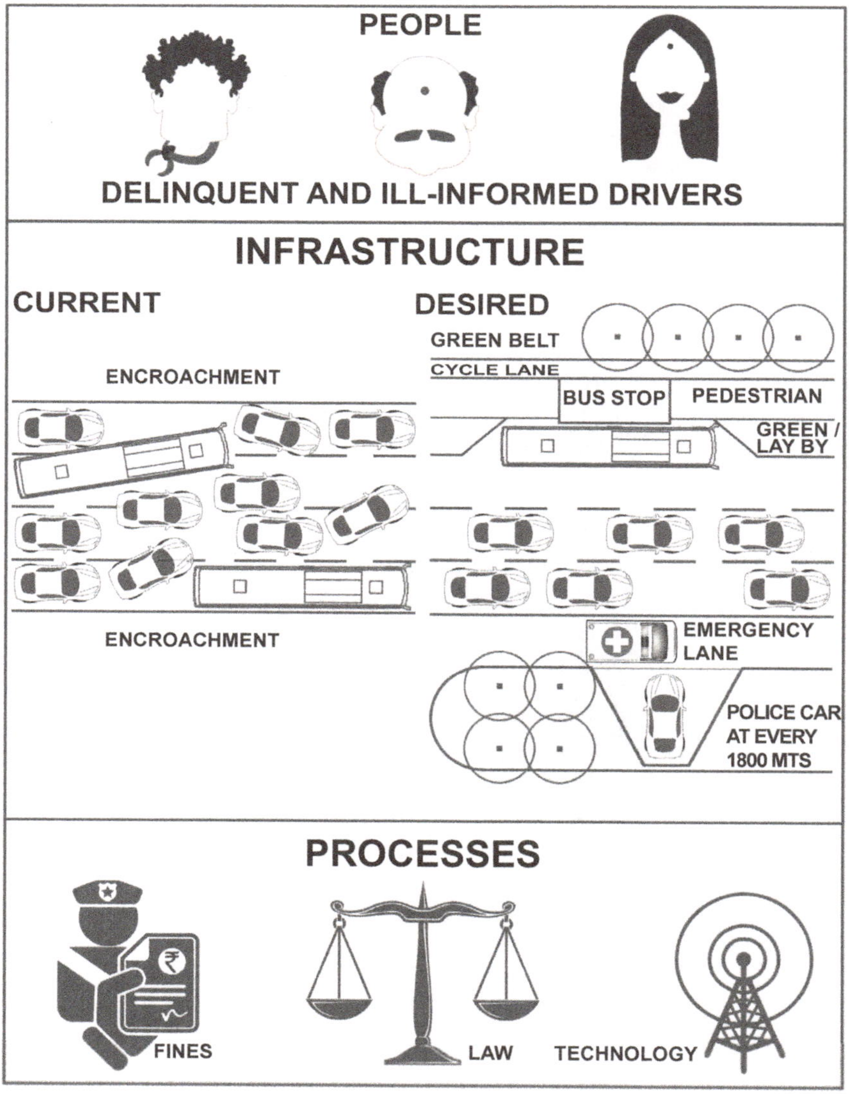

Aligning the Deliberately Delinquent Driver

Effective Enforcement – Key Component of Traffic Management

Effective enforcement of traffic rules is the most important requirement for traffic management. We can have the best rules of the road, but if these are not enforced effectively, there will continue to be an increase in traffic violations and fatal accidents.

Consider This

A traffic study carried out in the capital puts the number of average daily prosecutions by the Delhi Traffic Police at only 11,000 in comparison to the staggering 146 million traffic violations committed in the city every day – a prosecution rate of barely 0.007%.[35]

In India, while traffic violations such as drunken driving, jumping traffic lights and overspeeding attract stringent punishment and fines under the Motor Vehicles Act, enforcement of rules is abysmal. The sheer scale of traffic on city roads renders traditional physical policing, currently used to enforce compliance, both impossible and ineffective. In a situation such as this, increasing the physical number of policemen on the road makes only a marginal difference and tends, instead, to increase inefficiency and corruption by intensifying the possibility of physical interface between the derelict traffic cop and the offending driver.

Technology to Manage Scale

Modern technology has the ability to manage scale, speed and efficiency in ways that accomplish tasks faster and more effectively. Consider the numbers. Facebook uses modern computing to effectively manage more than 1 billion active users every month.[36] Similarly, American multinational Google is estimated to process over 3 billion search requests and about 24 petabytes of user-generated data every day.[37]

According to figures published in the *Delhi Statistical Handbook* released by the government's department of economics and statistics, the city has more mobile connections than people. Data shows that as of 31 March 2010, Delhi had a massive 2.83 crore mobile phone connections divided among a population of just 1.82 crore.[38] And while technology makes it possible for these connections to be monitored and managed with a degree of efficiency hitherto unknown in India, when it comes to traffic, even 10,000 policemen are unable to handle the traffic on the city's roads. Here, the difference lies not in the degree of efficiency between the average Delhi traffic policeman and his telecom counterpart but in the technology they deploy – while modern computing is used to support the telecom employee, the cop must rely on his baton to get the job done.

Countries in the West are increasingly using technology-based intelligent traffic solutions to redefine their urban traffic-management systems. At the heart of this technology is the ability to manage a large number of vehicles using integrated systems, techniques and tools. In India, although there have been technological improvements in almost every field, traffic-management technologies have remained primitive, continuing to depend on outdated models of physical policing and random checking.

As humans of the 21st century, we have the technology to make the management of any number of vehicles more than easy. The question to ask is why we (in India) are continuing to fly the Fokker of traffic-management methodologies when the rest of the world is flying Boeing 787 Dreamliner.

1,322 TRAFFIC VIOLATIONS IN 25 SECONDS

In a pointer to an overwhelming trend across the city, video footage of a small stretch at Delhi's Dhaula Kuan during the morning rush hour has revealed more than 1,322 traffic violations committed in 25 seconds. The footage, shot by the Institute for Road Traffic Education (IRTE), shows how almost all commuters violated traffic norms, turning the 4-lane carriageway into a 12-lane free-for-all with cars, two-wheelers, trucks and buses locked in a mad frenzy to get ahead. The video was screened at a road safety convention organized by the International Road Federation (IRF), where it left transport and safety experts (from India and abroad) stumped on how to deal with Delhi's traffic woes. Some observed that even best practices and technologies such as CCTV surveillance, which had been successful in other parts of the world, might fail to control traffic in Indian cities due to the sheer number of violations and the single-lane roads having to accommodate as many as three and four lanes of vehicles.[39]

In the context of India's roads – indisputably the most chaotic in the world – the only possible solution, therefore, is to find a strategic technology model capable of managing scale, which makes it possible to detect and penalize every traffic violation committed on the road, without the need for physical policing.

Some Might Argue

A smart technological solution that only engineers would understand is unlikely to be implementable in the Indian context. To this we submit that the solution being suggested here, although based on smart technologies, is very simple to understand and implement. Just read the next five pages

Consider:

Mrs Sharma from Tilak Nagar was busy chatting on her cell phone in the car, completely oblivious to her delinquent driver who was busy breaking every traffic rule it was possible to break, including jumping red lights and snake-driving to make sure Mrs Sharma reached her kitty on time, and honking to impress her with his efficiency.

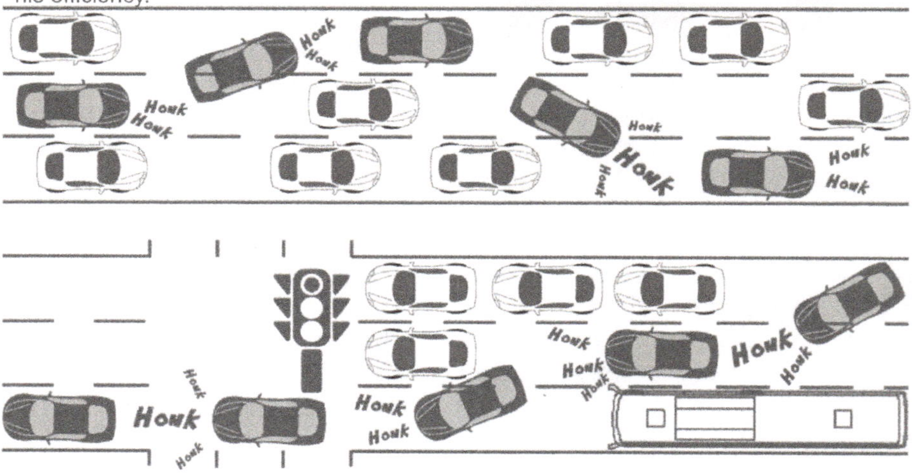

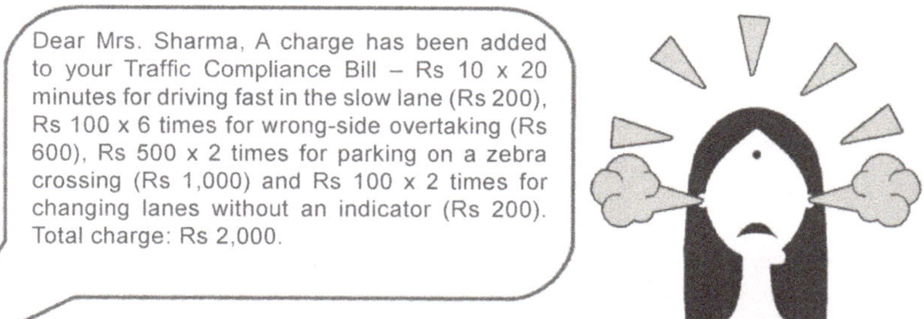

Now, Mrs Sharma sits up and watches her driver like a hawk because every time he breaks a traffic rule, she receives an SMS informing her of each traffic violation. Even before she had reached her kitty party where she had to shell out money for the lunch, her Traffic Compliance Bill had gone from Rs 1,936 to Rs 3,936, a whopping increase of Rs 2,000 in the space of one car journey.

The Solution

The Smart Citizen Card Model

The Smart Citizen Card Model (introduced in the context of controlling honking behaviour) offers an optimal and operationally effective system to monitor the individual traffic behaviour of every vehicle on the road and holds drivers accountable for every instance of rule violation.[40]

In its new avatar, the Smart Citizen Card Model uses Kinetic Coordinate Surveillance Technology to map the exact coordinates of every vehicle on the road and to track its movement (forwards, backwards and lateral), speed and distance from other vehicles through a set of five SIM cards installed in each corner and at the centre of every vehicle.

As an extension of the Honking Model, each Kinetic Card uses satellite-based navigation technologies or GPS to 'measure' movement (as opposed to honks) and therefore, to detect every traffic violation committed by the driver. A series of zigzag movements for instance would indicate snake driving while location and time information on vehicles could easily be used to detect speeding, wrong-side overtaking, jumping red lights or parking on zebra crossings.

Supplemented by a network of traffic cameras and sensors on arterial roads and highways – to corroborate data from the Kinetic Cards and detect secondary traffic offences such as drunk driving, mobile phone usage or driving without a seatbelt, the Smart Citizen Card Model makes it possible to monitor and record every traffic violation committed by the driver and transmit the information to receiving towers managed by operators authorized to charge for violations in the form of periodic Traffic Compliance Bills delivered directly to violators, as part of cell phone bills!

The Smart Citizen Card Model has the potential to detect and fine for every single one of the 1,322 traffic-rule violations caught on tape without the need for a single traffic policeman, thus revolutionizing traffic compliance, bringing about a paradigm shift in the management of traffic in Indian cities and fundamentally impacting the safety, capacity and convenience of the road network.

TECHNOLOGY TO MANAGE SCALE

KINETIC CO-ORDINATE SURVEILLANCE TECHNOLOGY

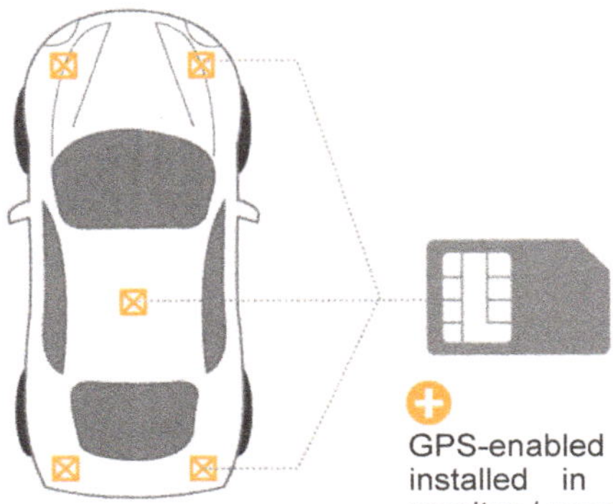

GPS-enabled SIM cards installed in each vehicle monitor / record every traffic violation commited by the driver.

Sensors installed at tamper-proof location in the cars monitor horizontal movement using sophisticated co-ordinate technology, to check for compliance, such as lane-driving and speed, and transmit data to the central monitoring station.

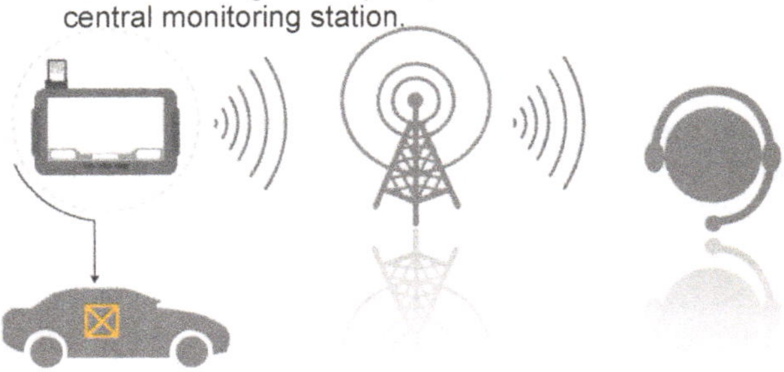

Central Monitoring Station generates real-time traffic violation statements, without error or prejudice, for millions of cars concurrently.

DOWN
WITH THE
BATON

KINETIC CO-ORDINATE SURVEILLANCE TECHNOLOGY

TRANSPARENCY
Reduces dependence on the police and other government personnel, and employs technology to convert enforcement to a rule-based (impersonal) transaction.

DOWN WITH THE BATON

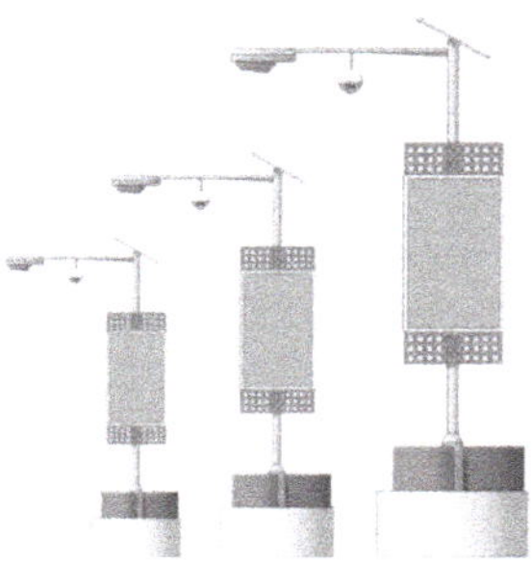

TRAFFIC CAMERAS
Installation of a system of traffic cameras and sensors on arterial roads and highways to supplement and corroborate data collected from the Smart Citizen Card.

We have observed that you are jumping too many red lights in the morning.

We assume that you are running late. How about getting up a little early?

You can also opt for our customized car wake-up service.

TRAFFIC TUTOR
Surrogate tutor is a means of informing drivers of the desired parameters of traffic behaviour.

Traffic Compliance Bill

The Traffic Tutor

While the Smart Citizen Card Model directly addresses the issue of the deliberately delinquent driver by enforcing compliance with traffic rules, the model also provides an optimal means of educating ill-informed drivers through the generation of periodic Traffic Compliance Bills specifying not only how and when a traffic rule was violated but also stating the rule itself for the information of the offender.

Research has shown that educational intervention can substantially reduce the rate of recurring violations. And while there is an assumption that anyone who has a driver's license is aware of traffic rules, there is no mechanism to check that drivers actually remember and follow them on a regular basis.

Transparency Becomes the Tutor

The Blood Test Report

Transparency in blood tests and home blood-pressure measuring tools have revolutionized health management. There was a time when only doctors could read blood-test reports. Now, thanks to a simple thing called the reference range, it is possible to quickly and easily understand a blood report without a medical degree. Often, the lab will include a small explanatory note at the bottom that explains the person's result in greater detail, or the need to corroborate it with further testing, allowing the patient to understand his own diagnosis without the intervention of a medical professional. Like the blood-test report, the Traffic Compliance Bill uses transparency to inform the offending driver, stating the violation (result) and explaining it in the context of the rule violated (reference range) in an attempt to improve understanding of the road environment and influence the offender to avoid committing further traffic violations.

The Traffic Compliance Bill, therefore, not only measures compliance and levies fines but also acts as a phenomenal surrogate tutor, a means of informing drivers of the desired parameters of driving behaviour.

TRAFFIC COMPLIANCE BILL

सत्यमेव जयते

Oct 2015

Car Number: DL3C A 4X72

To- Mr. I OWN THE ROAD

Traffic offences and fines-		Your Fine	Avg Fine	Best Citizen
Red light jumping	16x1000	16,000	2,000	0
Parked on zebra crossing	7x500	3,500	1,500	0
Wrong side driving	8mins x 2000	1,600	1,800	0
Parking on Pedestrian zone	3 x 5000	15,000	1,600	0
Snake driving	160mins x 100	1,600	1,000	0
Over speeding	200x500	10,000	0	0
Honking	200x1	200	100	0

Total	Rs 63,000	Rs 8,000	Rs 0

Minimum 10,000 to be paid immediately, balance in 60 EMIs.

Your Insurance Rating - 1.5/10

Your Position- Bottom 10%

Kindly pay before due date to avoid suspension of drivers license.

Non-payment could adversely impact your insurance premium, and a surcharge will be added to your petrol bill.

Yours sincerely.

N.K Radhaswamy

Traffic department- New Delhi

Transparency

As Dr Prakash D. Haveripeth notes in his paper 'Corruption in India and Its Combating', 'for the average person, a bribe is the most obvious evidence of corruption. In many countries, applicants for driver's licenses, building permits and birth certificates have learned to expect a surcharge from civil servants in order to obtain these documents.'[41] Similarly, the practice of paying money to police officers when a traffic offence has been committed is almost a norm. As noted, however, the consequences of corruption are more pervasive and profound than these bribes suggest. While systemic corruption undermines the credibility and authority of democratic institutions and counteracts good governance, what really taints the moral fabric of a nation is when the average citizen is able to circumvent the law and be a part of that corrupt transaction.

In India, drivers are fined for non-compliance with traffic rules only if a traffic policeman physically sees them violating the rule or in rare cases when a traffic camera records the misdemeanour. In the subsequent interaction between traffic cop and driver, even the most law-abiding citizen may choose to take the easy way out and pay a small bribe to get away with the offence. Bribery in these instances may be used to ensure that the offender escapes a stiffer penalty (a Rs 100 bribe is requested when the alternative is to pay a legitimate fine of five-to-ten times that amount). On a grand scale, the effect of corruption is that money intended for maintenance of roads and provision of traffic facilities is diverted for private gain. On an immediate level, when corrupt officials allow drivers who speed or who are driving vehicles that are not roadworthy to proceed with their journey, the consequences for other users are potentially disastrous. A breakdown of public trust in the integrity of traffic officials is also likely to be the result, leading to an increase in lawlessness among road users.

Corruption is a collusive mechanism; the greater the interaction between government officials and the public, the higher the rate of corruption will be. The solution is to introduce technology to separate the two parties from each other or to 'remove human interface'.

Research conducted by the Centre for Media Studies (Jawaharlal Nehru University) has shown that levels of corruption in the Indian Railways have fallen significantly since the computerization of the ticketing system.

R. Vaidyanathan succinctly writes in his blog *Bharatkalyan97*:

> anyone who has travelled in trains in the past will recollect the ubiquitous ticket collector who was the ultimate arbiter of seats and berths – at a price. In those days, recommendations to appoint a particular person as ticket examiner at major stations used to sometimes come from cabinet ministers in Delhi because it was a 'lucrative' position. But after the computerization of rail bookings, the role of railway minions has become minimal since even wait-listed tickets are upgraded through the system.[42]

By digitizing the enforcement of traffic rules and minimizing direct contact between the traffic cop and the offending driver, the Smart Citizen Card Model automatically reduces opportunities for corruption in the traffic ecosystem.

The model not only reduces dependence on the police and other government personnel, freeing them to concentrate on other issues of law and order, but also uses technology to convert enforcement to a rule-based (impersonal) transaction, eliminating position and power from the equation, which is often used by offenders to wiggle out of fines or to intimidate the police.

The Smart Citizen Card Model also brings about a certain institutionalization of transparency and accountability by means of the Traffic Compliance Bill, which provides an itemized account of all traffic violations, supplemented with photographs from traffic cameras, and giving drivers the opportunity to challenge a fine in case it is unfair or wrong.

Invertonomics

Inverting the Problem into an Opportunity

The underscore of the Smart Citizen Card Model is to control the problem (traffic violation) by monetizing it and inverting it into an opportunity for profit (money) and greater compliance, enabling private enterprise to manage the solution (mechanism of measurement) and drive it for revenue.[43]

The model allows for the government to auction operational licenses to private operators or concessionaires, authorizing them to install, manage and maintain telecom towers, issue Kinetic Cards and profit from the collection of fines for traffic offences.

Since traffic violations already attract stringent fines under the Motor Vehicles Act, it becomes necessary to find an alternate means of weaving an economic opportunity around traffic compliance to sustain the model and provide for the creation of an enduring, operationally efficient 'mechanism of measurement'.[44]

The question is whether this means that the average citizen on the road ends up paying heavier traffic fines to finance the measuring mechanism.

Consider This

In 2010, the collection of traffic fines in Nagpur increased by Rs 43,52,900 from the year before. Till 30 June of that year, a staggering 1,62,607 cases were registered against traffic violators and Rs 2,16,48,200 was recovered in fines.

Re-monetizing Traffic Violations

Cases of traffic violation are on the rise and so is the collection of fines, but statistics show that this is just the tip of the iceberg and that the number of cases registered cover less than 10% of the actual violations.[45]

The state suffers substantial losses in traffic-fine income as a result of poor enforcement of rules. In the current environment, many offenders fall through the net since it is simply not possible to check every driver via physical policing. Of those who do get caught, many end up bribing the cop with public funds that end up in the policeman's pocket rather than the government's coffers.

By providing a means of achieving near-perfect enforcement of traffic rules (75–90%, allowing for lacunae in the exigencies of collection), the Smart Citizen Card Model substantially increases income from traffic fines, in effect, remonetizing traffic violations and inverting them into an opportunity for profit. The premise being that since the purpose of the state is not to profit from traffic offences, but rather to use fines and other punitive measures to reduce traffic violations and create a positive road culture, a percentage of revenue from fines collected could be diverted to private operators for the management and control of traffic violations. Here, even if compliance levels remain the same, the technology makes it possible to check every offender each time he violates a traffic rule so that even if the private operator takes 50% of all recovered fines, the government still pockets substantially more than it did before, with its share of revenues (and some portion of the operator's) available for use in traffic-cop welfare, the installation of security cameras and sensors, and the maintenance and upgradation of the road network.

INFRASTRUCTURE
SECURITY CAMERAS
EMS
we save lives
EMERGENCY MEDICAL SERVICES
DIAL EMS 367
ACCESS TO EMS
EMS
CENTRAL MEDICAL DISPATCH
ambulance
AMBULANCES
reliance ambulance
PRIVITIZATION OF AMBULANCES
AIR AMBULANCE
CRV
CRASH RESCUE VEHICLES
PARAMEDICS
TRAFFIC COP WELFARE
PEDESTRIAN AND CYCLISTS SAFETY

The Money Trail

The 'Money Trail' allows for funds collected from traffic fines and the sale of Smart Citizen Cards to be ploughed back and used in the upgradation of the road infrastructure such as the construction of arterial roads, highways and bridges to improve links, the expansion of roads to reduce travel time and the establishment of special corridors to facilitate the swift and easy movement of public transport – transforming the Indian road network into one of the best and the most efficient in the world.

What the Money Trail also does is make available funds for the installation of a state-of-the-art, city-wide system of street cameras and sensors to boost safety and security, the establishment of an ultra-modern emergency medical services (EMS) network that will compete with the finest in the world in terms of first-responder ambulances, paramedics and state-of-the-art trauma and specialty care facilities, and the creation of an integrated pedestrian and cyclist fabric to ensure the welfare of the more vulnerable road users – paving the way for a safer and a more secure city.

Paving the Way to a Safer City

Installation of Security Cameras and Sensors

The idea is for the government to make it mandatory for private operators to use part of the money collected from fines and the sale of Kinetic Cards to install and maintain optical cameras and sensors across the city – on all arterial roads and highways. What this will do is support and substantiate the information collected from the Kinetic Cards by providing visual proof of traffic violations and facilitate the detection of criminal offences, making the city one of the most watched in the world and therefore address problems of security in more ways than one can comprehend.

In the current scenario, installing cameras involves large capital expenditure. More significantly, in the absence of proper mechanisms, there is no way to ensure that the cameras remain in working condition. The failure of the Intelligent Traffic System (ITS) installed by the Pune Municipal Corporation is a case in point. A recent compliance report placed before the High Court of Bombay in a public interest litigation (PIL) seeking better implementation of traffic norms reveals that even in Mumbai, only half of the total CCTV cameras installed in various parts of the city to monitor traffic remain functional.[46] The solution is then to use the economic opportunity created by monetizing traffic violations (and, by association, the cameras) to discharge obligations of safety and security for the city, shifting the burden of installing and managing the cameras from the public to the private sector and thus ensuring the creation of a perpetual, operationally efficient, security and surveillance system.[47] The CCTV surveillance is dealt in more detail under the head of 'Civic Cop' later in this chapter.

Used in conjunction with the police and other intelligence and security agencies, cameras and sensors can help prevent crime, ensure VIP safety and secure the city and its citizens in many ways. Cameras can capture images to enable the identification of vehicles and individuals involved in an offence or zoom in on and register individual faces utilizing facial recognition software, which automatically identifies suspects or known criminals from intelligence and police databases. Their precise movements can be tracked by camera from the point of entry into the city, helping thwart potential crimes and terrorist threats as part of a sophisticated 'ring of steel' around the city.

Defense experts say that surveillance cameras also serve as a huge deterrent to crime. A criminal who knows he will be filmed and possibly identified by a surveillance camera will often choose another target or decide not to carry out a planned crime at all.

Emergency Medical Services

With 18 fatalities every hour, India has the highest number of road accident deaths in the world. Of those injured in road mishaps, almost 80% receive no immediate medical care, with 60% dying as a result. Of these casualties, more than 50% can be saved if even basic emergency care is made available to them within the Golden Hour.[48]

The money trail generated by the Smart Citizen Card Model makes it possible to establish a world-class integrated network of emergency medical services around road-accident trauma consisting of advanced tertiary care hospitals at key locations, networked with pre-hospital–care ambulances and supplemented by seamless communication, centralized dispatch and medical direction. The idea is to provide appropriate and safe transport for the injured to a definitive health-care facility within the golden hour and timely diagnosis and treatment by a multidisciplinary team of health care professional – supported by appropriate resources – to diminish or eliminate the risk of death or permanent disability.

> The share of funds available for EMS would likely be to the tune of Rs 5 crore to Rs 20 crore per month, per city, generated entirely from moneys collected from traffic fines.

Privatizing First-Responder Ambulance Services

What the government could do is to make it obligatory for all large multispecialty hospitals to have a minimum of 10 to 20 EMS ambulances available within the circle of the golden hour – close enough that it takes only 60 minutes from the moment of injury to dispatch an ambulance to the scene; transport the victim back to the hospital; summon the appropriate surgical and support staff; and perform the necessary life-saving surgery. What this will do is make the roads and highways substantially safer and also create a self-sustaining emergency medical care ecosystem by generating a new revenue stream for the private hospital – that of the accident victim.

On the assumption that the cost of acquiring a first-responder ambulance is Rs 20 Lakh, amounting to an investment of Rs 3 crore for 15 vehicles; for a Rs 750 crore multi-specialty hospital that typically invests upwards of Rs 20 crore on each state-of-the-art operation theatre, the capital cost of the ambulances becomes a worthwhile investment towards securing future business. For the hospital, each ambulance functions as a mobile marketing executive – bringing in the victims of road accidents and therefore more business for the hospital. Equally, it might be possible for the government to offer private healthcare providers certain tax concession for surgeries and procedures conducted on accident victims rescued by their first responders, or some other linkage could be established to offset the cost of the ambulances and to incentivize private hospitals to become part of an integrated system of dispatch and emergency medical care.

Some Might Argue

Certain indigent persons rescued by the first responders and subsequently treated for their injuries may not be in a position to clear their medical bills. To this we submit that a substantial corpus for insurance can easily be created from the money trail to cover all such expenses.

Telephone Notification

Access to Emergency Medical Services

The first step towards the establishment of an integrated network of medical services is to set up a unified toll-free number for access to the services, reachable from all landlines and mobiles and to install vandal-proof emergency call boxes at every 5 kms on arterial roads and highways. Through these, road users in need of help can communicate with a centralized control room geared to dispatch first-responder ambulances, fire tenders and crash-rescue vehicles to accident sites.

Emergency Medical Dispatch

At the control room, an emergency operator (dispatcher) verifies the caller's location, determines the nature of the emergency, and decides which first response team should be notified and dispatched. To aid in the dispatch process, all first-responder units must be equipped with GPS locators that update the control room every 10 seconds on their position. Specialized dispatch software enables the control room to keep current status on unit as well as incident location, assisting the dispatcher in ranking the closest, most appropriate unit to respond to the call to ensure the shortest possible emergency response time. During emergencies, the dispatcher remains in constant radio communication with emergency units and officers at the scene to coordinate extraction, rescue and relief activities among all emergency personnel – fire, rescue, police and dispatchers.

First Responders – Ambulances

Critical to the safe and appropriate transit of victims to trauma-care facilities is the provision of advanced life-support ambulances (a minimum of four per 10 sq. kms of roads), available to respond to emergency service calls, 24 hours a day, 7 seven days a week.

Safety regulations require that each first-responder ambulance be manned by qualified Emergency Medical Technicians and equipped with state-of-the art pre-hospital emergency machines such as heart defibrillators, intravenous drips, splints, oxygen and drugs to meet the emergent needs of critically injured patients. This includes the deployment of 12 lead ECG with telemetry capabilities to help reduce the diagnostic time frame of cardiac incidents, increasing survival rates for heart attacks.

The primary role of the ambulance crew is to stabilize victims before they are transported to a hospital, in safely and without delay. To this end, all paramedic staff must be qualified to administer first aid and deal with an extensive range of emergencies, including profuse bleeding, crash injuries and cardiac arrests. The crew must also be highly skilled in advanced emergency driving so that they are able to move victims away from the traffic-accident site – as safely as possible – with the ambulance itself providing a safe and clinical working environment whilst allowing for maximum mobility.

Air Medical Transport

Even seconds can count in life-or-death emergencies, underscoring the importance of having an advanced air medical service to transport critically injured patients to trauma or specialty centres. In the case of a road-traffic accident, the air ambulance can land right at the scene of the incident and get the patient to the necessary hospital within a few minutes, thus saving valuable time. After receiving a call, specialized air medical crew must be trained and ready to be airborne within minutes, with each flight staffed around the clock by a trained emergency medical service pilot, nurses and paramedics and the equipment necessary for critical care assessment and treatment in flight.

Extraction from Accident Sites

Crash Rescue Vehicles (CRVs)

In the case of road-traffic accidents, ambulances alone are not sufficient in initiating a post-crash response as victims are often trapped inside the vehicle and need to be extricated with professional tools. In this scenario, rescue and relief operations must be supplemented by versatile crash rescue vehicles (CRVs), manned by trained operators and equipped with hydraulic rescue tools, fire-extinguishing apparatus and road-clearing equipment.

Pedestrian, Cyclist and Women's Safety

While, on the one hand, the Smart Citizen Card Model makes it possible to bring about much greater levels of pedestrian safety due to the effective enforcement of traffic rules, the model's money trail offers an unprecedented opportunity to create an integrated pedestrian and cyclist fabric to ensure the welfare of more vulnerable road users. The model allows for its Kinetic Coordinate Surveillance Technology to be used as an effective source of real-time data for developing and planning best practices to ensure pedestrian safety such as, for instance, the correlation between pedestrian deaths and the absence of red lights, pavements or over-bridges in particular locations.[49]

It also facilitates a safer environment for vulnerable women road users, with cameras and sensors making it easier to identify and serving as a deterrent to pedestrian as well as car-borne harassers and sexual predators.

Smart Citizen Card Model – Other Benefits

Economic Opportunity – Insurance

Auto theft constitutes a huge drain on insurance companies, decreasing their revenues and leading to increased premiums for their customers. The sector is also particularly susceptible to fraud with owners disposing of their vehicles and filing fraudulent theft reports with the police. In such instances, the vehicles are almost never retrieved and the owners end up gaining from both the sale and the insurance settlement.

Consider This

Statistics show that more than 40 vehicles are stolen in Delhi every day. In 2011, 14,668 motor vehicles were stolen in Delhi. According to Delhi Police data, only about 2,957 of these vehicles were recovered.

By making it possible to check the location of any vehicle, the Smart Citizen Card Model assists in reducing the incidence of auto theft and fraud, providing a significant benefit to insurance companies. The model can also support companies in verifying false claims and ascertaining responsibility for road accidents more effectively.

Revenue Model for Insurance Industry

As indirect beneficiaries of the Smart Citizen Card Model, insurance companies may choose to incentivize customers to install Kinetic Cards in their vehicles. Or companies could become potential stakeholders in the model itself, either by participating as shareholders or co-partners with telecom companies or purchasing relevant traffic information from operators, collected in the course of tracking traffic violations – creating an entirely new revenue stream for licensees.

Second-Hand Car Market

The Smart Citizen Card Model makes available the entire pedigree or history of every vehicle on the road, including information on mileage, location, service history and traffic fines, making it impossible to falsify information and bringing in a greater degree of transparency to the sale of used cars.

Benefit to Corporations

Information collected from Kinetic Cards can help large corporations assess the veracity of petrol claims and prevent misuse of fuel allowances (using highly specialized software to compute cost of petrol based on mileage). Data from Kinetic Cards can also be used to confirm if people with touring jobs have reported to sites as claimed or can be used to track delinquent drivers and employees.

Benefit to Taxation Authorities

By linking the purchase of petrol to the Kinetic Cards installed in every vehicle, the Smart Citizen Card Model allows operators to detect and record every petrol transaction, preventing vehicle owners from purchasing petrol in cash or otherwise evading taxation authorities by falsifying petrol expenses. Tax authorities could get an additional handle to be able to ascertain trends in under-reporting of income especially by small businessmen, often the most serious offenders.

Stakeholders

Current Ecosystem

As a powerful, key stakeholder with a high level of influence in the traffic-compliance environment, the government is the ineffective law enforcer resigned to low levels of compliance as a reality for India. In other instances, it is the corrupt functionary accountable for administering poor mechanisms for the dispensation of driving licenses. At a loss for highly efficient methods to resolve issues of traffic compliance, the government chooses to address the problem using outdated and primitive measures such as physical policing and random checking, resulting in low compliance rates and poor enforcement of traffic rules.

Of the multiple stakeholders involved in the traffic-compliance ecosystem, the group most directly impacted by the state's failure to enforce traffic rules is the citizen (road user) who is both cause agent and suffering stakeholder, vulnerable and at greater risk of accidents due to poor road-user behaviour and an inherent lack of awareness and education. As cause agent, the citizen stakeholder group is made up of a cross section of offender drivers – the driver caught in a bind, finding himself in a predominantly non-compliant and confusing environment when it comes to lane driving or following prescribed speeds; the casually delinquent driver when it comes to mobile-phone usage and traffic-signal compliance and the reckless driver (driven by a false sense of 'nothing can hurt me; accidents are for others') when it comes to drunken driving and driving without a seatbelt or helmet.

While the offender driver attempts to circumvent the law and avoid prosecution by paying a bribe, the police functions as a sort of Dr Jekyll and Mr Hyde, on the one hand, the sole operating force working to create some sort of compliance (the well-meaning cop with a modus operandi not designed to manage scale) and on the other the unintended beneficiaries of the disempowering collusion between the deliberately delinquent driver and the morally flexible policeman.

New Ecosystem

In the conceptual model provided by the Smart Citizen Card solution, the government transforms into the Brahma or the creator of change, creating an operating environment and road infrastructure that lends itself to convenient compliance and embracing the possibility of a 100% compliant future by enabling an empowering bhagidari between the citizen, private enterprise and itself. Here, the police functions in the capacity of a strong operating ally (as opposed to the sole enforcement agency), working in conjunction with private enterprise (Smart Card licensees) to ensure a smooth and effective implementation of the new traffic-compliance methodology, free to focus on other policing demands while simultaneously ensuring exponentially higher compliance levels.

The citizen driver thus becomes part of a transparent enabling environment that rewards compliance while holding drivers 100% accountable for every instance of traffic violation. Educated and more aware, he or she is presented with the opportunity to individually engage and comply with the solution, becoming empowered and more likely to be voluntarily compliant in a manner compatible with his own values and sense of justice.

Fundamental to the new ecosystem is the advent of private enterprise as the operator of the new methodology and of the technology itself, which serves as the scalable enabler of new systems and processes. As licensee, the operator works to create an environment that encourages compliance through the use of a creative combination of reward and charge. The key challenge being is to endear the new system to the citizen so that instead of a 'bad cop', the operator is seen as helpful, facilitating a positive experience for the average citizen on the street. What makes the difference is that even though the average citizen may receive a monthly traffic compliance bill of Rs 100 to Rs 500, what he or she notices is a huge change in the operating environment. The roads no longer have huge jams, people drive in single lanes and pedestrians can walk. They can see that the benefits outweigh the negatives. And, if a citizen is 100% compliant, he or she can pretty much run on a zero bill and might even be rewarded for following the rules – although, to begin with, 100% compliance is likely to be difficult, given the operating environment.

Driver's Licensing in India

Aligning the Ill-Informed Driver

Privatizing Driver's Licensing

Consider This

Mr Sharma goes to the Delhi road transport office to get a driver's license. As applicants head inside to do a battle with the bureaucracy, touts swarm around them, offering pain-free shortcuts through the red tape for just Rs 3,000. 'What do you want – a driver's license or learner's permit without a test?' a man asks Mr Sharma, identifying himself only as Raju. Like the other 'agents' at the front gate, Raju specializes in paying bribes to officials to help new drivers get behind the wheel without taking driving tests or filling out paperwork. Raju tells Mr Sharma that the driving test will have 50 multiple-choice questions. All he has to do is mark all the A options to pass the test. Now, imagine how skillfully crafted the test is – no matter how difficult the question paper, if you mark all A's, it will take you past the 40% mark. Mr Sharma takes the test, marks all A's and gets a driver's license for the bargain price of Rs 3,000.[50]

In India, the driver's licensing environment is all about going to touts.

Applicants often pay up to 2.5 times the official fee to cut red tape and speed up the process. These large extra-legal payments are not direct bribes to bureaucrats but instead payments to agents with the agents in turn paying the bureaucrats to bend the rules. Hiring an agent involves substantial extra costs but it assures the applicant of getting a license even without knowing how to drive or having to take a driving test. And while it is possible to obtain a license without hiring an agent, bureaucrats routinely create hurdles ('red tape') to encourage license candidates to use agents. The result is a distorted process geared towards corruption, one in which bureaucrats circumvent the single key feature of the licensing process – verifying that license applicants know how to drive and drivers, having obtained their licenses illegally, pay little attention to traffic laws, making India's roads some of the deadliest in the world.

Now, the idea is that if all this money is currently going towards bribes, it might as well be used to build a better infrastructure for training and licensing drivers.

Invertonomics

Inverting the Problem into an Opportunity

Driver's licenses are intended to ensure that only safe and knowledgeable drivers use the roads and therefore, it is only if you educate correctly that you can create the right kind of driver for the operating environment. An obvious way to cut down on corruption and increase the efficiency of the licensing process is to privatize driver's licensing services. One of the potential disadvantages of privatization, although there is evidence that licensing fees would remain competitive if market-driven, is higher costs for applicants. In the Indian context, however, since applicants are already compelled to make large extra-legal payments to obtain licenses, privatizing would simply serve to divert money paid as bribes from the babu to private enterprise for the establishment and management of efficient, well-oiled infrastructure for training and licensing drivers.

Here, once again, we are using the tool of INVERTONOMICS to control the problem by monetizing it and converting it into an opportunity for profit.

THE MAGIC OF INVERTONOMICS

THOOK - Rs 6,500 crore
$1 billion

PISS - Rs 13,000 crore
$2 billion

LITTERING - Rs 26,000 crore
$4 billion

TOTAL = $7 billion

CORPUS OF $70 BILLION
(Rs 4,55,000 CRORE)[51]

Revenue Model

Assuming that a private operator charges Rs 10,000 to train and test each applicant and to issue him a driver's license, at the rate of approximately 100 applicants per day, the private operator could easily generate up to Rs 10,00,000 a single day and close to Rs 3,00,00,000 per month. What this will do is not only enable private operators to set up phenomenal, state-of-the-art training and licensing facilities but also spawn a host of driving schools and a whole new service industry that can be used to create jobs and counter the problem of unemployment.

Some Might Argue

Why should private agencies be asked to enter into the essentially government domain of licensing? To this we submit that the government cannot be expected to rigorously test 55,00,000 drivers per city. So, if we are a nation of 5 to 6 crore drivers (across the 10 major cities), the government as policy the policymaker, can do only entry-level testing, which means that 90% of the existing stock of drivers will continue to behave and misbehave.

Some Might Argue

License fee of Rs 10,000 is too high and most citizens will not be able to afford it. To this we submit that there is an assumption that most people who are learning to drive own a vehicle and are capable of spending between Rs 5,000 and Rs 10,000 per month on petrol, which means that they can easily spend Rs 10,000 on a license. For those who are economically underprivileged and can show a EWS (economically weaker sections) certificate, which says that their income levels are below a certain threshold, the fee maybe subsidized to Rs 1,000. In the current environment, even those who can ill afford it are compelled to pay Rs 2,000 to Rs 3,000 rupees to get a driver's license – it is not as if corrupt officials exempt or give any concession to the poorer people.

Eye of the Needle

While the new training and licensing structure is geared towards preparing the new driver for the operating environment, it fails to take into account the existing unprepared driver who will clearly continue to wreak havoc. The solution, therefore, is to create a Pink Letter Day – say 30 June 2020 – on which all existing driving licenses will cease to be valid and much like doctors who must go through regular skill programmes, all drivers would have to go through the testing process to re-validate their driver's licenses. This would mean that every citizen – no matter their age, whether driving for 2 years or 30 – would have to get a re-validation of their driving license before that date. Considering that the spectrum of existing drivers is likely to be at multiple points on the learning curve, every driver must pass through the stringent training and testing process of the new licensing regime.

Some Might Argue

There is a possibility that the private licensing authority might also become corrupt. To this we submit that if we were to rate the corruption coefficient of the current training and licensing system on an index of 1 to 10, it would rate 9. Similarly, in terms of efficiency in teaching and entry-level testing, it would rate 2. Assuming that in the private licensing system, corruption drops from 9 to 4 and the level of education and testing goes from 2 to a 7, this would be enough to make a substantial difference to the system as a whole. In the new model, not only do we have much better entry-level testing and less corruption, we've generated employment and created a situation where existing drivers must re-qualify in order to be able to drive. Unlike in the current system, where if you have a driver's license you have it for life – even if the license does have a limited validity, the corrupt authority allows for the license to be renewed automatically on the payment of a small bribe. Also, if the private licensing authority is actually charging the citizen Rs 10,000 rupees for a driver's license, there is little opportunity for corruption – whatever capacity the citizen has to pay has already been sucked out of him. The citizen would rather study and do well on his test since he doesn't have the capacity to pay any more.

Aligning Traffic Infrastructure

Traffic data is a critical element in decision-making for the appropriate planning, design and management of road networks.

While the concept of forecasting the future use of road networks in terms of traffic loading and flow is an accepted approach worldwide, in India, the routine collection of traffic data has not been considered important for the development and management of the road system. The result is ad-hoc infrastructure assessment and planning and a road network that is itself not conducive to traffic compliance. In the absence of definitive traffic information and data, no government agency is able to come to a conclusion or make the simple decisions needed to resolve traffic issues. As a result, road assessment and development is based more on political self-interest and expedience than on what is good for the city. The prolonged flip flop on whether to continue or discontinue the controversial Bus Rapid Transit (BRT) system in Delhi, for instance, is a classic case of fractured decision-making and contrarian government agendas in the absence of conclusive traffic data and information.

The Bus Rapid Transit (BRT) System

The bus system in Delhi is vital – 60% of all commuters in Delhi travel by bus. The BRT was envisaged to give priority to and create dedicated corridors for buses in order to increase their speed, reliability and efficiency. After the implementation of the BRT, net transit time for buses carrying commuter traffic decreased substantially, and yet, the BRT came in for severe criticism due to the difficulty of access to bus platforms, which were in the middle of the road, junctions not being large enough to manage the huge volume of vehicles and the effect this all had on other motor traffic. Private vehicles, which constitute 90% of the traffic, were confined to two lanes of limited width while buses, which constitute only 2% of all motorized traffic-run in dedicated lanes, are often empty. In addition, underutilized pedestrian and cyclist tracks on either side took up valuable space that could have been easily used to create additional car lanes.

REAL-TIME FACTUAL DYNAMIC DATA		
2016	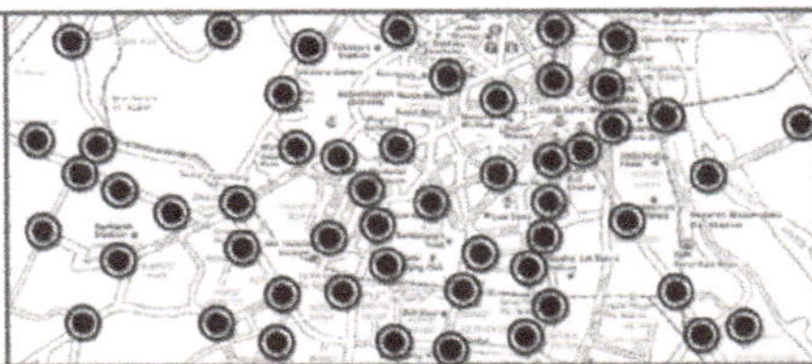	Points of conflict, severely compromising pedestrian safety. Jan: **260** Jul: **250**
2017	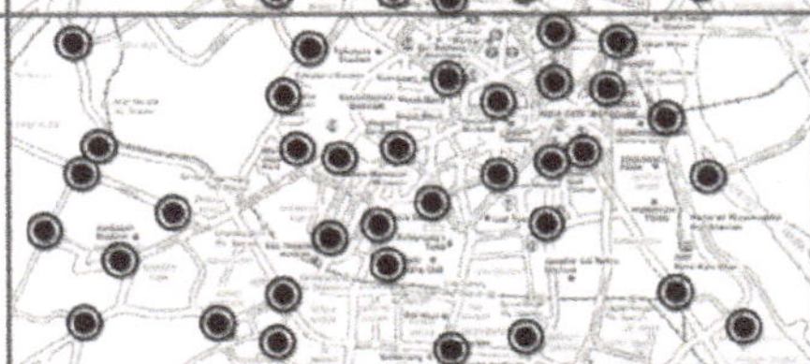	Jan: **200** Jul: **160**
2018		Jan: **100** Jul: **60**
2019		Jan: **40** Jul: **20**
2020		Jan: **2** Jul: **0**

Using the economic opportunity provided by Honking and Traffic Compliance, the Smart Citizen Card Model can generate a host of traffic data – such as the flow and volume of traffic, its composition and speed, origin and time to destination, points of congestion and waiting time at traffic lights – currently unavailable to government agencies, to enable them to better manage traffic, plan infrastructure and take traffic – related decisions. For instance, if the system records an unusual number of horns at a particular location, it would be easy to deduce that there is some glitch or hold-up in that area that is slowing traffic down and needs to be addressed.

In our cities, due to lack of lane driving, traffic is comparable to a turbulent flow. Laminar flow, on the other hand, is much more efficient and has the capacity to carry a larger volume of traffic. The moment traffic flows are mapped, simple computing will make it possible to tell where the constrictions lie and it will become easy for the relevant functionaries to resolve them more quickly and efficiently.

The rate of resolution of constrictions goes up with the availability of definitive data. Assuming that Delhi has 1,000 traffic constrictions, accurate statistical data will make it possible to resolve all of them in three to four years, create a safe, effective future infrastructure, and arrive at a far more scientifically managed traffic plan.

In the long run, better traffic also means savings on petrol and maintenance. Technology can make it possible to coordinate red lights so that drivers are likely to encounter only 2 red lights out of every 20 if they proceed at a specific speed or within the speed limit. This is not currently possible since there is no accurate traffic data available on the speed and density of vehicles along specific roads.

The Smart Citizen Card Model will throw out into the open the abysmal state of affairs and enable the government to restore or impact the areas of constriction and conflict with a certain degree of conviction backed by irrefutable data.

Consider This

The existing Rao Tula Ram half flyover, an atrocity inflicted on the city of Delhi by some influential people living along the stretch who didn't want to lose a part of the service lane in front of their homes (public land) to a dual-carriageway flyover. Strings were pulled to cut this flyover down to size on the drawing board. What followed was a nightmare of endless traffic jams and a farce enacted by the Public Works Department (PWD) and the traffic police in making it a two-way passage. While the PWD has already begun work on the construction of a new flyover that will decongest the area under pressure from the media and the public, the traffic mess on the Outer Ring Road due to the 'half flyover' continued for six long years, till the half flyover was completed to make a proper one.

Nearly 2,00,000 vehicles pass through the flyover every day, and with the right data, the government would have been well within their right to insist that residents move boundary walls back by 10 to 20 feet, or insist that the service lane be acquired to accommodate the flyover. Residents on the other hand, would have been unable to pressure the authorities and prevent the flyover from being expanded for the sake of the city.[52]

Pedestrian Safety and Walkability in Our Cities

Road Design Is Key to Pedestrian Safety

Walking is an essential human activity. In a sustainable city, walking should be safe for all citizens. However, in most Indian cities, walking can be more dangerous than driving. In Delhi, close to 1,000 people are run over by speeding vehicles every year while walking on or crossing busy streets. Despite civic agencies investing crores of rupees in subways and overbridges, Delhi's roads continue to be a death trap for pedestrians.

The Smart Citizen Card Model not only improves vehicular management but also makes it possible to enhance pedestrian safety, using processed traffic data to plan traffic infrastructure. Data on the number and location of pedestrian deaths, for instance, could help to determine potential locations of overbridges and subways, which would serve to reduce the number of deaths and injuries. While the Smart Citizen Card Model makes it possible to put in place various reactive measures, extensive proactive measures are also needed to ensure the safety of the average pedestrian. One such measure is the setting up of a centralized, empowered approving body called the Pedestrian Commission of India (PCI), which serves as the vanguard of pedestrian interests and which, like the NHAI (National Highways Authority of India) and the AAI (Airports Authority of India), functions as an instrument of advocacy and expertise to map and effect transformation in the existing pedestrian fabric of Indian cities.

Imagine an India...

... where sidewalks are as broad as roads with trees for shade and oxygen, pavements are well-lit, safe and secure and street furniture and vendor carts are appropriately designed for the local context and placed as not to transect free movement.

... where the random squalor of the soft shoulder littered with garbage, construction debris, exposed cables, unfinished public works, squatters, broken pavements and dysfunctional lights is suddenly transformed into a smooth, well-paved oasis of green grass, flowers and fountains.

... where shopkeepers, used-car sellers and sweet shops can no longer encroach into the rightful pedestrian space by extending shops or parking cars. Where vehicle owners can no longer park their cars on footpaths outside their homes, offices and in market places.

... where the citizens and the government participate together in an aligned manner to effect the 3 key objects of transformation – pedestrian safety, civic sensibility and urban aesthetics.

The Pedestrian Commission of India (PCI)

The first and most important step in the planning of any city is to conduct a pattern analysis of its different fabrics – the morphology of its buildings, high and low vehicular-density areas, public transport as well as pedestrian and cyclist network. The next step is to lay these one over the other to find where the pedestrian fabric is cut or transected by the other fabrics, isolate those areas and then detail them to a high degree to ensure that there are no conflict points.

So, to begin with, the city must be mapped.

In India, there is no centralized body responsible for mapping cities. Eicher, a private company, was the first to create geospatial maps for Delhi, followed by the Delhi State Spatial Data Infrastructure (DSSDI), a pioneering effort undertaken by the Delhi government.[53] Maps produced by the latter are not, however, available in the public domain. Additionally, no such effort exists on a nationwide level.

Even where the government has set up institutions for mapping, such as the Surveyor General of India, the nation's principal mapping and surveying agency, the maps produced are static and limited and the institutions concerned not empowered enough to have a say in or influence the way in which cities are developed. They are mere spectators, tasked with surveying and mapping the city.

In Indian cities, the pedestrian typically does not get more than 4 or 5 feet of pavement space, first because it is a budget issue and second because the perception towards pedestrians is almost discriminating – 'Oh, how pedestrian', as opposed to the best cities in the world where the roads are narrower than the pavements to encourage people to walk or cycle. In comes the PCI which ensures not only that there is a mapping of the existing fabrics but which is also empowered to create by-laws to protect pedestrians and provide them with adequate and safe walking spaces within the city.

It would become the responsibility of the PCI, in conjunction with the local municipality and land-owning agencies, to administer the pedestrian fabric, to ensure that it is not encroached upon and work with state transportation professionals and other stakeholders to address pedestrian safety issues through urban design and engineering solutions such as basic sidewalk design. It would also set up the rules and create different levels of pedestrian friendliness for various parts of the city as well as examine and approve all private and public infrastructure projects from the point of view of pedestrian safety.

The PCI would thus become the body of advocacy, innovation and legislation, the *mai-baap* of the pedestrian space. Any person or institution looking to construct anything within the city, or to use the pedestrian fabric for any purpose, would have to first seek its permission and also conform to the Pedestrian Master Plan, 2020, 30 and so on.

Foot Overbridges

Two alternate designs were suggested to the Delhi government using contextually appropriate urbanscape elements. The foot overbridges become much more and fulfill the promises of city-wide, clean toilets every kilometre, elevators and other universal accessibility features, legit space for the informal sector, canvasses for street art, Wi-Fi convenient shops for clean drinking water and selling of street food. There would be a dedicated space for an all-new Women's Security Force with an Eagles Vantage point, space for beat constables, CCTV, solar lights and visually refreshing flowerscape.

Additionally, these new structures that shall animate the roads every kilometre would become symbols of the city's public architecture and draw from local cultural symbols and design vocabularies to become elements of civic pride.

WOMEN'S SECURITY FORCE
CYCLE TRACK
WOMEN SECURITY FORCE

WI-FI ZONE WITH COFFEE SHOP
Cafe Wifi

ELEVATOR
SHOPS
TOILETS
WOMEN SECURITY FORCE

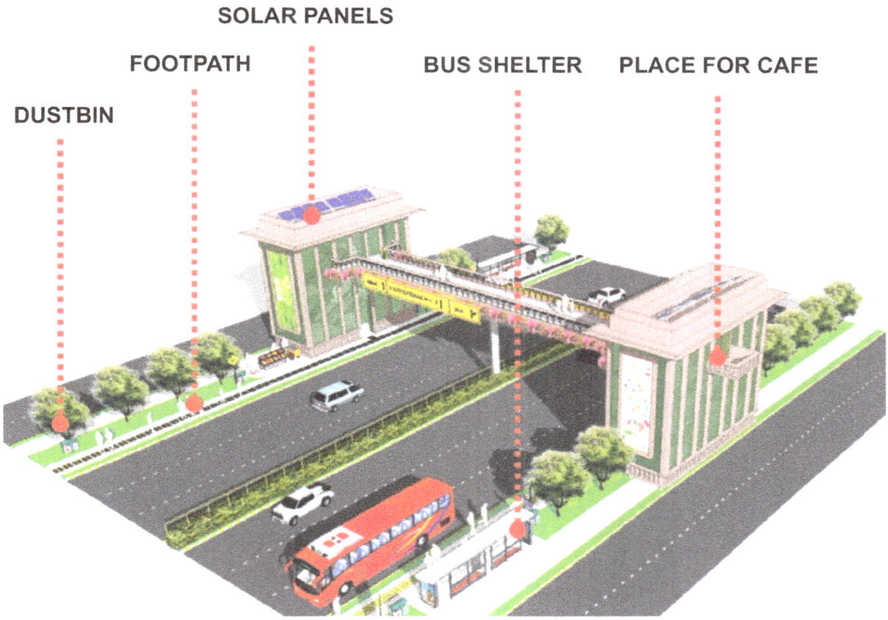
SOLAR PANELS
FOOTPATH
BUS SHELTER
PLACE FOR CAFE
DUSTBIN

INFORMAL
SECTOR
RECYCLE

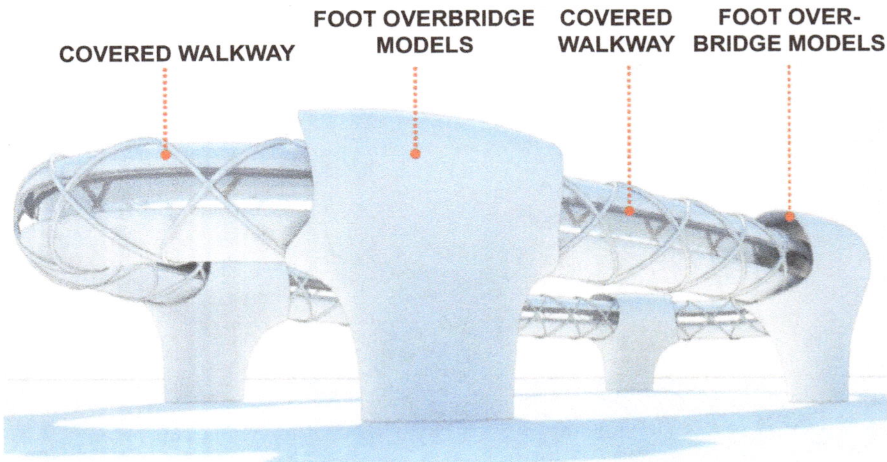

A new skywalk designed by the author has been recently constructed at ITO, Delhi's busiest crossing. It is being used by over 40,000 users daily and has become a visual icon for the city.

The Civic Cop

Since it is now the owner and administrator of the sidewalk, median and the pedestrian space, it becomes the responsibility of the PCI to provide better illumination on roads and streets, which is critical for cyclist and pedestrian safety. The PCI could go one step further and say that in addition to street lighting, they will install a CCTV camera as standard equipment on every light pole.

Consider This

The first widespread system of street lighting used piped coal gas as fuel and was started in London in the early 19th century. Since then it has become a standard civic amenity often mounted on a column or pole, either on the side of the road or within the median, to provide illumination, promote safety and security on roads and improve the quality of life by artificially extending the hours of light in which activity can take place.

Just as installing a light every 15 metres (on every street) must have seemed an expensive and absurd proposition 150 years ago, we are suggesting that a CCTV camera now becomes a standard fixture on every streetlight.

What this will do is create a comprehensive network of 'Eyes on the Street' and impact public safety in a fundamental way. What it will also do is allow the PCI to directly impact citizen behaviour on the sidewalk and in the pedestrian space by effecting the implementation of fines for five simple civic offences:

1. Littering
2. Defacing public property
3. Spitting
4. Urinating and defecating in public spaces
5. Harassment and inappropriate physical contact

Technology Model – How Is It Going to Work?

Clearly, if we are going to have a million cameras in a city, it is not possible for someone to be sitting and watching them 24×7. The system must, therefore, be based on a technology model that makes it possible to detect offences, identify defaulters and fine them with minimum human intervention.

Twin Tools for Identification

Facebook's facial recognition software, DeepFace, is now nearly as accurate as the human brain. DeepFace can look at two photos and irrespective of lighting or angle, tell with 97.25% accuracy whether the photos contain the same face. Humans can perform the same task with a marginally higher accuracy of 97.53%.[54] DeepFace is currently just a research project but in the near future, it could easily be used by the Civic Cop to look at a new photo and connect it to the name of an existing user and therefore, identify defaulters from among Facebook's 5 billion-strong database. Today, even mobile phone cameras can handle face recognition by upto 97% accuracy.

Now, it is possible that the defaulter may not be on Facebook. Even so, he or she may already be a part of the system through voter registration cards, Aadhar or the Jan Dhan Yojna, and therefore identifiable. This model is predicated on the fact that slowly, as the informal sector becomes regulated, everyone will have an identity and is going to be somewhere on the radar. Any person entering a city, for instance, whether on foot or through a railway station or bus stand, could potentially be asked for ID by the local police and if the person doesn't have one, the cop will create one for him or her on the spot.[55]

Even if we are not able to issue identity cards to 100% of the population and 20% is left out – most individuals today carry a phone and because it is a GPS-enabled entity – the phone could become a key tracker.

The assumption is that whoever is littering, urinating or defacing public property actually has a phone in his or her pocket. So the moment you do anything delinquent, not only does the Civic Cop capture the transgression on camera, it uses DeepFace facial recognition technology to identify the person and using the GPS to track the phone, confirming their presence at the scene of the offence. Within minutes, the system triggers an auto SMS / WhatsApp to your mobile saying that you have been photographed at Sarojini Nagar at 5:15 p.m., violating Rule 2a (littering and defacing public property), the fine for which is Rs 100 and will be charged with the next phone bill.

The Civic Cop thus becomes an instrument of the PCI, using CCTV cameras and pattern-recognition algorithms to effect civic order within the pedestrian space, in a manner otherwise improbable in the foreseeable future.

The Civic Cop

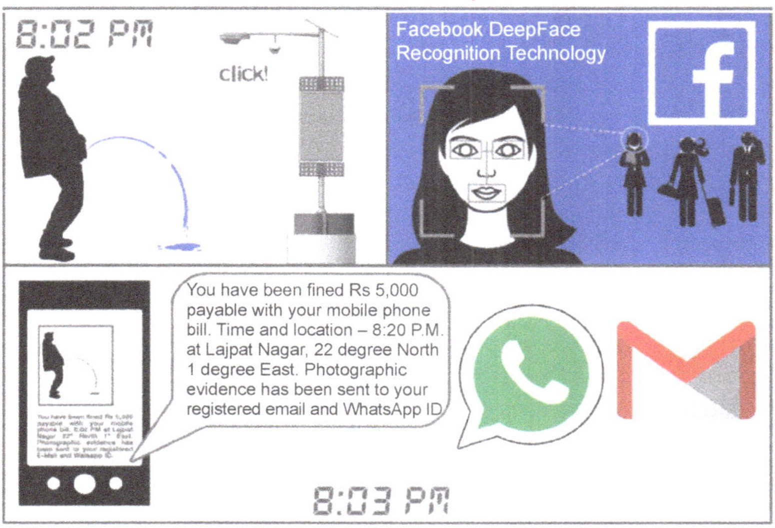

Corroborative Evidence for Criminal Offences

While it may not be possible for the PCI to levy direct fines in cases of eve -teasing and inappropriate physical contact (in India, sexual harassment is governed by the Criminal Procedural Code), what the Civic Cop will do is provide corroborative evidence and visual confirmation of these offences in the form of photos or video footage, making it easier for women to file FIRs and to bring offenders to book. This could potentially act as a huge deterrent to sexual offenders, many of who escape prosecution due to the lack of physical evidence. If a woman feels she is being harassed on a sidewalk, for instance, she could press an emergency button on her phone, allowing GPS to detect her location and the system to give her access to CCTV footage of the particular spot where the incident took place. The woman could then use the footage, at her discretion, to identify the offender and to file criminal charges.[56]

Revenue Model

Let us assume that in a population of 100 crore (this includes people in villages), there would likely be at least 20 crore civic offenders and that each offender would, on an average, run up penalties of Rs 100 per month. This would mean that the PCI stands to collect fines worth Rs 24,000 crore per year (20 crore people x Rs 100 per month x 12 months). The result is that the PCI starts to make money. It is no longer just a mapping body that examines and approves. It acquires teeth and is actually able to impact citizen behaviour in the public space and enforce some sort of discipline. It also acquires the capacity to impact pedestrian safety in a fundamental way, both as a funding agent – by using the funds at its disposal towards the installation of street lights, construction of pavements and the development of an appropriate pedestrian fabric – and as an agent of advocacy.

Revenue Model for Street Lighting

Assuming that the capitalized value of Rs 24,000 crore rupees is Rs 3,00,000 crore (at the rate of a 6% return on capital) and further that the cost of installing one streetlight – including the pole, foundation, lamp and CCTV camera is Rs 10,000. An investment of only Rs 1,00,000 crore will mean 10 crore streetlights across 50 cities or 20,00,000 street lights per city. For Delhi (one of the largest cities in India), which is approximately 1,600 sq. km or 16 x 105 sq. m, this would mean a streetlight and a CCTV camera every 27 sq. m, making it the one of the safest and most-watched cities in the world.

Providing street lighting is one of the most important and expensive responsibilities of a government or municipal body. While guidance for the lighting of public streets, roads and highways is provided in the Indian Standard (BIS, 1981), municipalities often fail to comply with them due to the expense of putting up streetlights. Now, suddenly, installing a light is no longer an expense. First because the PCI has sufficient funds to install streetlights in every town and city in India and second because the streetlight itself becomes a *kumau puttar* (revenue grosser).[57] Wherever a light is put up, it has a camera attached to it – the moment someone spits, urinates or litters, the light earns. So, very quickly, we find that the PCI is auctioning lights to concessionaires and say TATA or Reliance or a government SPV is installing 1,000 lights in J.P. Nagar, Andheri or Ballygunge in Kolkata because each light is bringing them money.

Here, again, we have used the tool of INVERTONOMICS to control the problem – inverting it into an opportunity for profit by creating a public–private partnership, which allows for the government to auction and sell licenses to concessionaires, to install, manage and maintain streetlights cum CCTV cameras and to profit from the collection of fines for various civic offences.

REVENUE MODEL FOR STREET LIGHTING

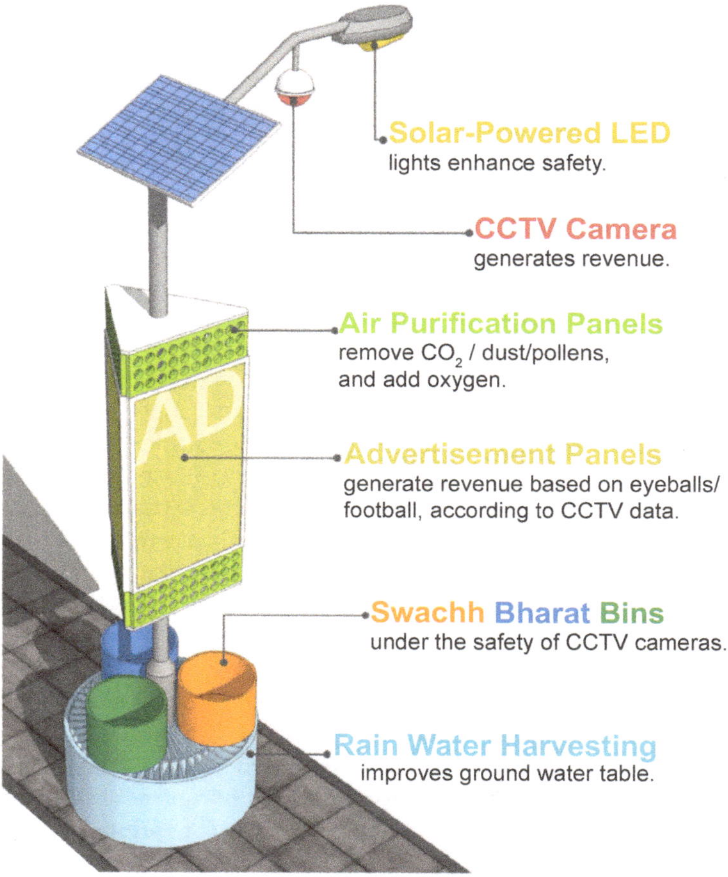

The Civic Cop model provides for the large capital expenditure involved in installing streetlights cum CCTV cameras and the operational expenditure involved in their maintenance. It also allows for proceeds from fines to be shared among the PCI, the Civic Cop Corporation (concessionaire), the municipality and the police, creating a synergistic model of action and enabling the PCI to operate through and in close collaboration with the various stakeholders in the system as a unified body. As discussed earlier in this chapter, even where CCTV cameras are installed, in the absence of proper mechanisms, there is often no way to ensure that they remain in working order.[58]

The solution is to introduce the CCTV camera in a manner that its creation as well as operation becomes positively remunerative to some party, creating an incentive to run it efficiently.[59] In the case of the Civic Cop, what the revenue-share model does is to align the interests of all stakeholders within the system and ensure that they support and remain positively wired to the continued operational goodness and success of the streetlight-cum-CCTV camera, because their earnings from fines depends on it.

What the PCI could also do is use the Civic Cop to fine for unauthorized parking on the pavement and within the pedestrian space. Let us assume that the Civic Cop fines for unauthorized parking at the rate of Rs 100 per minute and also informs the tow agency. The fines could potentially be levied through the Kinetic Cards already installed in every vehicle with proceeds being shared among the PCI, the Civic Cop Corporation (concessionaire), the municipality, police and (in this case) the Smart Citizen Card Corporation.

STREET PARKING

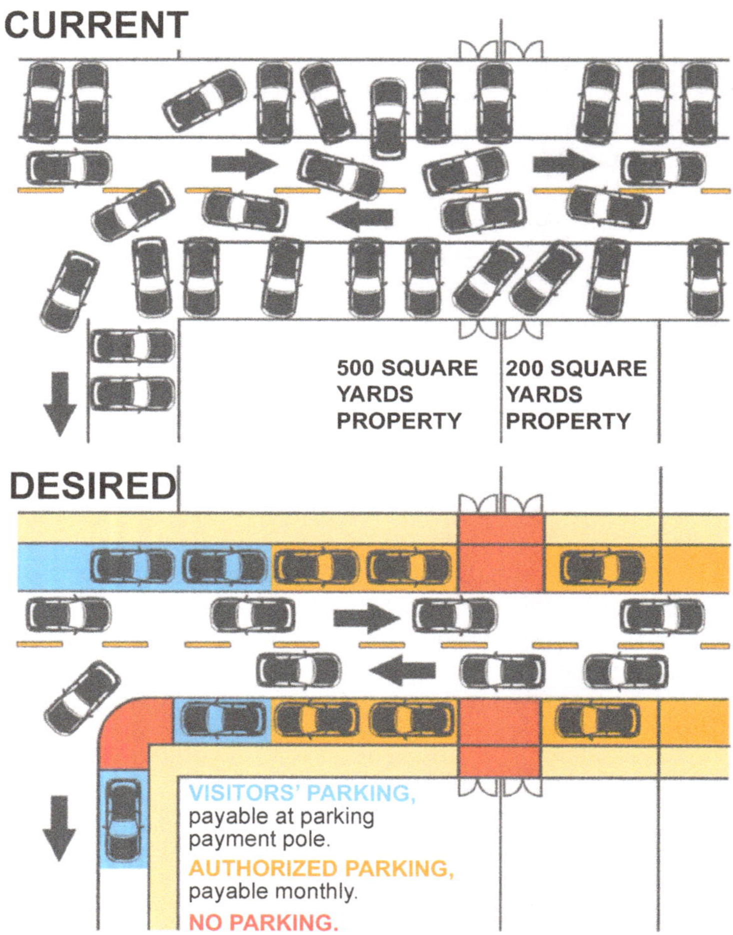

Some Might Argue

A punitive model of fining citizens for civic misdemeanours might draw the ire of the common man and therefore be untenable in a country where political parties lean heavily towards populism. It may therefore be expedient to propose an alternate (non-punitive) model around the CCTV camera cum streetlight that can run either individually or together with the Punitive Model (as discussed earlier).

The Non-punitive Enterprise Model operates on the premise that the data captured by the Civic Cop is likely to be extremely valuable and therefore commercially marketable to the insurance sector which loses crores of rupees every year to car thefts, burglaries and misreported vehicle accidents. The estimated size of non-life insurance in India is Rs 80,000 crore (growing at 9–11% annually). Revenues from the sale of data could, therefore, be easily used to fund the installation and operation of the streetlight cum CCTV camera across Indian cities and towns. Additionally, advertising panels mounted on the streetlights themselves could generate further funds to supplement the associated capital and operating expenditures.

In a posh colony, for instance, advertising rights to a cluster of, say, five poles could potentially be sold for Rs 15,000 per month to an SME looking for focused local publicity. In a less premium location, rights could be sold for as much as Rs 5,000 per month. Assuming that the capitalized value of an average of, say, Rs 10,000 per month for 5 ad panels would be between Rs 6 lakh to Rs 8 lakh, money available would be far in excess of the capital plus operational cost of 5 light poles (including the cost of relaying data to the Central Data Center).

The Enterprise Civic Cop Model could be a practical and viable solution towards fulfilling the promise of 15,00,000 CCTV cameras made by the recently elected AAP government in Delhi. Currently, one-tenth of 15 lakh cameras are being installed. This model can easily be replicated in tier-I and tier-II cities as well.

Low-Income Group (LIG)

The Civic Cop could also fine for parking on roads outside homes in residential colonies on a daily basis at the rate of, say, Rs 50 in LIG colonies to Rs 500 in posh colonies such as Vasant Vihar and Shanti Niketan in Delhi, Colaba in Mumbai or Alipore in Calcutta.

Let us assume, for instance, that you are parking outside your residence in Vasant Vihar, on the footpath, which is now owned by the PCI. You will be fined Rs 500 a day by the Civic Cop, which will capture your car there. If it is Lajpat Nagar, it may fine you less, say Rs 50 a day. The Civic Cop will post your fine on your Kinetic Cards; if you don't pay the fine, you won't get petrol, be allowed to use toll roads or park in authorized parking areas. If you own a car and you have no place to park it, you may even be willing to pay the fine for the privilege of parking on the footpath, at the rate of, say, Rs 15,000 a month.

Consider This

Very simply, people assume that the space outside their home belongs to them and that they have the first right to use it. It is endemic to our very culture that we have not understood the distinction between the interface of the public and the private, which is why our *jagran*s are so loud and we have no qualms about throwing garbage on the streets. The interface is always ours and yet not ours. So we will put Italian marble inside and maybe 3 feet outside our gates, and the rest will remain broken. We will use the footpath for parking, yet it is not our responsibility to keep it clean or free from encroachment. So now, since in any case one doesn't consider it theirs and legally it is not theirs, if one parks on the footpath, in comes the PCI and slaps a fine on them for encroaching on the fundamental rights of the pedestrian.

GUPTAJI HALWAI
SHARMA VEG
VERMA AUTO
EXIDE
PEDESTRIAN COMMISSION OF INDIA
CHALLAN
Dear Mr Gupta,
You have been found guilty of-
1) Encroachment
2) Littering on street.
3) Posing danger to pedestrians.
Fine payable-Rs 6,000.
Yours sincerely
PEDESTRIAN COMMISSION OF INDIA
CHALLAN
Dear Mr Sharma,
You have been found guilty of-
1) Encroachment
2) Littering on street.
Fine payable-Rs 3,000.
Yours sincerely
Yours sincerely
PEDESTRIAN COMMISSION OF INDIA
CHALLAN
Dear Mr Verma,
You have been found guilty of-
1) Encroachment
2) Littering on street.
3) Posing danger to pedestrians.
Fine payable-Rs 4,000
Yours sincerely
GUPTAJI HALWAI
SHARMA VEG
VERMA AUTO
EXIDE
FRESH
TASTY

For habitual offenders or people who rake up large amounts in unpaid fines – because you can't put a fine of Rs 5 or Rs 10,00,000 on a Kinetic Card, the PCI could easily say that on account of violation of the footpath, the house tax of a particular residence be doubled as penalty. The PCI sends the MCD a simple notice: 'House number xxx, violation of fundamental right of pedestrians, penalty on house tax levied xxx.' What this will do is push the citizen to comply with rules of the pavement and pedestrian space and pay civic fines regularly for the simple reason that if one does not pay their house tax, after a point, all civic amenities will be affected. One cannot, for instance, pay their electricity bill or get a lease deed registered, plus the penalty on unpaid house tax is a hefty 24% (compounded). The PCI could take it further and say that let the water and electricity bills also be made 5 times their amount. Although the government cannot, by law, deny one water and electricity, it can easily charge one more. Very simply, if one thinks that one can take away the fundamental rights of the pedestrian, the government can also act against one financially.

The Civic Cop could also be used to address the problem of the deliberately delinquent squatter such as the shopkeeper, the used-car seller and the sweet shop owner who regularly encroach on pedestrian paths with impunity.

CONSIDER THIS

Gupta Stores, whose shop is actually 8 ft x 8 ft, has taken over 50 ft x 50 ft of space in collusion with the local cops. Muthu Sweets has taken over the entire corridor in the local market for their display of Diwali sweets.

Often thinly disguised cases of land grab, this insidious occupation of pavements and sidewalks inhibits pedestrian passage and renders it hazardous due to the presence of illegal structures such as awnings, extensions and display cases; construction materials, dismantled cars and car parts (in the case of car sellers or workshops); and stoves, pans and other temporary cooking structures installed by hawkers and restaurant owners.

CONSIDER THIS

A two-year-old boy slipped from his mother's arms and fell into a *kadhai* of boiling oil after the mother was hit by an e-rickshaw in Trilokpuri, East Delhi. The child sustained 100% burns and died soon after. According to a report in the *Indian Express*, a local halwai was frying snacks in the *kadhai* on the roadside, encroaching the space meant for pedestrians, which led to the unfortunate incident.[60]

Now, all encroachment as well as collusion with local police will be caught thanks to the Civic Cop and daily fines will be levied. Incremental and unacceptable squatting will lead to exceptionally high fines through the incumbent's mobile phone bills and the suspension of local beat cops for complicity.

Finally, all hoardings and advertisements will come under the purview of the PCI and be installed on its territory. Currently, 95% of all hoardings are unlicensed and the money paid for putting them up (at stake is tens of thousands of crores) simply goes into the pocket of the local municipality and the police. Anyone can put up an advertisement or a hoarding anywhere with boards often obstructing traffic lights and street signs and collapsed hoardings posing a danger to pedestrians and street traffic.

Now, the Civic Cop will play watchdog and enforce compliance with simple and easy-to-follow norms. It will ensure that any sanction or permission for the installation of advertisements or hoardings is in strict compliance with the law and further that no hoarding which constitutes a danger, obstruction or nuisance to the free flow of traffic or to pedestrians is permitted to be erected. The PCI will collect license fees for the installation of all hoardings and advertisements, the proceeds of which will be shared with the municipality and the local police. Hoardings will, however, no longer go unreported due to the Civic Cop.

So suddenly, the PCI becomes the greatest lokpal to have ever been set free on city roads. It ensures that citizens start cleaning up their colonies, stop littering, urinating and defecating in public spaces, desist from putting up ad-hoc hoardings and advertisements and parking on footpaths. Homes are broken and rebuilt on stilts because now it is cheaper to spend on constructing parking than to pay four times house tax or people simply start buying fewer cars which leads to lower air pollution. Pavements and pedestrian pathways are clean, safe and well lit and the pedestrian finally gets his due – the right to walk and move around the city, safely and freely.

In this chapter, we observed how safety, convenience and capacity are all severely compromised in the current ecosystem.

The Smart Citizen Card aided by the Kinetic coordinates surveillance technology could fine incumbents for each instance of traffic-rules omission. The Traffic Bill would also act as a surrogate tutor. Most people read bills more carefully than rule-books!

The privatization of entry-level testing for drivers' licenses and a regime of triennial renewal for existing license holders would raise the median of the quality of drivers animating our roads.

The money trail from the fines, which would run into billions, would be shared among all the stakeholders and also fund road infrastructure expenditure as well as Emergency Response Systems.

PCI becomes the vanguard of the pedestrian space and using Civic Cop, the CCTV Pole effect fines on all instances of encroachments and delinquency in the pedestrian space.

PCI would make our cities walkable again!!

Chapter 4

SAFER CITIES

According to the National Crime Records
Bureau 2013 annual report, 24,293 rape
cases were reported across India in 2012.

Introduction

The Delhi Gang Rape

On 16 December 2012, a young physiotherapy intern and her male friend boarded a private bus in Delhi's Munirka colony, a journey that would end in horrible circumstances. Within the hour, a group of six men already on the bus had gang-raped the woman, brutally beaten her and her friend and left them to die on the side of a road. The young woman succumbed to her injuries 13 days later while undergoing emergency treatment in Singapore.

The 'December 16th gang rape', as it has come to be known, shocked a country often inured to such sexual violence.[61]

Within days of the story being reported, the citizens of Delhi had brought parts of the city to a standstill, protesting against the state and central governments for failing to provide adequate security for women. Thousands of demonstrators clashed with security forces over a period of weeks, braving lathi charges and water cannons despite the cold. The protestors demanded immediate action that the rapists be caught, tried and hanged and that better policing and stricter laws be brought in to create an environment of zero tolerance.[62]

In response to the protests, a high-level, judicial committee was set up to look into and suggest reforms to the existing laws against sexual offenders and as a result of its recommendations, proposals for several new laws were considered, 24×7 helplines were set up in several states and six new fast-track courts were created to hear rape cases in Delhi.[63]

Less than a year later, however, news broke of a 16-year-old girl having been gang-raped twice in two days in Madhyamgram, West Bengal: once, after a man conned her out of her home and later, when she dared to lodge a police complaint. Hoping that things had changed and that they would get justice (all but one of the 16 December rapists had been sentenced to death), the girl and her family had dared to report the incident to the police. Shockingly, the police did nothing. Two months later, the girl was set on fire by her assailants, at her home near Kolkata, to prevent her from testifying against them.[64]

At a memorial for the victim of the Delhi gang rape, held in December 2013, the press interviewed a young woman who had taken part in the protests a year earlier. She stated that while 'a welcome change is that the taboo on discussion of rape and sexual violence has been broken,' she saw 'absolutely no change in the rape culture and related brutality.'[65]

Such crimes are not going to go away. They may shock us momentarily but we are soon lulled back into a sense of complacency. So while every year, there may be an anniversary, an uproar and a demonstration at Jantar Mantar, these are all discordant actions and in the absence of synergy and a clear way forward, there is no way to measure if there has been any progress or to determine whether we are doing things that are actually making women safer.

Since December 2012, the focus has been on three possible remedies – stricter laws and punishment, better and increased policing and changing mindsets. Seven years on, while some action has been achieved on each of these fronts (for instance, some fast-track courts have been instituted and directives have been issued to police stations to ensure prompt filing of First Information Reports [FIRs]), similar incidents continue to take place with alarming regularity and the efficacy of instituted measures remains in doubt.

A report of the law ministry indicates that despite the centre asking all states to set up fast-track courts for the speedy trial of crimes against women and children, only 212 courts have been set up so far in the country. Of these none have come up in UP and Bihar, states which frequently report the highest number of rape cases.[66] Statistics, however, show that the six fast-track courts in Delhi were able to dispose of only 380 rape cases by 15 August 2013. In contrast, 2010 saw 707 cases being disposed of while 650 and 547 rape cases were decided upon in 2011 and 2012 respectively. What this effectively means is that the disposal rate of rape cases was actually higher when regular courts were deciding them.[67]

Clearly then, the question is not one of intent but of a lack of aligned action and a complete failure to understand the nature of the issue at hand, with measures taken not sufficient and often not appropriate to the scale of the problem, which begs the question: are we applying a Band-Aid to a gunshot wound?

Since December 2012, the focus has been on three possible remedies

1. Stricter laws and punishment

2. Better and increased policing

3. Changing mindsets

Despite these remedies, similar incidents continue to take place with alarming regularity and efficacy of instituted measures remain in doubt.

Statistics show that fast-track courts slow down justice.

Clearly then, the question is not one of intent but of a lack of aligned action and a complete failure to understand the nature of the issue at hand, with measures taken not sufficient and often not appropriate to the scale of the problem.

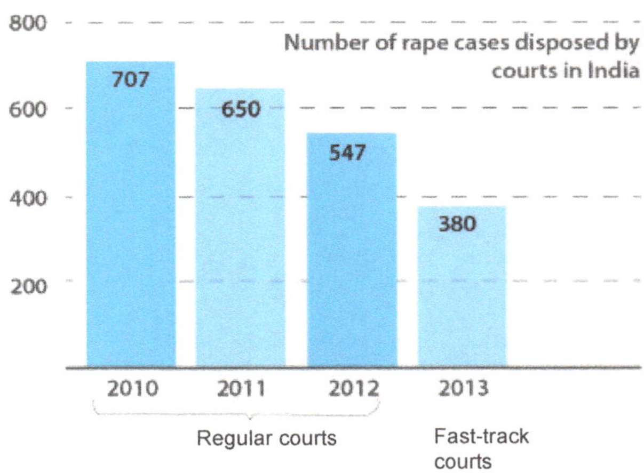

Creating a Mission for Safer Cities

While there is an urgent need for sustained government engagement on issues of gender-based violence, the only way to holistically impact the quotient of safety and security in Indian cities is for all three arms of society – the government, the institutions and the citizens – to come together and act in unison in the manner of a mission, much like they did for polio eradication.

Missions typically have a singular, measurable objective, a clear path with milestones, a timeline and most importantly, aligned action. In order to achieve the goal of 'we must be safe', we must have a unified action plan with clearly stated milestones, a well-defined path and all stakeholders working together in a manner that is both missionary and objective to align the actions of citizens, cities and communities. We must be future-ready with the capability to project and tackle the scale of issues that we are likely to be confronted with and not play catch-up as technology becomes more and more sophisticated and the stimulus for non-safety becomes higher and higher.

Addressing the Entire Bandwidth of Urban Safety and Security

Although heinous sexual offences against women tend to grab maximum eyeballs and media space, when we talk about safety and safer cities, it must be done in an inclusive manner which addresses the entire bandwidth of urban safety and transcends not just gender but also social boundaries. Whether it is pedestrians and cyclists, immigrant workers or the elderly, children who could be going to school or women tourists, the notion of urban safety and security must include every section of society and encompass the perception of India as a secure country and destination.

Crime against the Elderly

A recent annual report of the Delhi Police indicates that along with crimes against women, cases of crime against the elderly have seen a phenomenal rise in the last decade. According to the National Crime Records Bureau Report of 2010, 32,496 elderly were murdered and 5,836 cases of death not amounting to murder and kidnapping were reported from all over India between 2001 and 2010. Statistics indicate that a sizeable number of these crimes were committed by domestic helps who are without identification and known antecedents, and often engaged without any formal police verification.[68]

Lack of Pedestrian and Road Safety

Another area where safety is often a problem is the road network (as indicated in Chapter 3). As much as 11% of total global road injury deaths occur in India alone. These numbers are so high that they amount to wiping out almost half the equivalent population of a country like Iceland. Another disturbing trend is that while the total number of accidents has shown a slight downward dip over the last two decades, the proportion of fatal accidents is up from 18% in 2003 to 25% in 2012 (as per official data). More people are now dying in road accidents than ever before as Indian cities give more importance to high-speed roads for vehicles without ensuring safe access for pedestrians, cyclists and other vulnerable road users.

Even young, school-going children are not spared. In a particularly horrific instance, a young Lineshya and her cardiologist father, Pankaj Gupta, were crushed to death by a speeding bus while walking to the bus stop in Gurgaon in April 2014.[69]

Injuries and Fatalities at the Workplace

In India, rules that require accidents to be recorded are seldom obeyed and as a result, there are no reliable national statistics that show the numbers of workplace injuries and fatalities. The International Labor Organization estimates, however, that there were 47,000 deaths from occupational accidents in India in 2003 (the most recent year for which figures are available), an increase of 17% from a year earlier.[70]

The annual turnover of the Indian construction industry is about Rs 2,48,000 crore, which accounts for 11% of the national GDP. The sector employs almost 3.2 crore people, second only to the agricultural industry. However, construction workers are by far the most vulnerable segment of unorganized labour in the country.[71] The rate of fatal accidents in the industry is almost four to five times that of the manufacturing sector, with workers routinely exposed to a host of dangers, including hazardous substances such as asbestos, silicon and lead, and the serious threat of fire due to the storage and use of flammable substances and other disasters, caused as a result of collapse of structures and subsidence of the soil on which the construction activity is being carried out.[72]

Safety standards have always been an issue in India, but as the number and scale of the airports, toll roads, skyscrapers and mall projects increase, so the risk of tragedy rises. Big construction companies tend to train workers and provide for safety. But the industry remains dominated by small contractors who pay little attention to safety guidelines.[73] The result is a large number of undocumented casualties as workers are thrust onto construction sites with little training and no safety equipment.

The Price We Pay

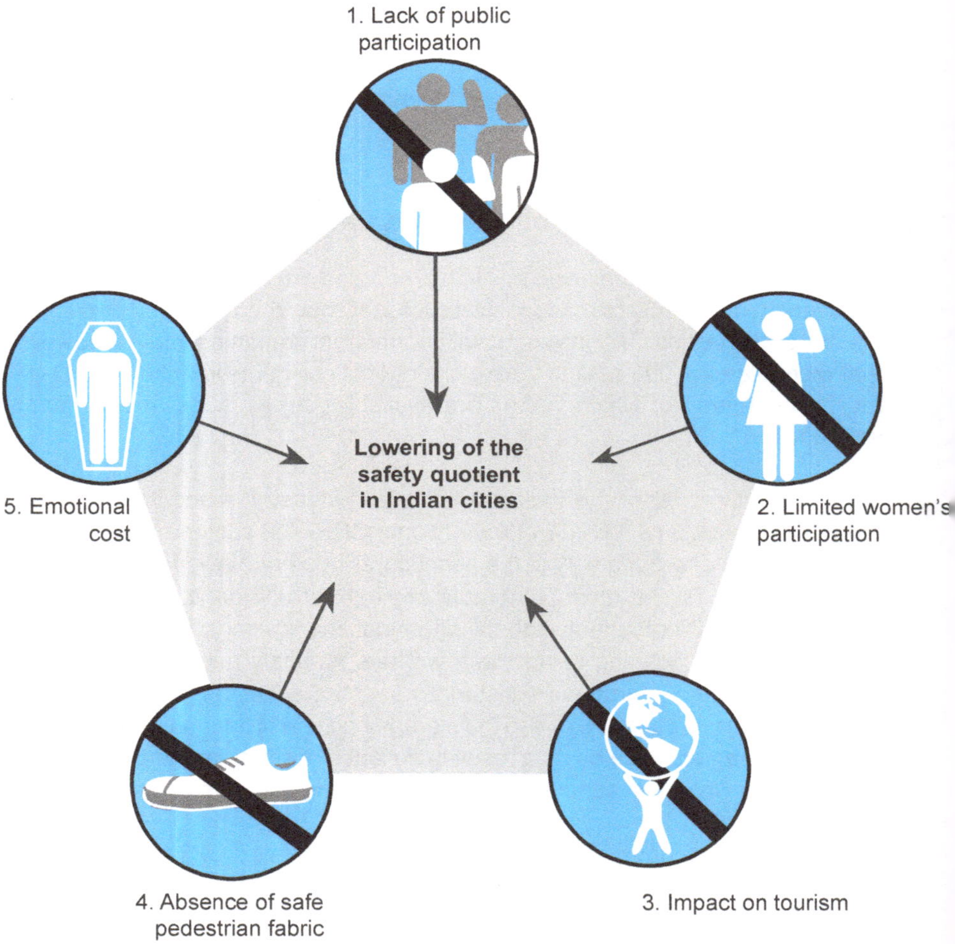

Urban safety and security is vital for citizen participation, engagement and access to services

In cities and urban areas in India and across the world, security has moved from being a social issue, affecting the well-being of individuals, to a serious developmental constraint. The lack of safety has the capacity to compromise the potential of entire societies, preventing the participation of citizens in active life, restricting their access to public services and locking them in a negative spiral of isolation and decay.

Lack of access to public spaces limits women's participation and self-expression

In the absence of a gendered approach to the expansion of urban spaces across cities and towns, women and girls are still unable to access the city on equal terms with men and boys.

Targeted simply because of their gender, women are exposed to daily harassment and sexual violence in public and community spaces. This takes place in and around schools, parks and workplaces, on streets and public transportation, in public-sanitation facilities, food- and water-distribution sites, or their own neighbourhoods. This limits their rights to public spaces, restricts their freedom of movement and reduces their ability to participate in school, work and public life and to enjoy cultural and recreational opportunities.

Impact on business, development and investment

At national and city levels, high homicide and violent crime rates are identified as major impediments to business, foreign investment and tourism, and also affect the willingness of people to invest in their own countries.

A recent study by the New Delhi–based Associated Chambers of Commerce & Industry of India (ASSOCHAM), for instance, has shown that in the three months after the 16 December gang rape, the number of foreigners travelling to India dropped by 25%, while the number of women tourists dropped by 35%. The study surveyed 1,200 tour operators across the country who agreed that 'concerns about the safety of women travelers' had impacted how foreign tourists viewed India.[74]

Inability to walk and access the city on foot

The Constitution of India guarantees every citizen the fundamental right to move freely throughout the country. Today, this right is violated in most urban areas as pedestrian infrastructure takes a backseat in the planning of Indian cities. Twenty-eight percent of all travel in urban India is done on foot and walking has the highest share of any other mode of transport. Despite these statistics, traditional Indian towns with mixed-use areas and walkable streets are being redeveloped to make way for unending roads that cater to private automobiles. Pedestrians are losing space on roads and sidewalks as on-street parking often takes precedence over pedestrian infrastructure. The result is severely compromised pedestrian safety, which effectively disenfranchises large sections of the population for whom walking is often the only option for mobility.[75]

Vulnerable Groups Violated and the Huge Emotional Cost

Apart from its impact on citizen participation, business and development, there is the huge emotional cost engendered by the absence of safety on the road network, at construction sites and in industry. Vulnerable groups must often bear the burden of huge medical expenses as well as loss of income due to death of or grievous injury to earning members. In the long term, the outcome is human cost compounded by financial debility, with aspects such as health, education and shelter being severely compromised.

1. FACELESS GOVERNMENT

Urban anonymity leads to higher crime rates

Citizens are invisible and so is the government

2. INADEQUATE SCALE OF GOVERNMENT RESPONSE

The pace of growth is outpacing the pace of planning

Ratio of police officers
Delhi - 120:10,000
World Average - 350: 10,000

3. PRONOUNCED SENSE OF THE OTHER

There is a sense of insecurity and perceived threat from anyone outside the immediate social strata that reflects in our responses to everyday phenomena which translates to a higher propensity for crime and violence against the perceived 'other'.

4. VIOLENCE OF HAVE-NOTS AGAINST HAVES

Where the distribution of education, health and employment are not available to all, it follows that the urban poor are forced to resort to crime and violence due to frustration and insecurity.

5. DERELICTION OF CHOICE OF SAFETY BY CITIZENS

In India, there is often a deliberate dereliction of this duty, with citizens choosing to subject themselves to the most unsafe circumstances.

The Problem

The lack of public safety has emerged as a social problem of great complexity and of significant importance affecting the quality of urban life in India. Before one can begin to talk of solutions, however, the first and most important step is to identify the issues that are leading to the lowering of the safety quotient in Indian cities.

Anonymity and a Faceless Government

Studies have shown that there is a steep rise in crime as population density rises from rural to urban areas. Safety in smaller communities is due to tighter networks and the increased likelihood of being caught or ostracized. In cities, anonymity, which is closely linked to a large immigrant workforce, breeds delinquency and a sense of freedom from inherited value systems and in the absence of accountability, the adoption of some disjointed, radical behaviour that allows the individual's basic instincts to guide him. This is compounded by little or no surveillance on the part of the authorities and the unavailability of corroborative evidence even in the wake of bona-fide efforts on the part of law-enforcement agencies, with the result that offenders often have no fear of the law, being seen or caught.

Citizens Are Invisible and So Is the Government

Another aspect of anonymity is little or no visibility of government functionaries. A beat constable, for instance, should, typically, be a familiar face in every community and know most inhabitants. This ensures that in the case of a crime or other emergency, members of the colony or neighbourhood are able to establish direct contact with the law-enforcement agency through him. In India, however, the numbers are so skewed and the functionaries so scarce that contact is only with the privileged few within the community, who use it to subvert the system rather than be governed by it. Only a combination of upscaling numbers and technology can resolve this mismatch of scales.

THE JANAMAITHRI SURAKSHA PROJECT

The Janamaithri (friends of public) Suraksha Project is an award-winning, community policing programme adopted by the Kerala Police, which aims to create a robust police–public interface by seeking the responsible participation of citizens in crime prevention at the level of the local community. The programme provides a beat officer for every residential area consisting of approximately 1,000 houses within a radius of 3 km, and a female constable detailed to every beat officer to ensure that the problems of women are addressed effectively. It requires that every officer knows at least one member of each family living on his beat along with the working habits and routines of the local people on a house-to-house basis. The programme also makes it mandatory for the beat officer to be available at least three days a week at a pre-announced place within the beat so anyone who wants to communicate anything to him can meet him there. The Janamaithri Suraksha Project has been tremendously successful in reducing crime rates in the communities in which it operates. It demonstrates that by creating a permanent mechanism for interaction with the public and by seeking their active participation in the performance of police duties, the process of law enforcement can become far more effective.

Pace of Growth and Inadequate Scale of Government Response

The pace of growth is outpacing the pace of planning. In Indian cities, the provision of facilities and services required to support large concentrations of population is lagging far behind the pace of urbanization. In most instances, planning and infrastructure follows inhabitation and growth (instead of the other way around), leading to unplanned initial settlements and then a game of shortsighted catch up by various arms of the government, such as the police, the municipality and the health agencies, in a typical desi, discordant manner of somehow managing the situation. The result is that the urban environment, particularly in larger cities, is deteriorating rapidly with a corresponding decrease in the quotient of safety and security. Data from the United Nations Office on Drugs and Crime from 2010 indicates, for instance, that in India, the police per capita is only 129 to every 1,00,000 citizens as compared to the worldwide average of 350, leading to a phenomenal increase in petty crime and violence across metros and urban areas.[76] It is a far cry from a predictive, proactive, planned approach where all agencies act in accordance with a laid-out master plan which is holistic, encompasses the concerns of all stakeholders and which has a longer term view with flexibilities well built in and key issues resolved.

Pluralism and a Pronounced Sense of the Other

India is the world's most plural society with dozens of ethnic and religious groups fragmented into a large number of sects, castes and sub-castes, coexisting within the extreme structuralism of the caste system. There is a prescriptive sense of 'our values' as opposed to 'their values' or 'our customs' as opposed to 'their customs'. The result is that cultures have thrived in silos and the whole sense of the other has taken birth in India. This sense of separation persists in our cities, reflected by the coexistence of many different sets of values in the same environment along with the belief that the other does not deserve the same kind of equality, respect and dignity. There is a sense of insecurity and perceived threat from anyone outside the immediate social stratum that is reflected in our responses to everyday phenomena, which translates to a higher propensity for crime and violence against the perceived 'other'.

What is missing is a shared 'civic identity' – a sense of citizenship and pride among the residents of a city. It is this collective identity or shared sense of belonging to a group along with a unified sense of appropriate behaviour guided by collective good which is the key to social order.

As a city, however, it is extremely important not only to have an exalted sense of what is appropriate behaviour for collective good but also that one cares for and empathizes with the other person on the street. Social order and empathy, together, are the bedrocks of good, safe and predictable environments. It is the inherent inability to understand and relate to the 'other' that leads to a lack of empathy. The result is that bystanders will rarely step forward to help victims of road accidents, or intervene and assist fellow citizens in the case of an attack or mishap, particularly when they perceive those persons as belonging to social groups or cultures other than their own.

Another aspect of collective identity is collective action. As citizens, we cannot always expect government agencies to rise to the occasion. In these instances, the government's inadequate response can often be filled by collective action on the part of citizens, which is critical.

Cases in point for collective action are community volunteers who, in many Western countries, serve as crossing guards and help young students walk to and from school safely.[77] Similarly, in India, in the places where residents' welfare associations (RWAs) are formed and fairly active, there is usually some definitive zone of action where they are able to act collectively, for instance, in the management of security and general cleanliness. We clearly see that wherever this sort of collective action or citizen *bhagidari* takes place, it impacts safety in a positive way. So issues such as installation of gates and management of colony's security are resolved, fencing is put up, guards are hired and the maintenance of general security maybe taken over from the government. This goes beyond mere citizenship; it is about finding the time, energy and inclination to act collectively and, therefore, to participate actively in the creation of a safe and secure environment.

Violence of Have-Nots against Haves

Social equity is the key to having a safe city. In the urban context, poverty reflects a lack of access to not just financial resources, but also to productive employment, basic services, effective and managed representation, and security and justice. Where the distribution of education, health and employment are not available to all, it follows that the urban poor often find themselves engaging in crime and violence due to frustration and insecurity.

Deliberate Dereliction of Choice of Safety by Citizens

It is the duty of citizens to take reasonable care to protect the health and safety of themselves and the people around them. In India, there is often a deliberate dereliction of this duty with citizens choosing to subject themselves to the most unsafe circumstances such as scaling medians and dividers, crossing high-speed roads without using zebra crossings, riding two-wheelers without helmets, driving without seat belts or under the influence of alcohol, and in the workplace, undertaking hazardous behaviour such as not reporting defects in machinery or choosing not to use safety equipment even when it is available.

CONSIDER THIS

In the Beas river tragedy, 24 engineering students from Hyderabad were drowned in an accident due to a sudden surge of river water released from an upstream hydroelectric project. Although the unfortunate incident could have been better managed by the dam authorities, it was also the result of careless action on the part of the students themselves – to climb up and sit precariously on a rock in the middle of a raging river.[78]

1. SAFETY FOR FEMALE CONSTRUCTION WORKERS

Female construction workers involved in the project by providing them with safe toilets, free health check-ups, midday meals and clean, well-lit accomodation.

2. SAFETY FOR ALL WOMEN

Citywalk is the first mall in India to offer dedicated nappy-changing stations for mothers with young children. As a first, the mall also provides for women parking attendants at key entry and exit points to enhance the feeling of comfort and safety for female patrons.

Prelude to the Solution

Select Citywalk – Case Study of a Mall

Let us begin by considering the case of Select Citywalk, a large retail and mixed land use project in Delhi, where the intent of the developer was to create a safe and convenient environment for women.

It is relevant here to underscore the clear choice that the developers of Select Citywalk made, to create a safe and enabling environment for women, as evinced by their willingness to undertake the extra expense necessary to achieve their purpose. At Citywalk, the commitment to safety has transcended social boundaries to include not just women shoppers within the mall but also female construction workers involved in the project, by providing them safe toilets, free health check-ups, midday meals and clean, well-lit accommodation.

Creating safety involves much more than simply responding to and preventing crime and violence. It requires the creation of an enabling environment in which women can move about safely, conveniently and without fear of violence or assault.

Conceived as a project in 2004, Select Citywalk was the first mall in India to offer dedicated nappy-changing stations for parents with young children. It was also the first to provide for women parking attendants at key entry and exit points to enhance the feeling of comfort and safety for female patrons.

Other design elements geared towards women include larger and more generous walkways (at the expense of retail space) to accommodate strollers and prams, and to allow women to walk about freely and without fear; higher lux levels in the parking and in stairwells; large, well-lit and highly visible lift lobbies; animated basements and carefully placed directional awareness signs to promote a sense of security, orientation and direction.

Safety has to be seen at every place and basement parking becomes one large area where women (and men) often feel insecure. So what is it that the developers of Select Citywalk did to make the parking safe?

It is a well-known fact of habitat design that criminal behaviour has a direct correlation with the built environment. Crime is less likely to occur in places that are clearly visible and within which activities can be easily seen. For instance, well-lit spaces with large windows or places where there are clear lines of sight and well-defined routes for people to easily enter and leave. It follows that transparency oversight – be it physical, functional or in a manner of connectedness through technology – or surveillance is a great way of ensuring safety.

The first step towards transparency is illumination. The architects of Select Citywalk, D.P.A Singapore and D.F.I. New Delhi, used much higher lux levels along with natural light filtered through a sophisticated system of skylights to ensure that areas such as the basement and the underground parking were secure and well lit.[79] Designers also ensured that lighting extended into the corners of parking stalls and that fixtures were carefully positioned to reduce glare, which can create problems for drivers due to the eye's inability to adjust rapidly to areas of light and darkness.

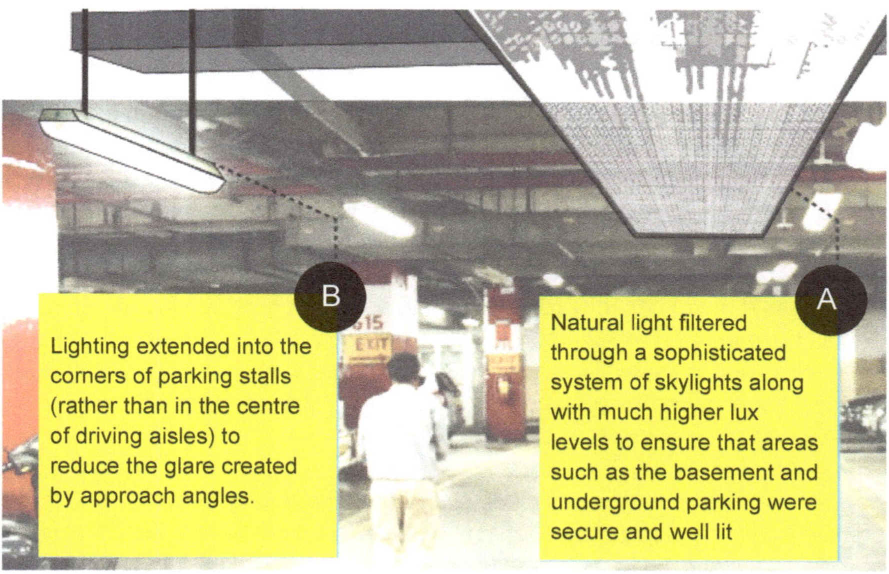

Experts consider natural surveillance to be the next most critical security design issue after lighting. People feel safer where they can be seen and heard by others and the essence of this 'eyes on the street' approach to planning and design is to increase opportunities for informal surveillance and to reduce the number of isolated places where crime can take place unseen.

At Citywalk, long-span construction and high ceilings were used to create openness and to enhance natural surveillance in the basement parking. Architects ensured that there were no dead-end parking areas, hidden nooks, corners or other potential hiding places which could attract persons with criminal intent. Lift lobbies, stairwells and waiting areas around escalators were purposefully designed with large plate glass windows to be well lit and spacious, making them clearly visible to patrons as well as security personnel stationed in the parking areas, limiting the possibility of both personal injury attacks and vandalism. Pedestrian paths were carefully planned to concentrate egress – bringing all pedestrians through one portal rather than allowing them to disperse through numerous exits, improving the ability to see and be seen by others. Similarly, vehicular entrance and egress were limited to a minimum number of locations, and attendant booths, parking offices and security stations were located where attendants could directly monitor activity.

C

Another means of increasing natural surveillance and transparency was to bring in retailers and small businesses into the basement.

Another means of increasing transparency was to bring retailers and small businesses into the basement. Patrons frequent such establishments even when activity in the parking is otherwise low, increasing opportunities for natural surveillance. There is also heightened vigilance on the part of owners and employees who have a vested interest in the security of the parking facility.

Studies have shown that an ability to find one's way with ease contributes to a sense of security and comfort in public areas. Within the Citywalk parking structure, signs and graphics were carefully placed to provide a clear sense of direction and orientation, allowing patrons to move quickly in and out of the parking structure, making them less vulnerable to attack. Additionally, a simple X and Y coordinate system boosted by colour-coded basements and parking bays was created to help drivers relocate their vehicles easily on return to the facility.

Other critical interventions in the environment included a bomb-resistant structural system and the construction of pressurized lift lobbies and stairwells as fire-safe zones, capable of holding several hundred people in the event of a fire, bomb scare or other disaster.

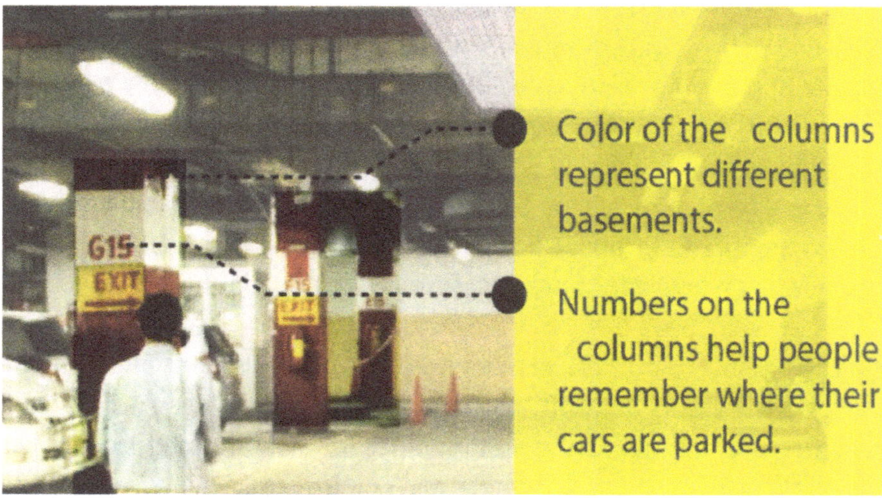

Select Citywalk also deploys state-of-the-art technology in the form of active security systems to enhance surveillance and oversight within the mall premises. Measures include comprehensive CCTV (in excess of 300, including some long-range focus cameras) and emergency communication coverage backed by a central control room, two-way intercom systems in elevators, stairwells and other enclosed areas, and sophisticated baggage scanners and hand-held explosive-detection devices at all entry points. Strict perimeter security and access control ensures that patrons on foot can only enter the premises through manned and 100% scanned entry points. Vehicular access to the parking area requires drivers to take a ticket on entry (often observed on a security camera) and interact with a booth attendant at exit, making the facility less attractive to criminals than one that is wide open and unattended. In addition, all entry and exit points are manned by highly visible, skilled security personnel, supplemented by dog squads trained to sniff out possible explosives.

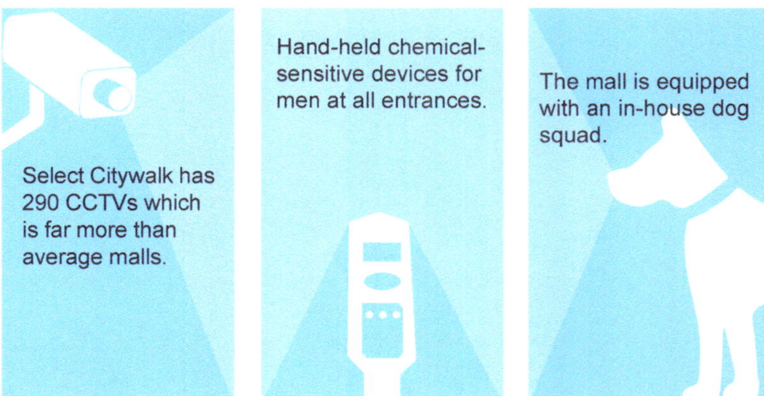

Select Citywalk was officially inaugurated in October 2007 by the former lieutenant governor of Delhi, Mr Tejinder Khanna. The mall has since won multiple awards for its safe development and the sense of safety and comfort that it has been able to give to women has translated to a greater number of footfalls and better business for the mall.

What Is It That Needs to Change?

The Three Measurable Domains of Action

The case of Select Citywalk clearly demonstrates how simple actions can translate very quickly to a safer and more secure environment. It also shows that in order to solve the problem of safer cities and to holistically impact the quotient of safety and security, we need to take action in three key domains:

1. Transforming Mindsets
2. Deployment of Technology
3. Interventions in Built Environment

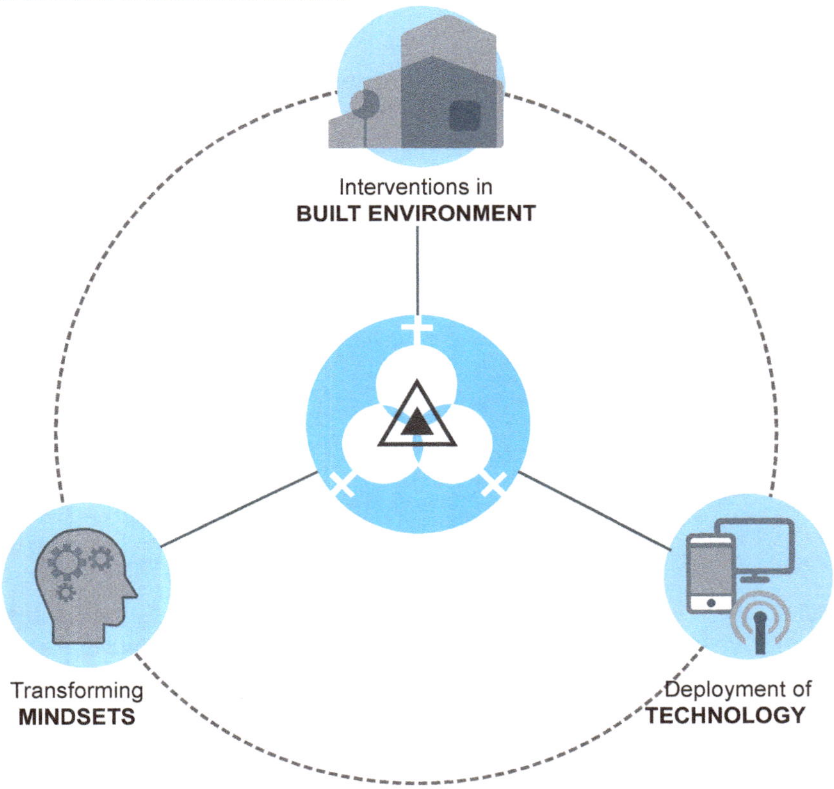

Transforming Mindsets

Safety is essentially a function of choice and intent: the choice of the average citizen who is vulnerable and wishes to be safe and the choice a community makes of increasing and maintaining a certain quotient of safety within the environment in which it exists. Below are some of the actions that can be taken to change this mindset:

a. Women's education
b. Gender sensitivity programmes in schools and colleges, within religious groups, corporates and the informal sector
c. Cop counsellers for vulnerable groups
d. Disrupting gender stereotypes
e. Community discourses on pluralism and the coexistence of differing value systems
f. Creating awareness – legal / medical / psychiatric counselors
g. Driving citizen engagement and involvement
h. Tax concessions for women-empowerment initiatives
i. Mandatory spending on women-empowerment projects as part of CSR initiatives

The first and the most important step towards creating safety, therefore, is to bring about a paradigm shift in the way that we, as a community, think about the issue of safety and security and drive a movement towards creating 'choice and intent' at the level of the average citizen – through awareness and education programmes in schools and colleges, within religious bodies, corporations and government institutions, and in the informal sector.

Some Might Argue

Tougher laws and expeditious justice is the only way to ensure that cities remain safe. To this we submit that while justice maybe the cornerstone of public safety, the bedrock of a safer city is 'every individual citizen's choice to be safe' based on the foundation of an appropriately built environment and the use of enabling technologies. The state and the citizens must work together to realize the dream of safer cities.

Similarly, the success of initiatives to address women's safety and security depends upon the transformation of social norms and the disruption of gender stereotypes that perpetuate inequality, discrimination and violence.

Gender-based policies for safer cities must aim to eliminate negative gender stereotypes, focus on empowering women to take leadership roles in different professions, business and local governance, and ensure a gendered approach to further planning and development. These policies must include, among other measures, regular gender sensitivity programmes and the mandatory implementation of Vishakha guidelines across businesses, corporations and government institutions, increasing the representation of women cops in cities and metros, and concessions for and the allocation of adequate resources to women's organizations and empowerment initiatives.

Gender Sensitivity Programmes

Although there is a rise in awareness and a conversation has begun around what gender equality means for the average person (the media, for instance, has taken up cudgels and this shift in mindset has begun to reflect in campaigns which portray women in alternate roles, at the workplace or as breadwinners), what is needed are regular gender sensitivity programmes within offices, businesses, corporations and government bodies, and as part of the curriculums of educational institutions. What the government could also do is have a gender sensitivity day, for instance, which every person and every community – whether it is the gurudwara, the mandir or the girjaghar – observes. This would not just be a woman's day where we may present the women in our lives with cards, gifts and flowers, but a day on which to conduct genuine introspection on what are the five things that we, as a community, are willing to do to commit ourselves to gender equality and changing our notions.

Sexual Harassment at the Workplace

Sexual harassment at the workplace has remained one of the central concerns of the women's movement in India since the early 1980s, when the Forum against Oppression of Women (Mumbai) took up the case against the sexual harassment of nurses in public and private hospitals by patients and their male relatives, ward-boys and other hospital staff; of air-hostesses by their colleagues and passengers; of teachers by their colleagues, principals and management representatives; of PhD students by their guides, and so on.

In 1997, the Supreme Court in *Vishaka and Others* v. *The State of Rajasthan and Others*, for the first time, acknowledged the gravity of sexual harassment in the workplace and laid down certain guidelines (Vishaka Guidelines), making it mandatory for employers to prevent the commission of acts of sexual harassment and to provide procedures for the resolution, settlement or prosecution of such offences. It was held by the Supreme Court that the guidelines issued were to be treated as law and further, they were to be strictly observed in all workplaces for the enforcement of the right to gender equality of the working woman.

It was only in 2013, after a span of 16 years, that India finally enacted the Sexual Harassment of Women at the Workplace (Prevention, Prohibition and Redressal) Act, 2013.The act makes it mandatory for all offices with 10 or more employees to have an internal complaints committee to address complaints of sexual harassment within a stipulated time or face a stiff penalty. The act provides for termination of service of the accused, withholding of promotions and increments and payment of reasonable compensation to the complainant in the event the harassment is proved. In case the allegations against the accused are found to be false or made with malicious intent, the act allows for the complainant to face similar penal provisions as those listed for the accused.[80]

Increasing the Number of Female Cops

Unhappy with the thin presence of women in the police force, a bench of the Delhi high court comprising Hon. Jus. N.V. Ramana (CJ) and Hon. Jus. Manmohan, has asked the centre why 50% of all Delhi Police personnel cannot be women.[81] Given the increasing number of crimes against women, we could go a step further and say that reservation for women cops should be applied to police across the country, and in areas where the safety situation is dire (especially in metros and cities), a separate Women's Security Force be raised to ensure the safety and security of the female population.

Just as you have the Border Security Force (BSF), which protects the border in times of peace and the Central Industrial Security Force (CISF), which is mandated to provide security for Public Sector Undertakings (PSUs), critical infrastructure installations and sensitive government buildings, we could easily have a corps of female security professionals for each city, which could be assembled and raised just to protect women. This would go a long way towards enhancing the feeling of safety and security for the average woman on the street as well as increasing sensitivity to and the understanding of women's issues on the part of the police force.

Gender Cop Counselors

In the current set-up, cops themselves are often not fully aware of the rules applicable in cases where the aggrieved person is a woman – what are the rights they have as women or how the rules need to be applied to them differently. So it is extremely important that every police station has a Gender Cop, a person with a psychology or psychiatry background whose job is to sensitize the police force from within and to interact with the woman citizen at the other end. Just as the beat constable's job is to know what is happening within his beat, the sole objective of the Gender Cop Counsellor would be to ensure the safety and the well-being of every woman within his or her domain.

'Mera Astitva Sirf Aapko Samarth Banane Ka Hai'

Let us say, for instance, that a Cop Counsellor were to conduct a Gender Sensitivity Programme at the gurudwara / mandir in Greater Kailash-2. The counsellor would, accordingly, address the women of the locality and tell them how to be aware, what are their rights under the law, what are they entitled to in different situations, and if they have any problem, if they are being harassed for dowry or if their husband is mistreating them, they can come to the police station and find them there. They will help to find solutions to their problems.

Generally, young women and girls are afraid of even entering a police station, let alone lodging a complaint or talking to a police officer. There is typically nobody within the police station who is willing to entertain these complaints properly, unless they know or have personal contact with the complainant or someone is known to the complainant. So now the women citizenry will start to feel that at least there is someone within the police station they can talk to or who will listen to their problems.[82]

Safety, however, is not just about gender. Social cohesion and integration are also critical elements for the creation of safer cities. Accordingly, policymakers and educationists must take up and address issues arising from ethnic, cultural and religious diversity in the Indian society and work towards creating a culture of tolerance, acceptance and respect – a seminal step towards inclusive growth and sustainable peace.

Consider This

In his autobiography *Wings of Fire*, A.P.J. Abdul Kalam, the former President of India, talks about how in the island town of Rameswaram where he grew up, the local Hindu priest, the maulvi and the padre met every week to discuss issues affecting their respective communities and attempted to come up with solutions together.[83]

Transformation of mindsets in the specific sphere of affinity for people of other faiths is only possible if there is genuine interfaith interaction between different communities. Therefore, it is extremely important that some forums be opened which are available for such dialogue to happen. Currently, the only interfaith interaction that happens is at Iftar parties where Hindus often go to eat kheer and other delicacies. Muslims, to some extent, have also begun to participate in Diwali – they send out greetings and gifts. This is a small area where simple things like greeting each other on the other's festivals can be seen as a sign of inclusion. In this respect, it is social media which has had a democratizing effect, with several leaders sending out greetings on Facebook and Twitter to ethnic groups other than their own.

Deployment of Technology

The convergence of various technologies plays a key role in the development of safer cities. From CCTVs, biometrics, license plate recognition and gunshot detection to advanced database systems and crisis-management centres, technology acts as a key enabler for law enforcement, emergency services and local decision makers to optimize their response to crisis situations.

Some recommended technological interventions for a safer city

Emergency buttons / Lux apps on cell phones

Smart cities – High situational awareness and collaborative technologies for greater interoperability between departments

Extensive CCTV / surveillance coverage

Moving from 'reactive to predictive' policies, using Predictive Analytics and Big Data based on density of population / individuals sensed through mobile phones

However, since safer city solutions incorporate a wide array of technologies, integration and interoperability is fundamental. What this means is that we must work towards creating Smart Cities – cities which have a high situational awareness and use collaborative technologies for greater inter-operability between departments. Smart Cities have a sophisticated, digital central nervous system, which enables the flow and immediate sharing of information between government departments and law-enforcement agencies, ensuring a higher degree of oversight, better coordination and shorter response times. While advanced database systems are changing the way in which intelligence is being gathered and processed, the emergence of smart technologies means that there are massive amounts of data from personal devices, social media networks, GPS technologies, CCTV footage and critical infrastructure to gather and interpret all the data. This analysis often provides intelligence on how to act or react to critical situations which is vital in keeping a city safe. By combining the latest big data technologies with predictive analytic capabilities, law-enforcement agencies can – for the first time – analyse large sets of data to generate important intelligence insights to accurately inform operational decision makers and even day-to-day policing.

The Emergency Button[84]

The Emergency Button is a simple technological tool, which can go a long way towards making citizens safer. It consists of an app that can be installed on your phone and which allows you to create a security group with anywhere from 2 to 20 people on it. The app exists as a button – either an actual button visible on the screen once you enter the app – which you can simply tap or a preselected key on your phone's keyboard, the hash key for instance, or any number from 0 to 9. In case of an emergency, you simply press the button twice and the app sends an automatic distress signal to all the people on your safety group through a series of WhatsApp messages. It also sends a default distress signal to the beat constable of your area or police station.

In the event of a distress signal, the probability is that at least one person on one's safety group would attempt to contact them and if one were to respond by saying 'Sorry, I pressed the button by mistake,' they would naturally be relieved that one is safe. If, however, one failed to answer, the person would have the option of triggering a 'not reachable' alarm on the app to which the beat constable would immediately respond by first locating the person's phone through GPS and then trying to find and help them. If they were not actually in distress and it were a false alarm, the beat constable would have the ability to fine the person – between Rs 1,000 to Rs 5,000, which could collectively go into a pool for whatever normally needs be done in terms of providing a phone or a GPS tracker to the beat constable.

Whether there are enough beat constables to make the app effective is a question that can only be answered when such a system is put in place, but certainly one would have created a two-level safety net: one consisting of one's immediate friends and family, the second being an emergency connection with the beat constable, who would also have the ability to know where the person or to trace one because he has a GPS tracker.

EMERGENCY BUTTON: Multiple Operating System

App for smartphones

Existing button can be replaced to incorporate the SOS button.
Long press # activates SOS

One-touch emergency button can be incorporated in new phones

EMERGENCY BUTTON: Two-step security net

Interventions in Built Environment

Well-lit streets and urbanscapes
Contiguous pedestrian fabric
Regulated informal sector
Directional awareness
Safe and clean public toilet infrastructure for women

According to findings from research conducted in Delhi as part of the multi-city Gender Inclusive Cities (GIC) Project (2009–2010), Delhi's dearth of public infrastructure, such as clean and safe public toilets for women, well-lit streets and proper pavements, is an important factor contributing to the lack of safety in the city.[85]

Within the course of the present publication, the authors have suggested and extensively discussed several measures that could potentially be used to impact each of these factors and bring about a significant transformation in the quotient of safety and security in Indian cities.

Chapter 5, for instance, tackles the issue of clean and safe public toilets. It introduces the notion of sanitation as a fundamental right and proposes the setting up of an autonomous authority called the Toilets Corporation of India (TCI) which, working in collaboration with municipalities across the country, fulfills its mandate to provide safe, clean and hygienic public toilets to the citizens of India.[86] Similarly, Chapter 3, Traffic Compliance, takes up the cause of the much-neglected pedestrian and advocates the creation of another empowered body called the Pedestrian Commission of India (PCI) to effect the fundamental right to safety of every pedestrian on a pan-India basis. As the nodal agency, the PCI uses domain expertise and a planned approach to examine the problem of pedestrian safety at the macro and micro levels and to come up with appropriate solutions for different local contexts, such as residential colonies, markets and shopping centers, metro stations, flyovers, highways, T-junctions and clover crossings.

As the owner and administrator of the sidewalk, the PCI becomes responsible for installing streetlights on roads and streets, which are critical for cyclist and pedestrian safety. It also becomes the vehicle for the setting up of an extensive network of CCTV cameras as standard fixtures on every light pole. What this does is create a sophisticated, grid-based system of street video surveillance, which has the potential to impact public safety in a fundamental way.

The PCI is envisaged as an autonomous body, empowered to fine for non-compliant behaviour on its own domain through the instrument of the Civic Cop (the extensive system of CCTV cameras set up by it), which makes it possible to detect civic offences, such as spitting, littering, urinating, eve teasing, unauthorized parking, encroachment and defacing public property on the pavement and within the pedestrian space.[87]

Regulating the Informal Sector

What the PCI could also do is use the model of the Civic Cop to regulate the informal sector, which animates the soft shoulder and the sidewalk in most Indian cities and towns.[88] There are an estimated 1 crore street vendors in the cities of India, functioning mostly in breach of urban laws which govern licensing, selling and zoning.[89] These vendors consist of a large immigrant population with a very different set of value systems, which thinks it is anonymous and therefore can do anything and get away with it.

For the PCI to come in and suddenly say that there will be no *puchka-wala*, no *mochi* and no *paan ki dukaan* on the sidewalk is simply not practical. As the *mai-baap* of the sidewalk and the soft shoulder, the PCI cannot ban or remove the informal sector, an economic reality, which provides productive employment and cheap goods and services to the urban poor. It must, therefore, find a way to regulate it.

In the current model, there is an interface of institutionalized corruption, which exists between the local cop and the informal sector. The solution, very simply, is to legitimize that relationship or interface.

So now, the local cop has a government-issued, hand-held machine with which he clicks a photograph of Raju and his helpers. He also takes their thumb impressions and uses the same machine to issue ID cards to the helpers and a Spot License to Raju, in return for which he tells Raju that 'chum, you need to do five things':

1. Give me photographs and thumb impressions of all your help
2. Put a proper dustbin next to your cart
3. Install a solar light
4. Put up a CCTV camera on top of your cart (supplied by the concessionaire / Civic Cop Corporation)
5. Make sure you are not conflicting with the pedestrian fabric

The cop cannot grant a Spot License without these five requirements being fulfilled. He has a small checklist which he ticks and which has his signature to indicate that he has checked that all five conditions have been met. The cop says that, 'money, I will still take, and you can pay me Rs 500 less, but if my boss comes and sees that there is no solar light and no dustbin, I will get suspended – so you better make sure these things are there.'

So the onus is now on the cop to make sure that the rules are being followed.

This ensures that the local cop enforces the rules and that he knows who every street vendor is. Similarly, Raju *golgappe-wala* knows and his helper who has come from, say, Jharkhand also knows that now they cannot do anything wrong because not only have their photos been clicked and their thumb impressions taken, there is also a CCTV camera installed on top of the cart.

AFTER PCI

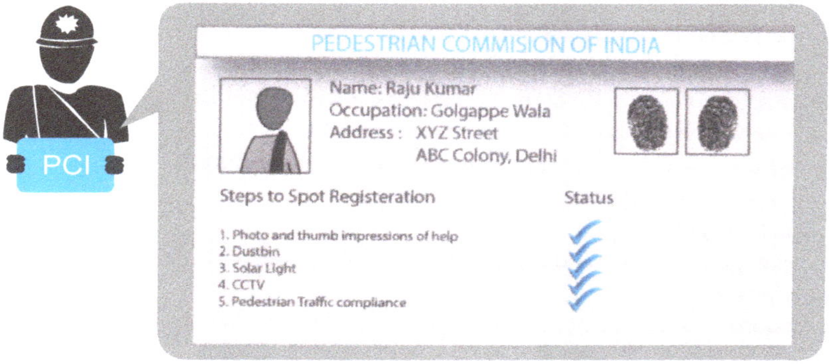

STEPS TO SPOT REGISTERATION

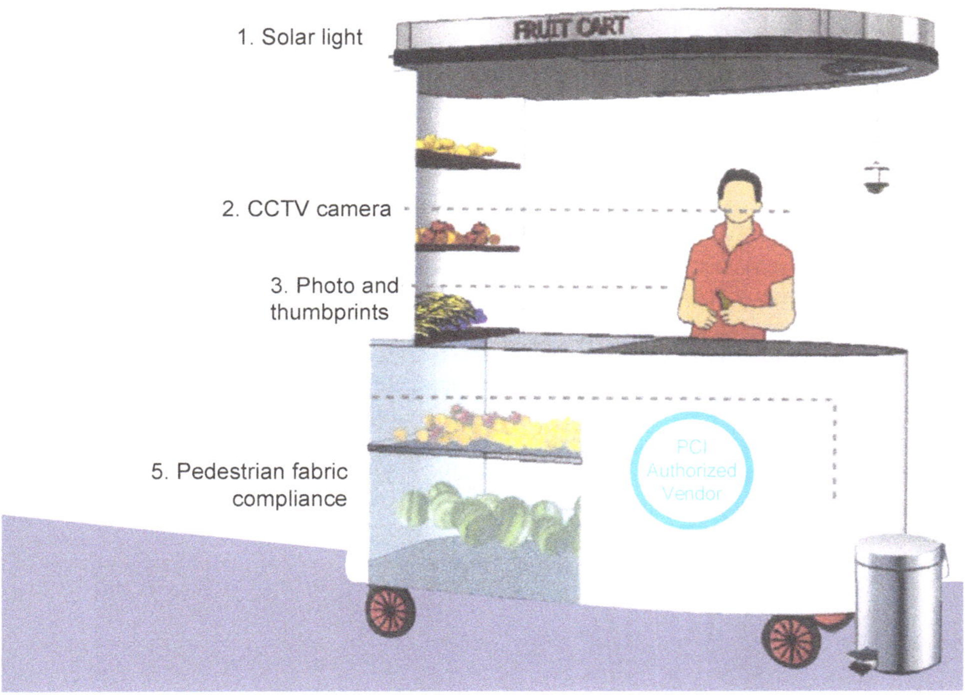

What this will do is legitimize the informal sector and also make them the 'eyes and ears' of the state on the street.

What we are saying is that every person wants to be a positive citizen provided you give him or her simple rules to follow. As it is, the informal sector functions under whatever operating environment the local beat constable puts in place. What we are doing is defining five simple rules, which ensure that the footpath is not encroached upon; every business has a dustbin, a solar light and a CCTV camera; and the owner of the business is not an anonymous someone but a known entity.

The result is that we have transformed a negative operating environment into an empowered, safe space for the informal sector, which gets a certain degree of legitimacy and becomes regulated. All it has to do is comply with certain simple, easy-to-follow rules even though it may or may not continue to pay the local cop.

REGULATING THE DOMESTIC SERVICES SECTOR

The Cop Licensing Model could easily be extended and used to create identities for the largely unregulated immigrant population that works in urban homes as domestic help. If you were to hire a new helper, for instance, you would simply inform the local beat constable who would come to your home and use his hand-held machine to take the worker's photo and biometrics and issue him or her a valid ID card. So now the local cop has a record of every cleaner, driver and helper who works in every house in his locality and the helper knows that if he commits a crime, he can be easily found because his photo and fingerprints are already with the police. This could go a long way towards making the elderly, who often find themselves dependent on domestic helps, feel safer and more secure.

Suddenly, now that there is a check, the footpath becomes a safer and cleaner place and even if Raju has to pay Rs 10,000 for a Spot License, which he was paying anyway, at least Raju golgappe-wala has now become legal. Also, once he has the license and has had it renewed three or four times, he has a much stronger locus standi to operate on the pavement, and the next time a new beat constable asks him for a higher sum, he can refuse to pay. Or he can refuse to pay a bribe altogether. Since the rule is so simple, he can just say: 'How can you not allow me to set up shop here when I have adhered to all the five requirements?'

Also, this way, someone becomes accountable. So now, if you find that the vendors in your colony are not following the rules, you can at least lodge a complaint against the beat constable and the station house officer (SHO), saying that 'Here are 20 photographs of the vendors in this area and how are they being allowed to get away with this when there is a clear policy?'

Here, the PCI is simply the agency that frames the rules. It could, for instance, provide three spots every 100 metres for the informal sector, along all arterial roads. In areas like Tughlakabad, which have a higher density of vendors, it would be cognizant of this fact and provide accordingly. The PCI could provide laybys to park the carts or widen the footpath to allow for the mochi or the paan-wala to sit there. It could also provide drainage points so that each cart's effluent goes directly into the gutter and does not litter the pavement.

The PCI also becomes the vehicle for the auction of solar lights and CCTV cameras (to be installed on vending carts) and the right to collect fines from them. A concessionaire could, for instance, identify 50 vendors within a certain area and say that he will install CCTV cameras on all of their carts or concessionaires could vie for the right to put up the cameras because they know that a Rs 2,000 camera will earn them Rs 5,00,000 every month.

Directional Awareness

It would also become the responsibility of the PCI to ensure that directional awareness signs and way-finding signage are aptly planned, installed and working in all cities.

Anywhere you travel in the world, street signs are always written in terms of the cardinal directions – North, South, East and West. In India, however, we have this concept of relative direction, which can be very confusing for anybody who is new to the city. The result is that visitors and tourists, because they are disoriented, must seek directions from strangers on the road or random taxi drivers and auto-wallas, when they might not actually need to seek directions otherwise, making them vulnerable to miscreants, theft and personal assault.

Consider This

In a particularly heinous instance, a Danish tourist was gang-raped in Delhi when she got lost and asked for directions to her hotel. Police officials said the 51-year-old woman was also robbed and beaten in the attack, which happened in the afternoon in the narrow streets near Connaught Place, a popular shopping centre and one of Delhi's tourist attractions.[90]

Very simply, therefore, the PCI must add scientific, Cartesian directions to street signs and ensure that road signs are based on a simple syntax that people can understand and orient themselves to and therefore be in a position to reach their destination safely.

Figuring out *WHAT* needs to be done is easy. The real challenge, however, is figuring out *HOW*!

Creating an Ecosystem for Safer Cities

Case Study 1 – The LEED Story

Let us consider the case of LEED, or Leadership in Energy and Environmental Design, a green building certification system that was successfully used to solve a similar problem – of how to make the built environment more energy efficient.

When American scientists began studying the leading causes of climate change, they found that the commercial and residential building sector accounted for almost 39% of the total carbon dioxide emissions in the United States.

Most of these emissions came from the combustion of fossil fuels required to provide heating, cooling and lighting and to power appliances and electrical equipment. The conclusion was, therefore, that by transforming the built environment to be more energy-efficient (by 'building green'), the building sector could play a major role in reducing the threat of climate change.[91]

The first step in this process was to define 'green buildings' by establishing certain standards of measurement for building performance and efficiency. Accordingly, in 1995, the US Green Building Council set up the LEED ratings system to measure how efficient a building really was by weighing and considering its contribution to energy savings, water efficiency and CO_2 emissions reduction.

Site selection | **Water efficiency** | **Energy and atmosphere**

Materials and resources

Indoor environmental quality

Innovation and design process

The next step was to publish the results of the measurement by granting pre- and commissioning-level certifications based on the ratings system and therefore to recognize projects that were implementing strategies for better environmental and health performance.

To receive a LEED certification, building projects must satisfy certain prerequisites and earn points in six main categories: site selection, water efficiency, energy and atmosphere, materials and resources, indoor environmental quality and innovation and design process. Points are awarded on a basic 100-point scale and credits are weighted to reflect their potential environmental impacts. There are four levels of certification – the number of points a project earns determines the level of LEED certification it will receive. Typical certification thresholds are certified (40–49 points), silver (50–59 points), gold (60–79 points) and platinum (80+ points).[92]

The objective of the certification was to promote the adoption of sustainable green building practices and to raise awareness of the benefits of building green and in the process, to discourage buildings from using excess energy and water and encourage them to generate less waste. By doing so, not only would they be more environment-friendly but also save owners and occupiers a considerable amount of money on operating costs.

Studies have shown that the average LEED-certified building uses 32% less electricity and saves 350 metric tons of CO_2 emissions annually, yielding buildings and communities that are environmentally responsible, cost less to operate and provide healthier work and living environments.[93] A report of the US Green Building Council indicates that (as of November 2013) the LEED footprint spanned 10.6 billion sq. ft, extending to nearly 60,000 green building projects across the globe.[94]

In India, numbers have crossed 833 million square feet under the aegis of the Indian Green Building Council, since the introduction of LEED in the year 2005.[95] Which would mean that within a period of less than 20 years, 10.6 billion sq. ft of built environment across the globe has been definitively transformed to become 30 to 40% more efficient in terms of energy savings, water use, reduction in CO_2 emissions and the stewardship of resources.

The question is, how did LEED achieve this transformation?

Very simply, what LEED did was to transform the building environment by introducing a unified scale of measurement based on certain health and environmental parameters and causing all stakeholders to align thought, intent and action towards the achievement of those parameters.

1. MEASURE the performance of built environment

2. Create TRANSPARENCY

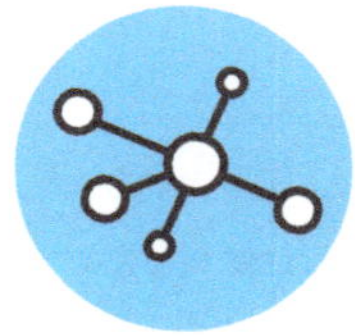

3. CONNECTEDNESS among the stakeholders of the building environment

First, LEED made it possible to measure the performance of each building, community or habitat on the basis of a pre-stated charter of goodness. Second, it created transparency by adopting the tool of dual certification (at the levels of intent and action) which offered compelling proof to owners, occupiers, peers and the public at large of how each building, community or habitat was performing on environmental parameters. The certificate allowed owners and developers to take advantage of a growing number of government incentives and to promote their projects (including buildings that were still in development) as 'LEED certified' to prospective buyers and tenants.

By creating transparency and therefore awareness of the benefits of 'building green' boosted by conferences, seminars and information published in the public domain, LEED succeeded in bringing about a certain connectedness among the stakeholders of the building environment. Connectedness informed users, making it possible for them to tell how one environment was better than the other, while transparency influenced intent and choice – owners and occupiers could now choose to live in greener buildings and therefore benefit by getting cleaner air and saving on energy while also doing minimal damage to the environment.

Measurement allowed stakeholders – architects, designers, builders, developers and vendors – to benchmark their performance with regard to others in the industry, within the same context and therefore, inspired aligned action at the level of thought, intent and execution.

The result was the creation of a whole new ecosystem geared towards 'building green' with owners and users increasingly aligned towards choosing buildings that conformed to higher and higher green standards, developers and builders correspondingly backing green projects with intent and money (transformation of mindsets), architects and designers upscaling their level of training and information to design buildings that performed better on environmental parameters and vendors aligning to the higher level of requirement to supply energy-efficient equipment such as LED bulbs (as opposed to CFL) and higher rated air conditioners which consumed less electricity (interventions in built environment and deployment of technology). The movement also gave rise to an entirely new stream of LEED Accredited Professionals, who with demonstrated expertise in green building and the LEED rating system were able to advise projects in meeting their LEED goals including, for instance, suggesting ways to earn LEED credits without extra cost, identifying means of offsetting certain expenses with savings in other areas and spotting opportunities for synergies in various projects.[96]

Therefore, by using the three tools of transformation – measurement, transparency and connectedness – LEED was able to align all stakeholders of the building environment, and to wire them to the success of the green movement.

Case Study 2 – The Energy Label

Another similar example of alignment is that of energy labelling. The energy label is a simple tool designed to help consumers compare appliances with similar characteristics on the basis of energy consumption. In India, the Standards & Labeling Program is administered by the Government of India and the objective of the programme as set out by the Bureau of Energy Efficiency (BEE) is the 'efficient use of energy and its conservation.'[97]

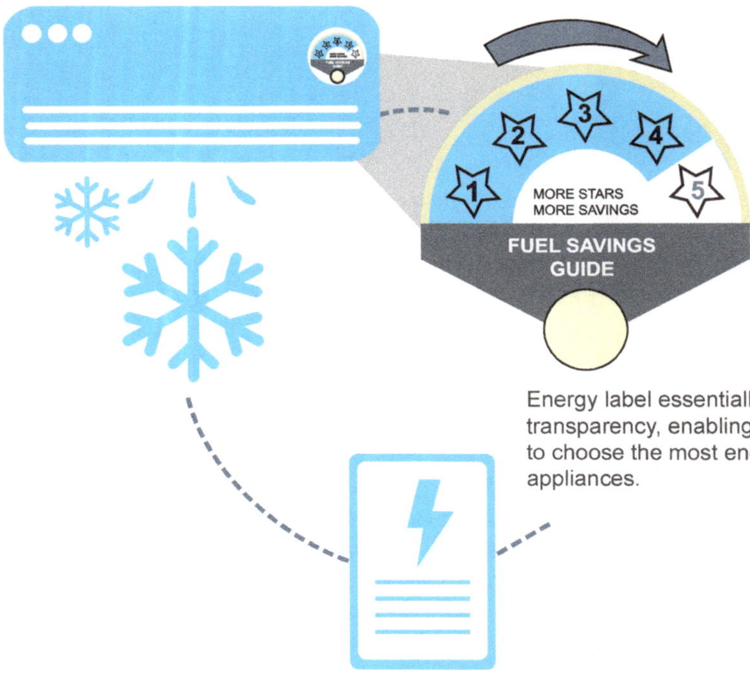

Energy label essentially promotes transparency, enabling consumers to choose the most energy-efficient appliances.

Therefore, reducing their electricity and power bills.

SOME MIGHT ARGUE

This whole business of transparency is theoretical and therefore futile. To this we submit that today, transparency is literally being lapped up by the consumer. Foods marked with nutritional information such as ingredients, number of calories and fat content have become very popular with shoppers who are typically willing to pay a premium for products that display this information. The result is that many entrepreneurs are using this opportunity to come up with food products, which are fresh, organic and more nutritious, and can therefore command a higher price. The Select Citywalk Mall, for instance, is in the process of launching a new food mart where every article will be marked not just with nutritional information but also the date on which its contents were harvested, packed and shipped. So now it will become possible to know that the mango you are eating was grown by a mango farmer named Rajkumar near Nashik in Maharashtra; that it was harvested in April 2015 and shipped in May 2015, first to Delhi and then to the shop from which you bought it.

In the case of air conditioners, for instance, minimum efficiency performance standards are prescribed by the BEE and each appliance is rated in terms of a set of stars from 1 to 5, with 5 stars being the most energy efficient and 1 being the least efficient. The first and most important step, therefore, is to be able to measure goodness on any parameter. In the case of air conditioners and other appliances, the parameter is energy efficiency and hence lower electricity and power bills. Before the labelling programme was introduced, consumers had no access to evergy-consumption information in respect to their household appliances. What existed, instead, was a vicious cycle in which consumers continued to purchase and use inefficient (often cheaper) appliances, which consumed more electricity while the inefficient appliances themselves continued to be available in the market resulting in the wasteful use of precious energy.

What the energy label essentially does is create transparency, enabling consumers to easily choose the most efficient appliances and therefore, to reduce their monthly energy bills. It follows that a buyer might actually choose to buy a higher rated air conditioner even though it costs Rs 5,000 more because he can figure out very quickly that the difference in operational cost between the 3-star and the 5-star air conditioner is Rs 1,000 a month (with the lower rated air conditioner being more expensive to run), so that in 5 months, he would have recovered the extra cost.

By creating transparency, the energy label aligns the intent and choice of the newly aware consumer who now prefers to buy the higher rated air conditioner. There is a corresponding alignment on the part of the manufacturer who must upscale to the higher level of requirement if he wants to continue selling air conditioners and on the part of the various sub-vendors who maybe supplying parts to the manufacturer. The result is the creation of a whole new ecosystem geared towards energy efficient air conditioners with the prices of higher rated air conditioners progressively decreasing as a result of higher demand and inefficient airconditioners disappearing from the market due to no demand, leading to a corresponding reduction in energy use and damage to the environment.

Imagine an India...

where safety is enshrined as a fundamental right in the Constitution.

where citizens have come together to act in unison in a manner that is both missionary and objective, to measure and impact the safety of their built environment.

where safety is a transparent and measurable parameter - a function of choice and collective action.

where government apathy and citizen haplessness have been transformed and replaced with a new ecosystem that engages both in an enduring partnership. One that empowers the citizens and the government with appropriate tools to impact the quotient of safety and enables both together, to be a part of the solution.

The Solution

The IWES

How can we follow the LEED example and put in place an ecosystem for measuring safety in Indian cities?

The idea is to create a 10-point rating system called the Index for Women's Empowerment and Safety (IWES), which could potentially be used to measure the quotient of safety and security in communities, organizations, corporations, government institutions and eventually cities, based on the goodness of performance on various parameters within the three key domains of:

- Transformation of mindsets
- Interventions in built environment
- Deployment of technology

Much like the LEED rating system, which over the last 20 years has revolutionized the green building movement, the IWES would seek to create a benchmark for the design, construction and operation of safer cities and to champion the movement towards 'women's empowerment and safety' using measurement, transparency and connectedness along with monetary incentives to drive change.

STEP 1

Government in consultation with civil society to set up an autonomous regulatory body called the Safety Council of India (SCI)

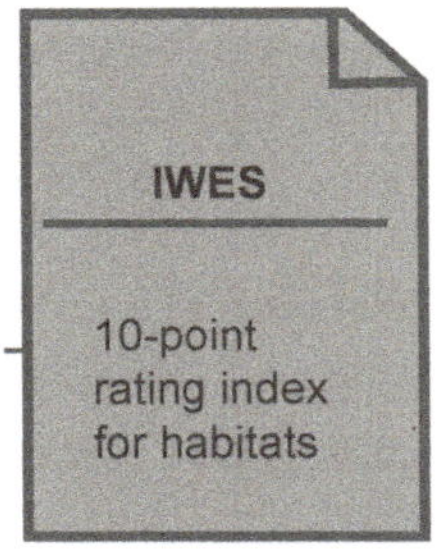

Members of the core body shall be responsible not only for establishing the parameters of goodness but also for ensuring the parameters remain dynamic – by adding, subtracting or editing the criteria or standard for each rating system – as may be required from time to time,based on an internal-review process.

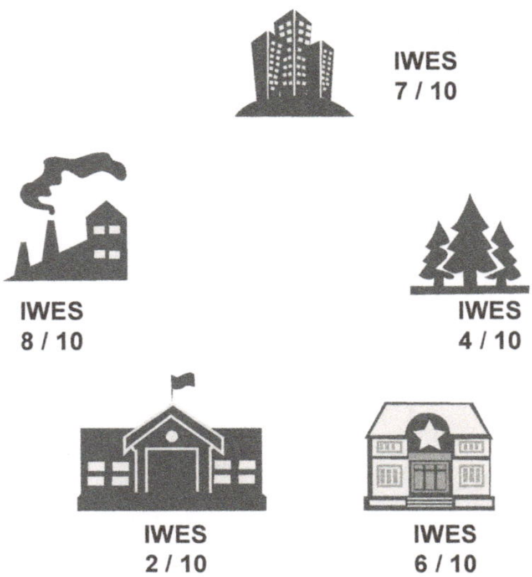

The Way Forward

The first step is for the government in consultation with civil society to set up an autonomous regulatory body called the Safety Council of India (SCI), which works together in collaboration with law-enforcement and other agencies, and fills its mandate of holistically impacting the quotient of safety and security in Indian cities.

As an apex body, the SCI will consist of a core group of experts drawn from various professional backgrounds, including (among others) lawyers, TV and media professionals, social activists, structural and fire advisors, architects, representatives of women's interest organizations, traffic, security and human resource consultants and lighting professionals, tasked with creating a 100-point charter of goodness that provides a set of 10-point ratings called IWES for different categories of habitat.

Potential habitat categories could include, for instance, multistoried apartments, gated colonies, commercial and mixed-land use, industry and corporations, educational institutions, recreational areas, roads, walkways and public parks, non-governmental organizations, government departments and public utilities, police stations and even judicial institutions – with each category governed by a separate set of criteria that addresses its unique requirements. Once an entity chooses a category or a rating system, therefore, it must use the appropriate criteria to guide design and operational decisions on its path to IWES certification.

Members of the core body will be responsible not only for establishing the parameters of goodness but also for ensuring the parameters remain dynamic – by adding, subtracting or editing the criteria or standard for each rating system, as may be required from time to time, based on an internal review process.

In addition to its core, expert body, the SCI will also train and certify a team of safety audit professionals, who as freelance 'safety' consultants will act as enabling agents or foot soldiers for the SCI.

It will be the responsibility of these accredited safety auditors to work with communities, corporates and organizations and to assist them in impacting and measuring their performance on the IWES. This would include helping entities to understand the process of application, fulfill the criteria for certification and submit the necessary paperwork to get their ratings from the SCI. What this will do is put in place an entirely new stream of safety professionals who can now make the business of safety a full-time profession.

The next step is for the government, through its instrument – the SCI – to make it mandatory for all tax entities to get an IWES rating, failing which they would be liable to pay a surcharge on their existing income tax bills.The SCI could also provide for a system of rewards or incentives in the form of concessions on income tax, depending on performance. A rating of 10 on the index, for instance, could garner an entity a concession of 1.5% while a rating of 9 could get a 1% concession.

STEP 2

Mandate for all habitat entities to get their IWES rating, failing which they would be liable to pay a surcharge on their existing property tax bills.

IWES INDEX	TAX
10	–2.0%
09	–1.5%
08	–1.0%
07	–0.5%
06	–0.0%
05	+1.0%
04 and below	+2.0%

Similarly, all habitat entities would also be required to get an IWES rating failing which they would be subject to penalties on municipal levies and property taxes. Entities would now be required to furnish their IWES ratings to local municipalities based on which they would get rewards (or penalties) on a scale of 0–10% on their annual property tax returns. Severe and recurrent dereliction of SCI norms could lead to further enhanced penalties or even cancellation of leases in the case of housing and other commercial projects. The idea is to create a powerful system of reward and penalty – a strong carrot-and-stick approach, necessary to galvanize an otherwise indifferent society into meaningful and sustained action.

The Carrot-and-Stick Approach

There are eight categories of residential colonies in Delhi – A, B, C, D, E, F, G, and H, as specified by the Municipal Corporation of Delhi (MCD), with circle rates and stamp duties in each colony varying, depending on the category of the colony or residential area.[98] In the current scenario, colonies actually prefer to be included within a lower category because then municipal levies as well as the stamp duty, in the case of purchase, sale and registration of properties, is much lower. The problem with this system is that it operates in reverse, effectively dis-incentivizing residents from improving their colonies, whether in terms of safety, cleanliness or other parameters, and therefore, being included within a higher category of residential area.

If, however, the government were to say that for a higher category of colony they would increase the number of sweepers per running length of road, or that for a safer or cleaner colony they would give a 5% concession on property tax, it could operate as a powerful incentive on residents to improve their surroundings.

In Anand Niketan, for instance, each block could get its own IWES rating and if their rating on the index was say 10, they could conceivably get a 10% concession on their municipal levies. Let us assume that for an apartment of a certain size, a resident pays a property tax of Rs 30,000 per year. A concession of 10% would mean a saving of Rs 3,000 per apartment and for the approximately 2,000 apartments in each block, a saving of nearly Rs 60,00,000. This amount could easily be invested by residents in putting up signage and fencing and making the colony safer and more secure. Suddenly there is a huge incentive to transform because residents can see that the money they save on municipal levies and taxes can be utilized to improve the colony and therefore, ratings. First, they would have created a safer, more secure space to live in and second, they would have been able to achieve this without any extra expenditure.

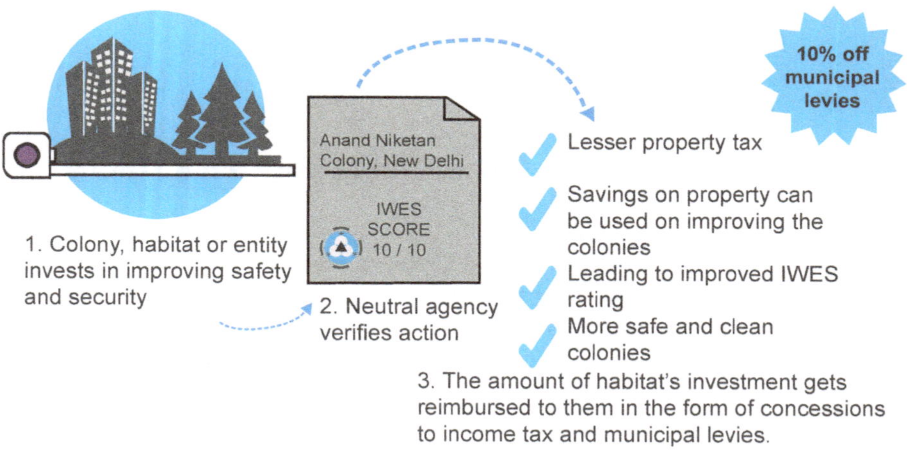

What this effectively means is that if a colony, habitat or entity were to invest in improving safety and security, the amount of their investment would be reimbursed to them, by the government, in the form of concessions to income tax and municipal levies. What we have done, therefore, is to create an alignment of thought (towards the notion of safety) by incentivizing action at the level of community, verifying that action through a neutral agency and finally completing the cycle by having that verified action, indirectly paid for by the government.

The next and final step is for the SCI to publish all IWES ratings on its website, Safetyadvisor.org, and additionally to require all tax and habitat entities to put their IWES ratings on their own websites, failing which they would be subject to various penalties. Correspondingly, for entities who perform well on the index and are entitled to a concession or incentive, they would receive the same only after publishing their ratings on their own websites. Let us assume, for instance, that an entity were to get a rating of 9 on the IWES. It would be required to duly publish its rating and only then become eligible for relief on income tax. If, however, the entity failed to publish its rating, it would lose its concession and instead be subject to a penalty on income tax, municipal levies or both.

This could act as a powerful incentive for entities to align and conform, particularly for larger organizations and corporations for whom municipal and other taxes and therefore savings are likely to be very large. What this will do is make the safety rating of each entity public information, creating a high degree of transparency and connectedness. It will also create the critical thing that comes out of measurement, transparency and connectedness, which is alignment.

In the case of sale or purchase of property, for instance, real estate website, magicbricks.com could, in addition to other information, also publish the safety rating of the colony or residential area in which each property is located.[99] A buyer who is in the process of evaluating two apartments, one in E-block and the other in F-block Vasant Vihar, could, therefore, easily compare the safety ratings of both blocks, which could influence his decision to purchase and down the line, impact property prices in a meaningful manner. This could potentially function as an additional impetus for colonies to put in the necessary safeguards and consequently to improve their ratings on the index.[100] MagicBricks, which is India's largest real estate website, already attempts to do its own safety audit and assign safety ratings to various localities where properties may be located. But now, the portal will be able to provide buyers with an 'accredited safety rating' that is reliable, transparent and universal as Punjabi Bagh in Delhi, JP Nagar in Bangalore and Alipore in Kolkata are all being mapped on a singular barometer of safety.

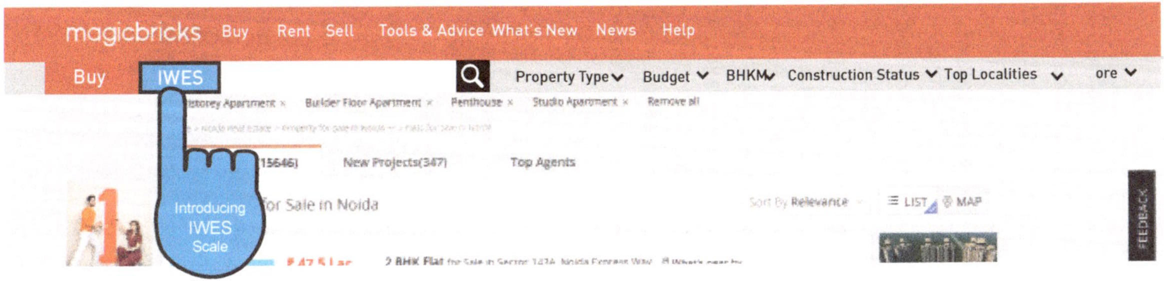

LOCALITY OVERVIEW

PROJECT GALLERY

Similarly, Naukri.com could, in addition to job and organization profiles, also furnish the IWES rating of each potential employer, impacting employment choices. Job seekers could now compare the safety ratings of potential employers and choose to work in an organization with a higher rating, forcing companies to align to the notion of safety and imbibe transformational steps within their premises whether to do with gender sensitivity programmes, better illumination in parking lots or enhanced safety training.

Enabling Informed Decision-Making

The IWES could potentially also be applied to cities with websites such as Tripadvisor.com furnishing safety ratings for each city or town. Mysore, a relatively safe city, for instance, could be rated 8 on the scale while Digha in West Bengal might rate only 6. This would reflect the state of safety and security in each area very lucidly to the consumer and have the capacity to impact tourism, business and investment for these cities in the long run.

Job seekers could now compare the safety ratings of potential employers and choose to work in an organization with a higher rating, forcing companies to align to the notions of safety and to imbibe transformational steps.

Enabling Safe Cities

The IWES could also impact the political system by spawning an entirely new agenda for elections. A candidate for an RWA election, for instance, could potentially promise that if he or she was voted to power, so and so colony would be upgraded to get a rating of 10 on the IWES. Similarly, in the case of elections to the municipality or the state legislature, the current campaign narrative is all about what is wrong. Even if an incumbent politician wanted to say, for instance, that while the problems may not have been fully resolved, there has been some positive progression, he or she has no way of showing this progress and therefore, it becomes very easy for persons in the opposition to create a hype around 'nothing has happened'. Within the ecosystem of the IWES, however, progress becomes measurable and transparent and the political party is able to say with certainty that while we started at x, we are now at position y. The result is that political parties begin to align and suddenly, because it is measurable, safety and security becomes part of the manifesto.

The IWES could potentially also be applied to cities with websites such as Tripadvisor.com furnishing safety ratings for each city or town. This would reflect the state of safety and security in each area very lucidly to the reader and have the capacity to impact tourism, business and investment for these cities in the long run.

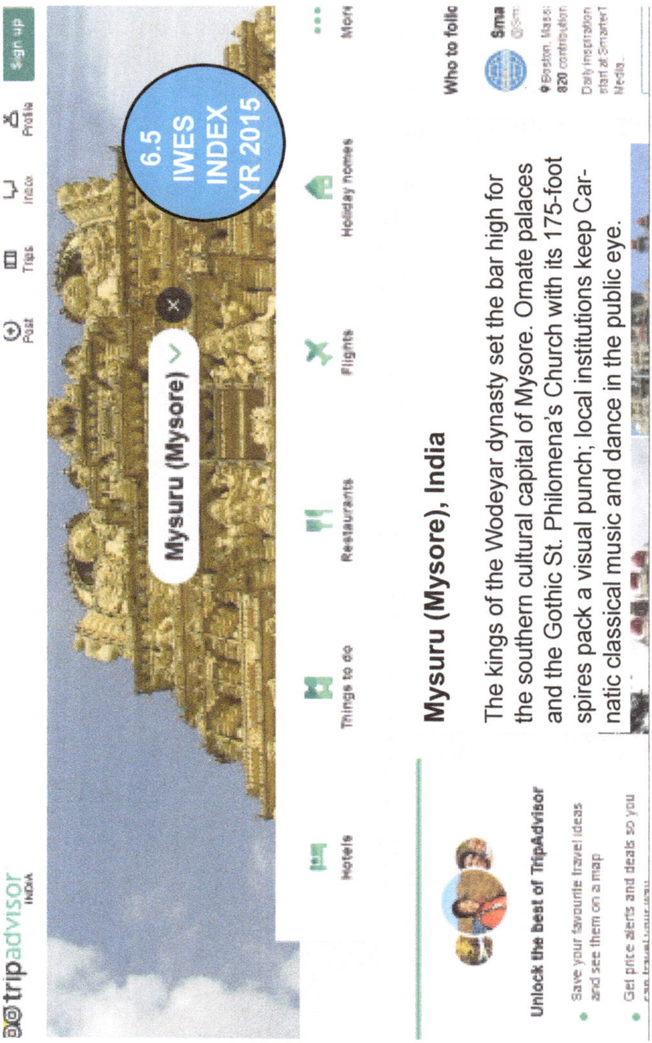

IWES Checklist

What the SCI could also do (to mitigate and transform these attitudes) is to frame a 'transformation of mindsets' checklist, which varies from one entity type to another, to benchmark and measure the performance of each individual, organization or city with respect to the quotient of safety and women's empowerment. A simple checklist for individual citizens could read, for instance, as follows:

IWES Checklist for Citizens

(Mandatory for filing of income tax / Aadhar application / school admission / car registration / gas connection / property registration. To be co-signed by 5 persons living in the locality of the applicant including one gazetted officer)

(As a reader, you may attempt answering this checklist)

Women's Empowerment
Have you ever given or accepted dowry for your own or your relative's marriage? ***Yes / No***

If yes, then:
Did you demand it overtly? ***Yes / No***
Did you accept / give it passively and not offer resistance because you didn't feel your individual case mattered in the larger scheme? ***Yes / No***

Do you support equal opportunity for women at home and in the workplace and in terms of access to education and the right to work? ***Yes / No***

If yes, then:
How many (in percentage) of the women in your family have the same or higher education than you?
How many women in your family find adequate financial security and acknowledgement for work either at home or at the workplace?

What is the percentage of women in your workplace?

What is the percentage of women at senior decision-making levels in your workplace?

Do you support equal rights to inheritance for women? **Yes / No**
If yes, then:

Did you receive / share with your siblings an equal share in your ancestral wealth?
Have you willed / agreed to bequeath your assets equally to your male and female children / grandchildren in writing?

What is the distribution of jobs and responsibilities in your household? Do you cook and help with household activities (if male) / do the male members of your household help with housework (if female)? **Yes / No**

Do you support freedom of movement and free clothing choices for women?
Yes / No

Have you ever intervened in the wake of some women rights being subverted?
And so on…

The idea is to create a simple 10-point checklist which could be used to determine an individual's rating on the IWES and therefore his or her eligibility for tax concessions, school admissions or a premium gas connection. The checklist could potentially be tailored for different regions and communities to make each individual think and transform for his or herself and to genuinely impact people at whichever point on the transformation curve they currently find themselves. The checklist would further have the potential to reach out to more than 50% of the general population, considering that most people would require to engage with at least one of the authorities – taxation, schools, Aadhar – at some point.

Revenue Model

Safety Council of India

The SCI could potentially charge a one-time fee for rating an entity plus an annual fee for revalidation of certification. There are roughly 4 crore tax assesses in India and let us assume that they would each pay between Rs 200 to Rs 20,000 for certification, depending upon the size of the entity. On an average, therefore, each entity would pay the SCI a fee of Rs 5,000 to get a rating, amounting to a collection of Rs 20,000 crore 4 crore assesses × Rs 5,000). The SCI could also collect an annual renewal fee from each of its members, which at the rate of approximately 10% of the one-time charge, would amount to an additional Rs 2,000 per year.

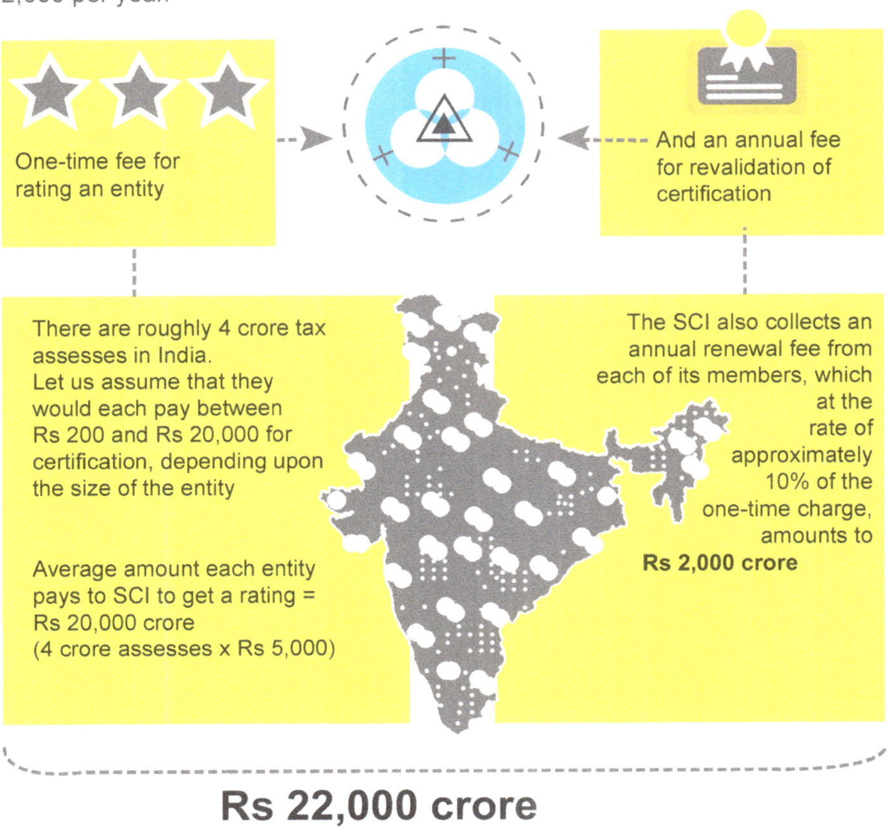

The SCI would, therefore, have at its disposal, the massive sum of Rs 22,000 crore, plus an additional Rs 2,000 crore per year, which amount would be more than sufficient for it to run its operations and also to promote safety as a funding agent and as an agency of advocacy. With this kind of capital, the SCI could potentially run not only separate expert bodies for each state (30 states x 100 members each) but also create customized criteria for various entities depending on geographical location, size, stage of evolution and so on.

Safety Audit Professionals

The SCI will offer accreditations at various levels to persons who demonstrate in-depth knowledge of the IWES rating system and of safety practices and strategies in general. These accredited safety professionals will act as freelance consultants to educate, handhold and assist entities in getting SCI certifications as well as recommend and supervise necessary interventions in built environment, deployment of technology and transformation of mindsets. For these services they would be entitled to charge anywhere between Rs 5,000 for a small company to Rs 20,00,000 for a large corporation. What this will do is create a new professional stream, an alternate career where persons can earn a considerable amount of money after making a minimal investment towards training and accreditation.

In the case of a small company that needs to get an IWES rating, for instance, it would be required to pay a fee of say Rs 5,000 to get a certificate. In addition, it could bring in a safety auditor who would typically charge between Rs 5,000 and Rs 20,000 and in return educate the company on the application process and the parameters with which they would be required to comply. He or she would inspect the premises to ensure that, for instance, it was well illuminated, that there was a safe toilet and an emergency exit was available in case of a fire or other disaster. The auditor could potentially also suggest and help put in place various other measures to improve the safety rating of the company and create a plan for upscaling the rating.

Industry

Total direct taxes collected by Government of India from individuals and corporates on a yearly basis is approximately Rs 4,00,000 crore to Rs 6,00,000 crore. Assuming that there is a 2% surcharge for non-compliance with the IWES rating system and a corresponding 0–2% incentive for good performance, at stake is Rs 4,000 crore per year (at the rate of roughly 1% of Rs 4,00,000 crore), which sum if invested towards safety could give a tremendous boost to the security and gender initiatives economy as well as the manufacturing industry for safety products. It could also generate huge demand and consultancy work for the new stream of safety audit professionals.

Similarly, annual municipal taxes for all Indian cities and states combined would be in the vicinity of Rs 35,000 crore to Rs 50,000 crore. If 10% is available as a concession in the case of good performance, then an amount of Rs 3,500 crore to Rs 5,000 crore would be available with the public to be invested towards improving safety and security, incentivizing industry to invest in research and development and production capabilities for safety products such as pavers, blinkers, pedestrian bands, fluorescent paint for evening illumination, energy-efficient lamps, pedestrian overbridges, CCTV and surveillance products, SCI-approved furniture, swings-and-play equipment for schools and playgrounds, street-vendor carts and cop spot-licensing products, grab bars and non-slip floors for toilets, and anti-slip strips for staircases.

What this will do is spawn an entirely new manufacturing industry for safety products as entities and individuals become increasingly aligned to the notion of safety and begin to invest more and more money towards making their surroundings more secure.

Safetyadvisor.org

As the website for the SCI, www.Safetyadvisor.org will function as an online destination, which not only lists the IWES ratings of various entities, such as hotels, restaurants, malls, police stations and schools, much like tripadvisor.com, but also provides for citizen participation in the form of real-time reviews of these entities, thereby becoming the 'the instrument of transparency as well as the instrument of connect.'

SCI to publish all IWES ratings on its website **Safetyadvisor.org**

A citizen may choose to review a police station and post that while the premises of the station were neat, clean and well lit, and that the constable on duty was very polite, he or she was made to wait 2 hours to file an FIR. The SHO of the police station could then respond and assure the citizen that certain processes have since been put in place and that the incident will not be repeated.

Similarly, in the case of a mall, a customer may write that on such and such date, she parked in the third basement next to pillar G and she found that the lights in that area were not functioning. The result would be that the manager of the mall would respond immediately, apologizing and assuring the customer that the lights would be replaced right away. The reviewer thus becomes a citizen journalist on Safetyadvisor.org, which creates a live, real-time, conversation and feedback mechanism between stakeholders, and transforms the role of the consumer from a passive to a more active audience.

This will create an interactive forum where stakeholders can interact with each other over specific transaction points and therefore generate connectedness at a level that no government can possibly do. So not only does the customer report that the light is not working, the manager responds by saying that it will be fixed and finally also posts that it has been fixed, completing the transaction. Safetyadvisor.org operates as a phenomenal surrogate tutor for entities, ensuring a perpetually high level of alertness and responsiveness to issues of safety and women's empowerment. It also gives birth to a Live Ecosystem of Safety within which institutions and entities of all types can benchmark themselves with regard to others of their type and work towards upscaling their safety performance on the basis of a pre-stated charter. The challenge is to create a multilingual platform that enables a wider demographic presence and ensures that everyone, including the most vulnerable groups, have access to information as well as the confidence to participate in this 'Connectedness for Transformation' mission.

Consider This

The Delhi Dialogue Commission, a 9-member panel, headed by chief minister Arvind Kejriwal, set up to implement the AAP government's 'vision' for the city of Delhi. The mission of the Delhi Dialogues Commission was to deliver on a 70- point agenda collated through the Delhi Dialogues, a series of mini conclaves organized by the AAP in the run-up to the assembly election, which paired experts, academicians and bureaucrats, and which empowered the average citizen to make suggestions on how to transform Delhi into a world-class city.

While the Delhi Dialogue Commission was a great way to create policy based on local feedback, to implement it would have required a forum such as Safetyadvisor.org which could bring together connectedness, transparency and measurement in a positively enabling environment and which connects the citizen *locally* with the concerned government official. Safetyadvisor.org is a very scalable model, which allows the government to think at a policy level and also to act in a very focussed, local manner, which is something that all governments must want to do.

Some Might Argue

In democratic societies, it is typically the media which plays the role of watchdog by highlighting important issues and helping to shape public opinion and therefore pushing the state and its institutions to respond and take action. To this we submit that the media tends to look at only sporadic and grave instances and lacks the capacity to impact other types of inadequacies. Safetyadvisor.org, on the other hand, offers a powerful, real-time tool that seeks to use social media to create an ongoing communication and feedback mechanism between the citizens and the state, enabling localized and immediate action (or reaction) based on every transaction. This is a sustainable and scalable model that does not rely on sensationalism and has the capacity to work at all levels of the transformation curve.

Revenue Model

Safety advisor's value proposition lies in its extensive listings of the IWES ratings of various entities. Safetyadvisor.org creates and offers itself as a massive library of resources in the hands of the average citizen, helping them make intelligent choices on careers, habitats, educational institutions, hospitals and online retailers (among others) on the basis of safety parameters. Whenever any transaction takes place – whether a family is choosing a school for a child, or they're choosing where to go and watch a movie, where to buy a house or seek employment, their paramount concern is safety. Even if they're looking at Shaadi.com, it could be a parameter to see where the prospective groom stays and how safe that place is (if women can be concerned with whether prospective grooms have toilets, they can also be concerned with safety). The result is simply that there are so many eyeballs chasing Safetyadvisor.com that there is likely to be huge advertising money riding on it.

Statistics show that full-year 2011 revenues for tripadvisor.com, which relies on a similar user-generated content model, were $637.1 million, a 31% increase over full year 2010.With 50 million unique monthly visitors and 20 million members, Tripadvisor operates mainly on a 'cost per click' model simply because of the large numbers of views it gets.[101] Numbers show that the search-engine giant Google racked up advertising revenues of 43.7 billion dollars in the year 2012, based on a similar pay-per-click model.[102] Safety is such a critical parameter in today's world, whether it is furniture for schools, non-slip tiles, phones which now come with emergency buttons or even cars (so far we have limited the concept to habitats but the concept could be extended to the automobile industry) that it is possible that Safetyadvisor.org could get even a million hits a day and therefore generate enormous advertising money for the SCI.

Another potential revenue stream could be other websites such as Naukri.com, Magicbricks.com and Shaadi.com, which may be willing to purchase online data from Safetyadvisor.org. Let us say that there are 4 lakh entities listed on Safetyadvisor.org of which 1 lakh are real estate habitats of interest to Magicbricks.com.

Magic Bricks may be willing to pay for that data, so that the IWES ratings of those 1 lakh entities could be automatically culled and transposed on its website (as opposed to being manually fed) via a cross linkage between the portals. So suddenly Safetyadvisor.org is sitting on very valuable data that any transactional website may want to pay for. Naukri.com may pay to pick up the IWES ratings of all potential employers listed on its website, for instance, or Flipkart may want to know the ratings of all the places to which they are supplying goods.

The IWES along with Safetyadvisor.org has the potential to transform the quotient of safety and security in Indian cities. More fundamentally it offers a great opportunity for citizens to come together and participate in a meaningful way in the Mission for Safety.

Some Might Argue

It will take generations of education in a pluralistic society like India for any effective transformation to become visible. To this we submit that in this age of handheld, mobile communication, adaptation to technology and associated transformations in human behaviour have demonstrated unimaginable pace. Consider this. Villagers in UP and Bihar who have barely any electricity are more than willing to pay Rs 5 a day to a local entrepreneur to charge their phones through DG power so that they can use Facebook and WhatsApp. WhatsApp has in fact become the instant photo-sharing platform of choice at all levels of society, from the upmarket city dweller to the local shop owner in a small town; even illiterate labour is seen using it. Such is the outreach of mobile technology; it is the greatest leveler one has seen in recent times. Considering the criticality of safety as a parameter in today's world, Safetyadvisor.org will likely reach the 1 million subscribers' mark within the first two years of operation and once it does, it will find buoyancy and leave no room for opacity and inaction. Whether it is a habitat or a tax entity, it will either be safe and find public traction or unsafe and, therefore, create public ire and opportunity for action. Together, we the citizens and the state can transform the quotient of safety in the cities of India forever.

Leapfrogging to a Much Higher Level of Safety

In conclusion, we use the tool of INVERTONOMICS, and set in motion a movement towards safety by providing communities with an objective system of measurement and bringing together all stakeholders into a positive, action-oriented ecosystem that is likely to show visible results within the first year of its operation, with 20–30% habitats becoming extremely safe within the first 2 years to universal coverage within 10 years.

The idea, however, is not just to achieve incremental progress but to create a methodology that makes it possible to leapfrog to a much higher level of safety that can actually set a precedent for other nations and societies to emulate.

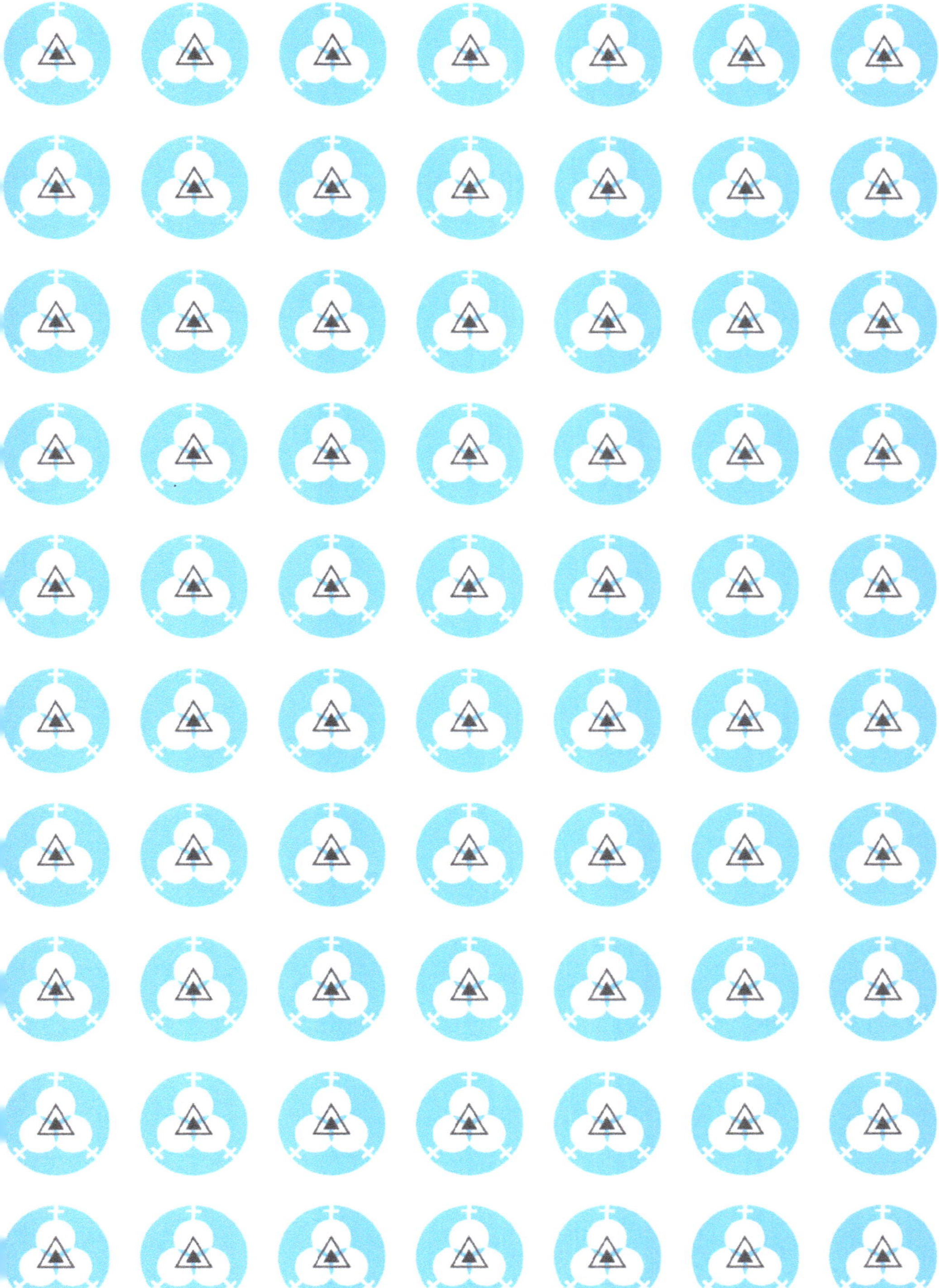

Prelude to the Dream

When the founding fathers of independent India created a dream for the nation and its people, they enshrined it in the Preamble of 'The Constitution of India.'

It was resolved that India be constituted as a sovereign, socialist, secular, democratic Republic, securing for its citizens justice, liberty, equality and fraternity.

Much has been accomplished ... and in line with the dream they set us on.

The notion of a vibrant, pluralistic, democratic India that most of us take for granted draws its strength from the Constitution and is effected through the key institutions of the Legislature, the Executive and the Judiciary at both centre and state levels. Institutions like The Armed Forces, RBI, Election Commission, Civil Services, Revenue Services, ISRO DRDO, SEBI, Stock Exchange, AAI, PTI, TRAI, LIC, SBI, Municipalities, Panchayats, Educational Institutions Such as the armed forces, the Reserve Bank of India, the Election Commission, the Civil Services, the Revenue Services, Indian Space Research Organization, Defense Research and Development Organization Securities and Exchange Board of India, National Stock Exchange, Airports Authority of India, Press Trust of India, Telecom Regulatory Authority of India, Life Insurance Corporation of India, State Bank of India, Municipalities, Panchayats, educational institutions – such as Indian Institutes of Technology, National Institutes of Technology, Indian Institutes of Science, Indian Institutes of Management – and various government and private universities have also made sterling contributions. Outside of the institutional framework, private enterprises, media, civil society, NGOs, farmers, small businesses, bollywood and general citizens at large. All have severally and collectively endeared to the idea of India and made it a live and palpable entity.

Now, in this ideas-age of hyper-scalable technologies, the time has come to reaffirm and renew our pledges and to create institutions which effect the dream of a Great India with a missionary sense of urgency.

To effect the dream, we must state it, and as a nation agree to a 'unified dream'. Then we must identify the institutions and legislative interventions that would be necessary to accomplish the dream.

A dream is being put forth through this book, as also the institutions and models that would fulfill the objective. The details of the solution are captured in a chapter-wise manner and can be read one at a time and in skip sequence.

A dream must be told in a charged, emotional manner and read in a lofty tone. Allow me to present **the dream of a great India**.

The Dream of a Great India

Imagine an Inclusive India

Where equality is more than a word in the Constitution, and is visible as equal access to opportunity, education and dignity.

Where social equity becomes synonymous with patriotism, replacing the centuries-old feudal currencies of privilege...

Where equitable distribution of wealth as a goal is a measurable and transparent index called Index of Equity, administered through the offices of the Equity Foundation of India. A credible barometer and guiding light for fulfillment of the Constitution.

Imagine an Inspired India

Where civic pride and inspired citizenship become the new narrative and participative volunteerism replaces passive denizenship.

Where collective good and individual action find unprecedented alignment and become key instruments of nation-building.

Where a sense of self-regulation and moral rectitude prevail and are further emboldened by a new technology–based 'civic cop' that judiciously and expeditiously fines instances of non-compliance in an effective and non-intrusive manner, at a scale hitherto unimaginable, to usher in an era of active principled citizenship.

Imagine a Pluralistic India

Where pluralism finds a new meaning and the majority celebrates and shares the joys of the minority's festivals not out of political correctness but out of a genuine sense of affinity to the festival as being part of a shared heritage.

Where the 'forces of assimilation' far outweigh those of otherization and the mainstream view includes the concurrent multidimensionality of our reality, whether of religion, gender, caste or geography, to effectively pursue our paths along our shared destiny.

Where the traditional faultlines of religion and caste fade and give way to a binding consciousness of Indianess that is soaked in the milieu of karmic connectedness and oneness of existences.

Imagine an Ethical India

Where meritocracy and fair play replaces favouritism.

Where enterprise and accountability find encouragement and come forth to become powerful vehicles of state management.

Where excellence and innovation become the new engines of transformation, creating global corporations with distinctive intellectual horsepower, financial muscle and an expansive spirit to pursue and effect greatness and together as a nation strive to have 50 firms in Fortune 500 by 2030.

Imagine a Purposeful India

Where government apathy and citizen haplessness have been transformed and replaced with a new ecosystem approach that engages both in an enduring partnership and enables both together to be a part of the solution.

Where problems like air pollution, noise pollution, cleanliness, waste management are solved with a smartness and efficiency that is exemplary, and only possible when government institutions and citizens align their individual actions towards collective good.

Where the missionary zeal of problem-solving sees the coming together scientists, social entrepreneurs, bureaucrats, politicians and citizens who work in unison to affect tangible and measurable changes along a stated path and with predetermined milestones much like the successful polio-eradication programme. They could now embark on programmes to make India's cities safe through new initiatives like the 'Safety Council of India' and 'Pedestrian Commission of India' that could help India leapfrog into the future.

Imagine a Patriotic India

Where the consciousness of one India comes alive in the Indian diaspora, the urban citizen and the bharatwasi, who individually and together contribute vigorously to the cause of nation-building.

Where the loving patriotism of a soldier, the empathetic devotion of a saint meets hard-working commitment of the farmer, coming together to effect a transformation that is based on humanity and sound principles of public administration.

Where the citizen understands and abides by the expected role play... Not just in sporadic exercise of vote but also in honest dispensation of all the duties that are required of him as a citizen.

Imagine a Just India

Where non-violence and civil discourse are the prime tools for dispute resolution for all internal and external instances of disagreement, while having enough gumption and muscle to rebut any offense with befitting firmness.

Where the justice system is sovereign, fair and free of prejudice to apply firmly, equally and expeditiously to all, and reaffirm the supremacy of righteousness and fair play. Where the capacity of adjudication is upscaled to meet the growing and expansive needs of India to ensure social justice, civil justice and gender justice is real for all Indians alike.

Where the right to safety is affected by better policing, predictive analytics and smarter emergency response systems to stem crime before it happens.

Where institutions like the SCI shall affect the median of safety preparedness through IWES, that is, the index of women empowerment and safety, and an army of safety auditors, to help India become safe and just.

Imagine a Clean India

Where cleanliness exalts from being next to godliness to becoming synonymous with good living ... and the Cleanliness Council of India becomes the government's instrument to affect physical and attitudinal changes to ensure people do not litter or spit in public spaces and the Toilets Corporation of India that would ensure universal access to public sanitation becomes a reality by 2020.

Where cleanliness is a measureable and transparent Index of Clean Environment (ICE) a 100-/10-point index of goodness assessed by the Swachh Bharat Mission through its accredited government and corporate institutions. These the cleanliness auditor would rate for small, medium and large habitat entities like schools, colonies, malls, offices etc. to affect cleanliness in an objective and measureable manner.

Where solid waste management reaches new heights under the aegis of the Smart Waste Management Corporations ... waste handlers have new-found dignity and security... And the whole city participates willingly in waste segregation and recycling because of unique incentivized recycling ecosystem that creates a new aspirational 'Currency of Garbage'.

Imagine a Healthy India

Where the right of access to better quality food is implementable because of a new ecosystem of food procurement and storage introduced by the Cocoon Corporation India that would reduce food wastage to under 5% and do away with the need for extensive preservatives and usher in a new era of quality food availability.

Where the right of access to healthcare of international quality at nominal prices becomes a reality aided by health insurance schemes, fair-price pharmacies, rejuvenated traditional healthcare practices and an expansive high-quality health infrastructure that uses state-of-the-art technologies to map disease surveillance and health administration by creating a digital health nervous system for India and tax incentive to make India the health capital of the world.

Where fitness becomes a national obsession and access to sports academies and fitness infrastructure at rural and urban level gets a new push, ushering in a new era of enhances longevity.

Imagine an Empowered India

Where quality education is available to all through a renewed public education system that relies heavily on assisted digital education and incentivized under the Mukhya Mantri Swarn Shikshak Evam Shiksha Abhiyan programmes for performing teachers with special focus on rural and suburban school infrastructure, enhanced focus on skill training, skill upgradation in tune with the requirements of our times through real-time versions of Rural-Naukri.com. This could unleash a new era of collaboration between industry and aspiring rural citizens. We need to tailor a country-scale Kerala model to be able to deliver a highly trained and ethical workforce to the world.

Where institutions of higher learning and excellence are incentivized to innovate and pursue seminal research and create global patents and products under the Pradhan Mantri Nav Nirman Kosh, where annually Rs 10,000 crore is distributed as awards and support in exchange of equity to innovators to fuel a wealth-creation and innovation era that can potentially change the wealth fortunes of the entire nation. All we need is 3 unicorns like Google to change the wealth landscape of our nation.

Where girl-child education and women's empowerment find unprecedented focus and a simple tweak in the income tax laws that allow for a say 10% rebate on tax in case one-fourth in household income is deposited in the wife's account, or similar schemes hinged on the logic that financial empowerment is key to women empowerment.

Imagine a Rejuvenated Bharat

Where a revolution in farming techniques, food storage, food trading and food processing is aided by the Cocoon Corporation of India – a state-of-the-art farm produce storage and shipment company – and by Foodie, a new agro-produce online exchange that would dematerialize agricultural produce, which will now be stored in bar-coded cocoons, and create a new buzzing rural marketplace that would greatly benefit the farmers financially and make them a part of the mainstream white economy.

Where rural governance infrastructure would get a fillip, thanks to the 6,500 Offices of Bharat, a brand new 30-acres block-level governance infrastructure built at a cost of Rs 6,50,000 crore over a three-year period and earning the government Rs 30,000 to Rs 50,000 crore annually. This Office of Bharat shall comprise six pillars, administrative infrastructure, agricultural and rural commerce infrastructure, educational infrastructure, transport infrastructure, sports infrastructure and health infrastructure. Together it would infuse a new life in Bharat and greatly enhance governance, farmer wealth, small rural entrepreneurship, access to education and access to quality sports, among others. This would also enable the widening of the tax net which is key to the transformation of Bharat. This singularly can usher in the era of the 'golden goose'... India would once again be 'Sone ki Chidiya'!!

Imagine an Aesthetic India

Where urban aesthetics, city skylines and streetscapes present a coherent contextual visual character replete with well-articulated, refined and yet playful elements that transform our cities from being unsightly to becoming delightful, physical portraits of our culture and our times.

Where the richness of indigenous arts, crafts and culture finds renewed patronage and willingly embraces the liberating universal influences of technology to create a new paradigm for Indian arts and culture that is soaked in the local milieu and yet, is progressive and global in character.

Where the average citizen's engagement with arts as a vehicle of self-expression and playfulness goes beyond mere recreation and festivity to being one of respect and patronage. The quotient of happiness in a society is positively correlated to the richness of its arts. For a great India to be possible, we need to integrate our artists and artisans into the progressive economy of our nation.

Chapter 5

CURRENCY OF GARBAGE

The world's dirtiest cities [103]

01. Baku, Azerbaijan
02. Dhaka, Bangladesh
03. Antananarivo, Madagascar
04. Port au Prince, Haiti
05. Mexico City, Mexico
06. Addis Ababa, Ethiopia

07. Mumbai, India

08. Baghdad, Iraq
09. Almaty, Kazakhstan
10. Brazzaville, Congo
11. Ndjamena, Chad
12. Dar es Salaam, Tanzania
13. Bangui, Central African Republic
14. Moscow, Russia
15. Ouagadougou, Burkina Faso
16. Bamako, Mali
17. Pointe Noire, Congo
18. Lome, Togo
19. Conakry, Guinea Republic
20. Nouakchott, Mauritania
21. Niamey, Niger
22. Luanda, Angola
23. Maputo, Mozambique

24. New Delhi, India

25. Port Harcourt, Nigeria

Can India be squeaky clean in our lifetime?

Yes. It can.

Introduction

India's former environment minister, Jairam Ramesh, has never been shy about speaking his mind. So, when he decided to weigh in on the country's growing garbage and pollution problem, it wasn't surprising that his message hit home. It was November 2009; just a few weeks earlier, US President Barack Obama had been announced as the recipient of the Nobel Peace Prize. Everyone was talking about it. Always the willing lightning rod, Jairam chose his words for maximum impact.

'Our cities are the dirtiest cities of the world. If there is a Nobel Prize for dirt and filth, India will win it, no doubt,' Jairam told the audience that had gathered for the release of the Green India 2047 report by The Energy Research Institute (TERI).[104]

Jairam's comments naturally found detractors. The opposition derided him for tarnishing India's reputation. The 2009 Copenhagen Climate Summit was only days away and India had been under pressure to reduce its pollution. Many, though, knew he was right.

More recently, the honourable Prime Minister Narendra Modi took up the issue of solid waste management very seriously and launched the Swachh Bharat Abhiyan. The initiative is laudable, and a step in the right direction.

Major cities such as Delhi and Mumbai are facing a garbage nightmare. The waste at some of Delhi's landfills now reaches over 30 metres in height. That's 10 metres more than the allowed limit.[105] For an idea of just how big these sites are, imagine standing next to a 10-storey high mountain of smelly, putrid waste that is spread across 150 acres. Many municipalities also try to incinerate their garbage, which adds to air pollution. In addition, a lot of garbage that doesn't get collected or falls off trucks tends to clog up storm-water drains, leading to flooding during the monsoons.

Mumbai may be even worse off. Ahead of the last monsoons, the city's municipal corporation decided to unclog drains and rivers to prevent flooding. The silt and waste that was dredged out was sent to the newly opened Kanjur Marg dumping ground. According to the *Hindustan Times*, the site filled up within just two months.[106] For a city desperately short of land, the situation is grim. It's hardly surprising then that our overburdened landfills have become an ecological and health nightmare. These dumps are not only breeding grounds for diseases, they are also a fire hazard, thanks to the methane generated by all the decomposing waste.

There is also a grave impact on the lives of thousands of young children who scavenge in these dumps for a living. Not only do the unsanitary conditions take a toll on their health, but the long-term opportunity costs of not attending school affects their well-being.

However, if you take a closer look, the problem is not that a city like Delhi generates thousands of tons of waste each day. The real problem is that most of what we thoughtlessly discard may not be garbage at all. While a longer-term transformation through education is welcome and certainly a part of the solution, it would take far too long to have a meaningful effect on the immediate problem. We need ideas that will have an impact within this generation.

If we approached this problem from a different angle, food and other organic matter, paper, plastics, metals and other recyclable materials – the bulk of household waste – could be eliminated from landfills entirely. But how do you get citizens who usually throw their litter out of the window or onto the road to collect, segregate and dispose of their garbage properly for recycling? What could possibly drive them to change these long-ingrained bad habits?

We have reduced our street kids to scavenging urchins.

The Problem

Systemic Issues

In most cities, garbage is collected from homes by young boys and girls who go from house to house every morning. They take the garbage to the local waste dump, where they forage for small items they can sell to small-time recyclers for a few rupees.

The garbage lies rotting and smelling in the open neighbourhood waste dumps until municipal vans come by to pick it up. These vans often have open tops, which means wherever they go, they are followed by a trail of foul smell and refuse that falls out of the truck.

Almost all the garbage is taken to giant landfills, where it is simply dumped in the open, creating mountains of putrid waste that becomes a breeding ground for diseases, and the place literally becomes wasted land.

Delhi alone generates 9,000 tons of waste everyday;[107] that's enough to fill 600 garbage trucks. The problem of waste management and littering extends to every city and town in the country.

The city of Mumbai generates roughly 6,000 tons of garbage every day[108] or about 400 truckloads-worth. Bangalore generates 4,000 tons or about 265 truckloads every day.[109] It's easy to see how these numbers add up over the months and years.

Delhi is now planning 10 new landfill sites.[110] It does not have a choice. The High Court of Delhi recently banned dumping of any new garbage at three of the four existing locations because they were grossly overburdened. What's more, they had already outlived their lifespan by several years. The news for the future is worse. By 2024, Delhi will be generating 17,000 tons of waste daily; that's a 52% increase.[111]

Mr Malhotra, D. LITT.

This species treats public spaces like a private dustbin. He'll chuck paper plates out of his car and wrappers on the street. Using insights from his Doctorate in Littering, he defends his actions by saying he pays taxes that employ street sweepers to clean up his mess.

Mrs Swamy, NIMBY

Mrs Swamy is a pious housewife. Every morning she sweeps her home, collects the litter and then dumps it over her garden wall into the back alley. A classic NIMBY (Not In My Backyard), Mrs Swamy doesn't really care what the neighbourhood looks like as long as her own home is spic-and-span.

Dr Bose, The Non-segregator

Dr Bose, an eminent surgeon, is well aware of the problems of littering. He keeps his home clean and actively works in the RWA to make sure no one litters. Unfortunately, because no recycling programme exists, all of Dr Bose's garbage goes into one big bag, which gets sent to the landfill. 'I'd love to recycle,' he says, 'but it just seems like such a chore. This is so much easier.'

What if people were paid to segregate their garbage?

The Solution

Imagine a situation in which an overwhelming portion of the city's waste never goes to a landfill. In fact, not only would most of the garbage be recycled, people would actually willingly participate in such a programme! So how do we get there?

Well, what if people were paid – yes, paid – to segregate all their garbage for recycling?

Before I introduce the system to you, it would be good to see how some alternative solutions to our current waste-management problem are working on the ground.

The Kabaadiwalla

You wouldn't be surprised to know that almost all homes from poor one-room tenements to six-bedroom villas already practice some form of recycling. Most Indians engage with this system through their kabaadiwalla. A man comes around once a month, collects old newspapers and magazines that have been piling up, and pays householders to take them off their hands. Irrespective of financial status, every home places value in the money they earn from the kabaadiwalla. The going rate is about Rs 5 – Rs 6 per kilo. The kabaadiwalla sells these papers to small businesses who either recycle it into pulp or use it to make products such as paper plates or paper bags.

But paper is far from the only waste that can be recycled. Organic waste from cooking, plastics and even metals can all find new life after you're done using them. Unfortunately, not all of these get picked up or disposed of in a manner that will ensure they reach a recycler.

The Vasant Kunj Case Study

To overcome this problem, the residents of Sector B4 in Vasant Kunj, an affluent Delhi neighbourhood, started a novel project. They had a constant problem of overflowing garbage at their local waste dump. Since it was located near the local park, it meant residents avoided the park because of the stench. So, in March 2013, the local RWA came up with a novel approach to end the problem. All residents of the block began segregating their waste into separate wet and dry bins. These bins were collected by local rag-pickers who earned Rs 80 a month per home.

The wet waste was taken to a local plant nursery where it was composted into manure. There, the rag-pickers used the manure to grow chilies, aborigines, tomatoes and mint in pots, which was then given to the residents who participated in the programme.

The dry waste was taken to the local dump, which is now 45–50% less burdened and does not smell. The project currently covers about half the residents and the RWA hopes that, thanks to its success, it will be extended to all residents in the near future.

NCR Waste Matters – A Public Group on Facebook

A highly motivated and energetic community of volunteers is spreading awareness and taking action on issues of resource optimization, segregation at source, recycling and organic composting. Monica Khanna Gulati, the founder of this brilliant initiative, is bringing together experts and professional agencies, and coaching first-time enthusiasts to manage waste through segregation and composting at individual, home, and community level.

The Currency of Garbage

While the Kabaadiwalla system and the pilot project in Vasant Kunj are encouraging, they're both plagued by the same problem – a lack of scale. However, there is a way to efficiently and quickly scale up such recycling efforts into a city-wide and even nation-wide campaign.

It all begins with a set of three 'smart' garbage cans, provided for free to each home by the Smart Waste Corporation or SWC. The green can is for organic waste. The blue can take in recyclables, such as paper, plastics and metals. A third, orange can is reserved for any non-recyclables such as leather, thermocol or synthetic rubber products.

Each can is embedded with a special SIM card that identifies it to the family whose home it belongs to. The SIM card also allows the can to be tracked in transit. For each kilo of recyclable material deposited in these cans, the SWC credits the owner with a certain number of points or cash. These credits can be used at stores to get discounts or special deals, or they can even be used to pay utility bills such as electricity and water.

The segregated garbage is taken into a Zonal Collection Centre (or ZCC) where it is checked and weighed to assess how many points the owner will be credited with.

From there, all recyclable materials are moved to third-party recycling units, a waste-to-energy power plant, or sent to the city landfill.

The SWC is able to credit points or cash to users' accounts because it will earn substantial sums of revenue from its operations. The largest source of revenue would come from the sale of all recyclable materials to professional recycling companies. If a single kilo of newsprint fetches Rs 6, imagine what a few thousand tons of newsprint each year can fetch. Additional revenues can be earned by selling garbage as fuel to waste-to-energy power plants.

Another major source of revenue would be the garbage cans themselves. Companies can sign up to have their ads displayed on each can. From the companies' perspective, it would be akin to having three small billboards in every home. What's more, since the cans are collected and sorted by zones, businesses can even choose to advertise in only specific zones or across the whole city. The advertisement contract could run for one week or even a month. After that it can be replaced by a new advertiser when the cans reach the ZCC.

The ZCC itself will serve many purposes. It will be the central depot and distribution point for all segregated and recyclable garbage that is generated in the area. It will also serve as a store where customers can buy recycled products that were created by processing their own garbage. A visitors' centre will allow children from neighbourhood schools to study how garbage can be converted into something valuable, helping them appreciate the inherent value of all things.

In effect, you now have an incentive system for the owner to not only dispose of his garbage correctly, but also organize it into recyclable and non-recyclable materials. You would have also created an incentive for private or public–private partnerships to set up a city-wide collection and distribution system of segregated garbage.

Such a system would ensure that all materials are put through their maximum life-cycle. It would rid our cities of garbage, unburden existing landfills, thereby improving health and sanitary conditions, and reduce the demand for hundreds of acres of valuable, vacant land to be converted into a garbage heap.

The System in Action

Since the waste is now being segregated, your cans at home won't fill up as fast as they used to. This means citizens would not have to prepare their garbage for disposal every day. What's more, each can would be designed to seal properly with an airtight lid. This way, families would not have to worry about any smell in their house or garbage falling out of the can while it is being moved around.

The garbage collector now comes around every three or four days. And it's not so bad for him either. Instead of fending for himself, he is now employed by the SWC; a 'collection agent' if you will. And since this is now an opportunity for proper employment, you would have an incentive for parents themselves to do this work rather than send their children to work in unsanitary and unhygienic conditions as illegal child labourers.

Every time the garbage is collected from a family's home, the collection man will replace the full cans with three empty ones. These would also have SIM cards embedded within to identify them as belonging to the same family. The garbage man carries the full cans to his cart and from there to a local, well-maintained and sanitized collection point. From here, larger trucks will carry the full cans to the ZCC. This is quite unlike the old method where open dumpers were used to transport garbage, dropping trails of trash on city roads. At the ZCC, all the garbage from Mr Malhotra's home and all other homes in Lajpat Nagar are checked for correctness of segregation. Machines would automatically open the cans, remove the garbage and subject the waste to a simple electronic scan. This machine would be able to check what kind of waste has been deposited in each can and automatically re-sort waste that has not been correctly segregated. The correctly sorted garbage would then be weighed.

This process would eliminate attempts to cheat the system by citizens who add objects such as rocks to try and earn more credits. It would also help in forming a check for citizens who don't correctly sort their waste. Any improperly sorted garbage would result in negative credits, which is a further incentive to sort waste correctly. Moreover, since the entire process is electronic and automatic, citizens can be assured of not being cheated in any way.

How the System Works

Let's say our friend Mr Malhotra, D. Litt. segregates his waste in the right can.

A garbage van from the SWC stops by thrice a week to pick up the cans and replaces them with three new ones.

From there, it takes the cans to the local collection point, where all cans from the neighborhood are collected. From there, they are taken to the zonal collection point.

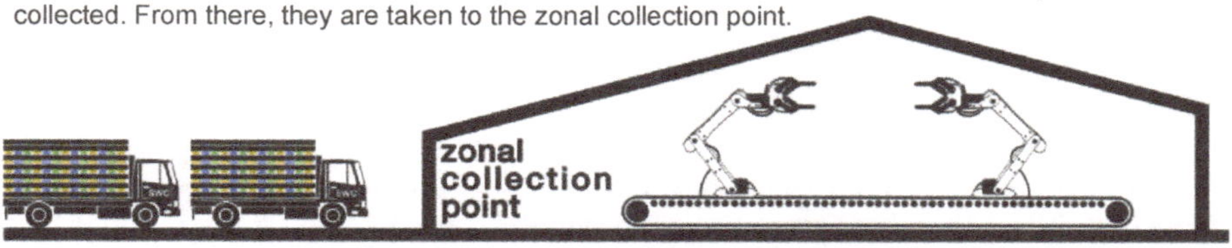

At the Zonal Collection Point, Mr Malhotra's garbage is emptied, scanned for correct segregation and then weighed. The system automatically logs Mr Malhotra's latest contribution and credits his account based on how much recyclable material was sent in. Simultaneously, it generates an analysis of that day's garbage segregation, which will be included in his month-end report so he can improve his efforts.

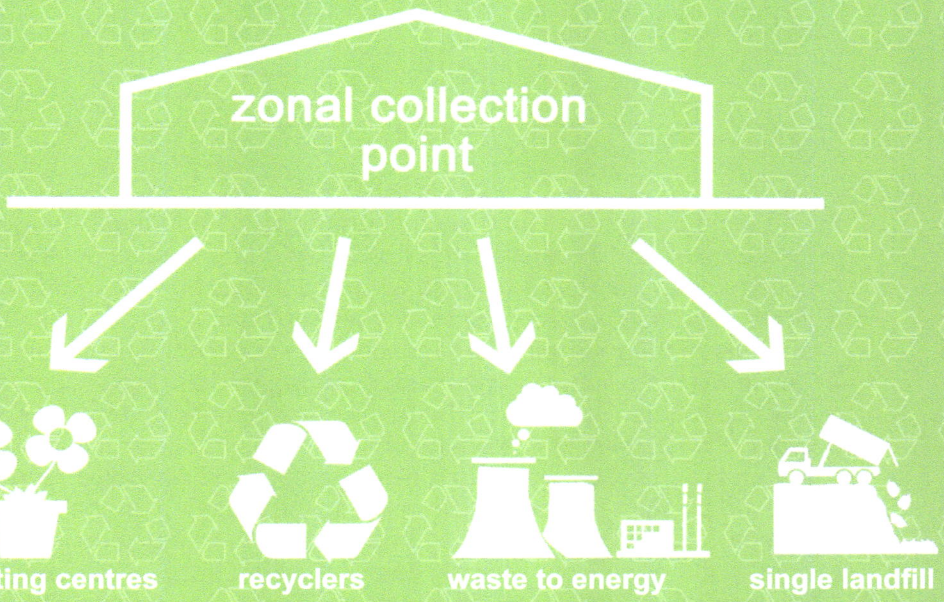

ne recyclable or organic garbage is distributed from the ZCP to composting centres, recyclers or waste-to-energy plants ne rest is sent to a single landfill, which is now able to operate quite effectively due to the greatly reduced load.

the end of the month, Mr Malhotra uses his points to buy his groceries, pay his bills or even top up his mobile credit. His cellent garbage segregation for that month earns him a further five percent discount at the neighbourhood Big Bazaar. I mes just in time to help him replace his old microwave oven.

e recyclers send some of their recycled products back to the ZCP where a shop sells them back to the public. Products n vary from things such as recycled notebooks to metal artwork, or even compost bags for home gardens.

Some Might Argue

The technology to validate such segregation and sorting is simply too complex and expensive. It is not. In fact, a Norwegian company called Titech has been building such machines for more than 15 years. Garbage is placed on a conveyor belt and it passes through a series of infrared, electromagnetic and spectroscopic scanners. These tell the computer what kind of garbage is passing through at any given time. So, if a PET bottle has accidentally gotten into the organic waste pile, the computer commands a robotic arm to knock it from the conveyor belt into a nearby trough, which would feed it into the plastics section.These machines, depending on their size, can process 30 tons of garbage per hour.[112] Working in two eight-hour shifts each day, it would take only 18–20 zonal centres to process all of Delhi's current garbage output. As the city grows, more zonal centres can be added.[113,114]

The system automatically records all this data from the correctness or segregation to weight, every time Mr Malhotra's garbage is deposited. It then makes calculations and stores them in Mr Malhotra's account until the end of the month. At the end of the month, his household would receive a reward statement from the SWC. This statement would read as follows:

Dear Mr Malhotra,

Thank you for segregating your waste this month. You generated 35 kilos of organic waste, 20 kilos of plastics and 10 kilos of non-recyclable waste. Your account has been credited with 285 credits. Your effort is highly-appreciated!

However, there are some steps you could consider to improve your segregation.

- Avoid depositing plastic PET bottles in the green can as they are not organic materials. Please use the blue can for PET bottles.
- While Diwali diyas are biodegradable, they take several years to break down. Please deposit them in the Orange can, not the green can.

Attached below is a detailed data sheet, which will help you compare how your family's recycling efforts compare to other citizens from your city.

Garbage Generated for October 2013 (lower is better)

City Averages	Percentage of Population	Your total: 65 kilos
>200 kilos	5%	
150 - 200 kilos	15%	
100 - 150 kilos	20%	
50 - 100 kilos	50%	
0 - 50 kilos	10%	

Segregation Accuracy for October 2013 (higher is better)

City Averages	Percentage of population	Shopping benefits at partner outlets	Your accuracy: 76%
90 - 100%	5%	10% off	
80 – 90%	15%	8% off	
70 – 80%	40%	6% off	
60 – 70%	20%	5% off	
50 – 60%	10%	4% off	
<50%	10%	No Discounts	

We hope you continue to set a great example with efficient recycling, and leave a clean and green city for your children to enjoy.

Sincerely,

The Smart Waste Corporation

Inverting the Problem into an Opportunity

The SWC would not only send a reward statement, stating exactly how many points have been awarded to Mr Malhotra's account, it would also let him know how he can improve his efforts by acting as his surrogate recycling tutor. The statement can be generated in English, Hindi, Punjabi, Tamil or whatever language might be applicable.

In addition to this, Mr Malhotra's monthly living expenses would be subsidized, thanks to the points he earns. If the SWMC is able to find enough merchant partners, he would be able to purchase everything from electronics to home appliances, food, clothing, fuel and possibly even tickets for movies or buses and metros, using these credits.

Furthermore, depending upon how well Mr Malhotra has been segregating his waste relative to the rest of his locality, the SWMC could incentivize him to improve his efforts with further rewards. For instance, Big Bazaar could say 'If you're in the top 10 percentile of the Smart Waste Management System ratings, we will give you an additional 5% discount on purchases for that month. If you're in the top 20 percentile, we'll give you a 3% discount,' and so on.

> **"Don't Waste in Haste,
> Segregate Your Waste!"**
>
> –*Seerat Chauhan*

Some Might Argue

It is easier to implement strict waste disposal laws such as those in effect in Switzerland.[115] Anyone who wishes to have their garbage picked up needs to buy stickers that cost €1 each. They must put one sticker on every bag of garbage if they want the garbage man to pick it up from their home. If there is no sticker, the garbage would lie there unattended. In effect, the less you dispose of, the less you pay. This has led to people recycling much more of their garbage to avoid paying.

This system works in Switzerland because civic maturity is higher there due to the advanced standard of living. In India, it would lead to people throwing their garbage over the neighbour's wall or disposing of it in a public park. Such high standards of civic maturity have yet to arrive here. That is why an incentive system, rather than one based on penalties, might be the fastest and most efficient way to get people to clean up. What's more, since it is self-sustaining, it can create viable jobs and income for the city. Finally, as we all know, clever citizens always find ways to circumvent laws. The smart technology and automation built into this process will make it virtually impossible to game the system.

The Way Forward

Legislation and PSU Management

To begin with, the municipality or state government would have to pass laws making the pre-segregation of garbage in all homes compulsory. It then needs to create the enabling infrastructure to support such a law. City authorities must create SWCs in their respective cities. These are government-owned PSUs that operate on a profit-and-loss basis. If necessary, they can list themselves on local stock markets to raise revenue for buying new infrastructure, such as better trucks and the garbage-sorting machines. As PSUs they would also enjoy favourable loans from banks and other lending institutions to purchase some capital equipment.

A very important challenge would be carefully managing the handover of staff from existing municipal bodies to the SWC. As far as possible, existing municipal staff should be absorbed directly into the SWC on long-term contracts. Any employees whose positions may be made redundant as a result of rationalization of the workforce should be absorbed seamlessly into other government departments or be provided with secure jobs in the expanded ecosystem. For example, some could be retrained to operate as recyclers. Others could be trained to operate the equipment. Any hardships that result from this transition should be compensated fairly.

Private Partnerships

City authorities will also have to hold license auctions to bring in private partners for the project. Some licenses that would be required include those for mobile service providers who would provide the tracking and ID infrastructure, recycling partners who receive the city's pre-segregated refuse to turn into recycled materials, retailers who sell recycled materials such as Full Circle Recycling, incentive partners who will participate in the scheme to offer customer benefits. Tenders will also need to be floated for technology partners who will supply the segregation checking equipment, garbage cans and new trucks.

In addition, licenses will need to be auctioned for waste-to-energy power plant systems operators.

THE STAKEHOLDERS

Old system

itizens

pose off their garbage in a haphazard anner. Some throw it at the local waste mp. Others leave it on the streets outside ir home to be picked up, while many rely litter the streets.

Garbage Collectors

Mostly disorganised labourers who work f less than minimum wage. They have r rights or benefits and are exposed direct to the garbage since they cannot affo proper protective clothing.

ag-Pickers and Manual avengers

d city dumps and landfills in the hopes of ding materials that they may sell for a few ees. They are all exposed to dangerous d unsanitary conditions and diseases. ny are young children who miss out on ool and a healthy childhood.

Municipal Authorities

transport waste from the garbage dumps open trucks, which often leak garbage ar foul smells as they move along. They dum everything in landfills, which are filling u quickly and are already at breaking point.

lew system

itizens

regate garbage in their homes, earn ards for proper segregation & recyclable terial collected

arbage Collectors

perly employed and paid a decent wage. ey work with full protective gear in itary conditions. They pick up garbage s from homes in carts or vans to deposit ocal collection centres.

ag-Pickers and Manual avengers

n garbage dumps no longer operational, y can work in far less unsanitary ditions by acting as collection agents ing litter of the streets in specially igned bags and depositing it at the ghbourhood collection centre.

Smart Waste Corporation

A public sector undertaking o public-private partnership, it collects & sorts garbage that is sent in by garbage collectors. Analyses garbage for prope segregation, weighs properly segregatec garbage, generates report of segregatior for each user. Separates recyclable anc non-recyclable materials. Sells recyclable material to recycling plants. Sends non-recyclable material to landfills or sells to waste-to-energy plants as fuel. Arranges marketing with incentive partners.

Full Circle Recycling' Retailers

'his retail shop is located on the premises of ach ZCC. They act as a retail outlet for itizens who want to buy products such as arden manure, paper products, handicrafts nd other art work, created from materials ecycled from the city's garbage.

City Municipal Corporati

Transports garbage between zonal stati and landfills, manages landfills, aucti licenses for management of the er programme and earns revenues from process.

Mobile Service Providers

Mobile service providers are a critical part of ne puzzle. Their infrastructure will help rack and locate each family's garbage ans. Their back-end billing processes will lso help in tracking and storing information or each customer to generate their monthly ecycling statements.

Incentive Partners/ Advertisers

This is a win-win for businesses s as retailers and public trans departments. They partner with the prog as it gives them a captive market includes the whole city's population. accepting the credits generated by Waste Management Programme, citizens enjoy discounts on their goods and serv

Waste-to-Power Plants

uy recyclable waste from the Waste Management Corporation to use as an ever-ready fuel for their power plants. This urther reduces the burden on landfills.

Recyclers

This group is ensured of a steady reliable stream of raw material and c not have to take up the headache of so and segregating it themselves. As a re there are substantial operational sav for recyclers.

All thanks to pre-segregation, the entire ecosystem has greatly expand Besides a cleaner, more sustainable city, the system has also creat thousands of new jobs.

The Bigger Picture

Let's shift focus to how many problems this system has solved.

1. You would have taken care of the biggest headache of any recycling effort by creating an incentive to segregate the garbage at its source.

2. There would be no unprofessional littering of waste during transit thanks to the tightly sealed lids of the cans.

3. You don't have open-air garbage collection points which are smelly, rotten places with scavengers and rodents hanging around.

4. We would have created a system where we can use the biodegradable waste to set up neighbourhood composting centres. All the biodegradable waste can be recycled to make compost and sold to the same citizens or the government for their home gardens or public parks.

5. Waste paper, plastics and metals could also be recycled, thus reducing the consumption of valuable natural resources such as trees, oil and minerals, respectively.

6. Whatever cannot possibly be recycled can be shipped to the city landfill which will store whatever is left. This way, at least 80–90% of the waste would be re-cycled or used in a productive manner.

7. It would also be possible for some of the waste to not just be sent to the landfill but to fuel a waste-to-energy power plant, which would generate electricity for the city.

The End of Manual Scavenging

Now we shift our focus to the other aspect of littering. You might have noticed that at a lot of airports, there is a system where you put in a coin and you take a trolley, which gets unlocked from the row. If you return the trolley to a row in the parking lot, or as you get into a cab, you get your coin back. Most of us, however, leave the trolley at the gate or in the car park.

If you go to the airport, you'll find a lot of people who are essentially unemployed or working overtime just collecting trolleys from all over the terminal and putting them back to collect the coins. If they spend three hours doing this, and return maybe 50 trolleys, they've made Rs 100 that day. This is roughly equal to the minimum wage and amounts to Rs 3,000 a month. For just a few hours of work per day, this is a handy additional income.

How does this translate to garbage? Right now, rag-pickers live and work in tragically unhygienic and inhuman conditions. They are essentially no better than manual scavengers. Now, with the new system, littering the streets may itself become unlikely.

However, if you do litter, the same people who used to eke out a living scavenging in unsanitary and hazardous garbage dumps would now pick litter off the roads as contracted agents of the SWC.

Even if they pick up 10 kilos of litter a day and deposit it at the neighbourhood garbage collection centre in a pre-segregated manner, it would be enough to subsidize at least two square meals a day. Assuming they earn Rs 5 per kilo of recyclable waste, the garbage collectors will earn up to Rs 50 per day. A simple meal at a roadside stall costs between Rs 20 to Rs 25. In this manner, they might even have a few rupees left over for other expenses.

This way, there is even an incentive for people to actually take litter off the streets, unlike municipal sweepers who merely collect the waste and pile it by the side of the road.

Waste-to-Energy

One of the unexplored aspects of segregating waste is transforming it into energy. Several technologies exist that incinerate organic waste and convert the energy into electricity using roughly the same process as burning coal or gas. The only drawback is that since organic waste is not strictly a fuel, it burns less efficiently than coal. A small pilot project in Surat will aim to generate 12 MW of power out of 600 tons of waste.[116] As the technology improves, higher efficiencies are expected.

Delhi produces 9,000 tons of waste daily. If the same plant that has been planned for Surat was brought to Delhi, and the city fed it 20% of its waste, it would produce roughly 36 MW of power. That's enough to light up several government office buildings, and eliminate a significant portion of waste that would otherwise go straight to a landfill.

Such a proposal is not new to Delhi.[117] Currently Delhi has two waste-to-energy plants at the Ghazipur and Okhla landfill sites. Ghazipur uses around 2,000 tons of garbage and produces 12MW of energy. A third waste-to-energy plant is being planned in Narela. However, it is awaiting approval from Delhi Pollution Control Committee. Smaller decentralized waste-to-energy plants outside the city are more desirable than large behemoths within it. With the new SWC, this will be quite easy to do.

Some Might Argue

The affluent class, which generates disproportionate amounts of waste, would not bother with segregating their garbage. The argument is that the pay-off is simply too insignificant for them and they wouldn't have the time or patience to bother with it. On the contrary, the attraction of such a programme for the affluent class would be very different. They have a stake in maintaining a clean and litter-free neighbourhood for reasons of aesthetics and keeping the value of their property from falling. A programme to rid the city of garbage and litter would mesh well with these goals. Also, most affluent families have domestic help, who already take care of garbage disposal. Training them to dispose of litter in the right can would only take a few minutes. At any rate, with the current system now the only way of disposing of one's garbage, families would have to segregate their waste before leaving it for collection. Failure to do so over a period of time would result in penalties.

Creating Social Change

Today, even if citizens want to participate in a proper recycling effort, they are powerless to affect change. The entire system has been poorly designed and is creaking and breaking as a result.

With the advent of the SWC, citizens would have both an incentive and an opportunity to do the right thing and responsibly dispose of their waste. Such a change in attitudes and incentives would help citizens transition their worldview from one of rampant consumerism to one where they begin to see a holistic picture of the world around them. They will begin to see the inherent value in all things, even something as mundane as garbage.

With this system, an empty wrapper, envelope or cardboard box starts looking like a unit of currency. It might look like 10 paise, Rs 5, or Rs 10. The moment it is no longer a worthless thing, it will not be thrown away on the roads.

We would have rid the roads and the streets and the gullies of India from 80% of their litter that no municipality will ever clean. We would have struck at the very source of this problem.

We would have converted garbage into currency.

Chapter 6

TOILETS

THE GREAT INDIAN INCONVENIENCE

Of 24.66 Mn Households in India

Only 3.2%
use public toilets

49.8%
defecate in open

46.9%
have toilets

I AM A CITIZEN OF MODERN INDIA!

WHY SHOULDN'T THE CONSTITUTION ENSHRINE WITHIN IT 'MY RIGHT TO SANITATION'?

TOILET CORPORATION OF INDIA
Central/national body driven by a unified goal – to provide safe, clean and hygienic

Introduction

We Don't Need Temples, We Need Toilets!

Cleanliness maybe next to godliness, but in India, sanitation and toilet statistics continue to raise a stink. Only 46.9% of India's 2.466 crore households have toilets while 49.8% of the population, nearly half of India's 120 crore people, still defecate in the open – squatting on roadsides, in agricultural fields or at railway tracks; the remaining 3.2% use public toilets.

According to data from the National Census (2011), the percentage of households in rural India with access to television and telephones exceeds the percentage of households with access to toilet facilities.[118] This, notwithstanding that the Indian government has spent close to Rs 1,25,000 crore on water and sanitation projects in the last 20 years. While some strides have been made in rural sanitation with projects such as the Nirmal Bharat Abhiyan (previously the Total Sanitation Campaign), the situation in cities and urban areas remains problematic and unaddressed.[119,120]

On 2 October 2014, Prime Minister Narendra Modi launched the Swachh Bharat Abhiyan, a five-year flagship mission intended to put an end to open defecation and adopt better SWM practices. The government constructed 86 million toilets since and brought down the number of persons who defecate in the open from 550 million to 150 million. It is a laudable initiative and has certainly galvanized action in this domain.

Linfen in China offers a significant lesson to Indian cities. It shows that simple, but vital things such as public toilets are as critical as any large infrastructure project to make cities livable. For a long time, Linfen was one of the worst cities in the world to live in. But in the last 4 years, it has turned around dramatically, recently winning the UN-Habitat's International Best Practices award for the Asia Pacific region.

At the core of Linfen's revival and the reason for it receiving worldwide attention is the city's 'toilet revolution' that began in 2008. Concerned by the poor quality and numbers of public toilets – only 12 for a population of 6,00,000 – the government constructed and retrofitted 200 toilets in and around the city. Smart design led to changing public perceptions and the toilets are now used about 2 crore times every year. In contrast, Indian cities, which are grossly under-equipped in terms of public toilets, have shown little urgency to improve the situation. Chennai, for instance, which needs about 6,000 public toilets, has only 714 and Nagpur, which needs more than 3,000 toilets, has 318.[121] Bangalore, a city with a population of 85,00,000 people, has about 500 public toilets, which makes it 1 toilet for every 17,000 people.

CITY	POPULATION	PUBLIC TOILETS
Bangalore	8.5 Million	500
Chennai	4.3 Million	714
Nagpur	2.1 Million	318

In any developed country you visit across the world, you normally find toilets available within a 3-to-5 minute walking distance. Typically, you have them at metro and gas stations, in the basements of restaurants or on the sidewalk. In India, however, you consider yourself fortunate if you can find a public toilet at all. Even where toilets do exist, if you were to look at the average loo in an Indian city, they are unhygienic, dilapidated and completely unusable. Talk to any woman on the street and they say they'd rather not go to the loo at all than use a public toilet.

The general consensus is that it is about quality and not just quantity. 'Forget enough toilets, I wish the ones we have in the city were usable,' says Shagun D, a women's activist working with the NGO Vimochana. Parvathy Jaya, a media professional, shares similar sentiments. 'Yes, we do need more public toilets in the city. But more than toilets, we need clean toilets. The ones that we have currently are unusable because of the condition they are in right now.'[122]

To make matters worse, in the absence of janitors or other female staff, it is often unsafe for women to venture into a public toilet even during the day. In our cities, women's safety has been a hot-button issue and requires urgent attention. But without improvements in the toilet situation, women in Indian cities say they're not going to be safe.

The Problem

Even where toilets do exist or capital is available and projects are set up for the construction of such civic amenities, the sustainability of public toilets is often disregarded and, in the long run, they become unsafe and unhygienic and are subsequently abandoned or closed down due to lack of maintenance.

Research has shown that the absence of public toilets results in increased street urination, creating conditions for the spread of water-borne diseases. Less visible, but as virulent is the effect on women who, in response to the lack of toilets, are likely to 'hold on', leading to urine (and pathogen) retention, bladder distension and an increasing propensity for continence problems.

The result is that in Indian cities, women, the elderly and people with disabilities may have to choose where to go or simply not go out at all for fear of there being no toilet when they need one.[123]

Of Pees and Queues

An inclusive, accessible and sustainable city begins with the public toilet.

Providing toilets to the 1.5 crore urban households that do not have them is a priority and organizations such as Sulabh have done well to build low-cost and easy-to-maintain toilets to address the problem of inadequate toilet numbers at the household level. However, it is equally important to provide toilets in public places. These are an integral part of the civic amenities and those who actively use the city need them. What is needed is a scaled up and concerted effort to not only increase numbers but also to improve the status of the public toilet and turn this everyday public amenity into an object of civic pride.[124]

Existing Models

Challenges and Successes

With liberalization has come the belief that many civic services such as sanitation and water can be delivered through public–private partnerships and that the onus for these services need not be borne by the government alone. The private sector has discovered that there might even be profits in this area and NGOs working on sanitation have realized that they can intervene in the design and delivery of sanitation services. A cogent example of a public–private sanitation model is the Sulabh Shauchalya, a simple 'twin-pit, pour–flush toilet' that has brought about a minor revolution in the availability of toilet facilities in many parts of India.

The Sulabh model has generated substantial revenues and the pay-per-use model it introduced has caught on. Every Indian city has tried variations on the theme. The main issue here is how a toilet block can pay for itself (capital expenditure) as well as cover its operations and maintenance costs (operating expenditure). On paper, this seems workable. Municipalities give the land for such public toilets free and more often than not, water and electricity are also free or heavily subsidized. However, although Sulabh continues to make profits out of its toilets, other efforts have met with indifferent success.[125]

One reason Sulabh makes profits is because its toilet blocks are usually built in areas with a dense footfall such as train and bus stations or important city junctions. The toilets are heavily used and generate considerable daily revenue. It is estimated that they can cover their construction costs (capital expenditure) in less than a year. This surplus can then be used to maintain or operate the toilets (operational expenditure) and also to cross-subsidize those built in slums where people cannot pay as much and the use is not so heavy.

In recent years, the Delhi government, through the municipal corporations, has attempted to rope in advertising agencies and award them with build, own, operate and transfer (BOOT) contracts to construct public toilets. The idea was that the agencies would invest in the construction and maintenance of the toilets and in return get free advertising space on the toilet structure.

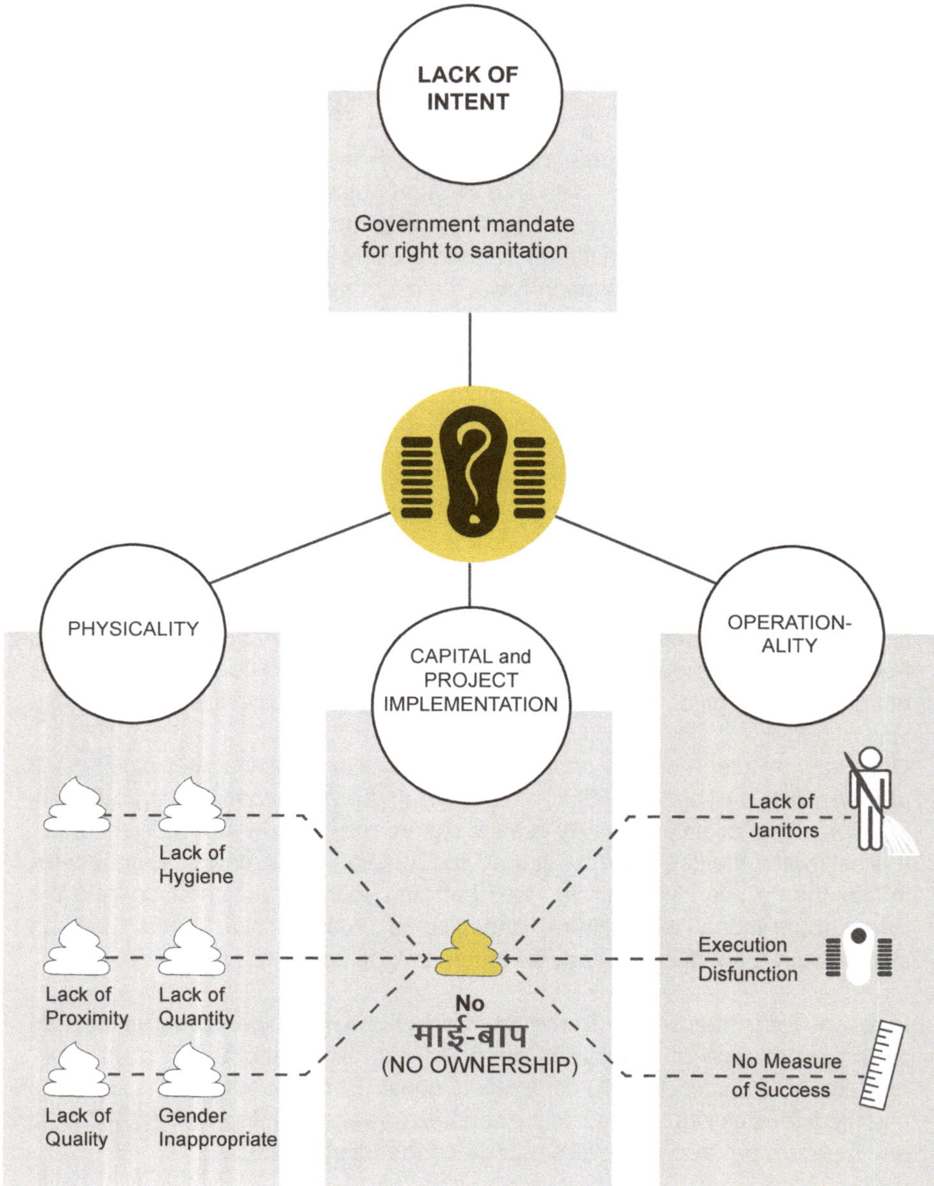
LACK OF INTENT
Government mandate for right to sanitation
PHYSICALITY
CAPITAL and PROJECT IMPLEMENTATION
OPERATION-ALITY
Lack of Hygiene
Lack of Proximity
Lack of Quantity
Lack of Quality
Gender Inappropriate
No माई-बाप (NO OWNERSHIP)
Lack of Janitors
Execution Disfunction
No Measure of Success

In these structures, typically, the entrance to the toilet was designed to be from the rear with the front of the building given over to advertising space, creating issues of safety and security, particularly for women users.

Also, in the absence of janitors or cleaning staff, the toilets were filthy and the entrance to the premises was often choked by debris, stray dogs and human waste. The problem was that once the advertising agency got the real estate in terms of critical surfaces for advertisements and hoardings and recovered its capital expenditure, it really had no interest in running the public toilet. It was more an obligation than something that could generate revenue for the agency and even if it were contractually required to put a janitor in each toilet, there was a possibility of collusion with the authorities to avoid responsibility.

It may be said that while the solution succeeded in the infusion of capital and therefore took care of some aspects of funding and construction, it failed on account of other elements such as safety, hygiene and access – in short, it failed to provide for the operating expenditure of the toilet

The solution would then seem to be to provide not only for the capital expenditure, but also the operating expenditure of the public toilet by adopting (for instance) the pay-per-use model and introducing the public toilet in a manner that its creation as well as operation becomes positively remunerative to some party.

The problem is that there really is no mai–baap of the public loo – someone who is interested in and benefits from the success of the public toilet.[126] The absence of a *mai–baap* is generic to most of India's infrastructural deficits. In Delhi's lush Jahanpanah forest park, for instance, the Delhi Development Authority (DDA) has done a brilliant job of creating portacabins with pay-per-use toilets. But in the absence of an agency that benefits from the success of these public facilities or is wired to ensure that they work, the toilets are broken down and in no condition to be used.

The conclusion, therefore, is that it is only if there is an agency that not only benefits from the creation and operation of the public toilet but which is also wired to its cleanliness and hygiene that a natural system of checks and balances is created which ensures its sustained operational goodness.

The Solution

Make Loos Your Business

The idea is to create a business model around the public toilet by auctioning BOOT licenses for public toilet structures to coffee shops in return for prime retail space in marketplaces across Indian cities. The government leases prime land to the coffee shop, which invests in the construction and maintenance of the public toilet and in the process of sharing premises with it, becomes automatically wired to its success. The coffee shop recovers the operating expenditure of the toilet in terms of costs as well as some profit on the basis of a pay-per-use model from people every time they use the loo. It also acquires the right to sublease extra space on either side of the toilet and to sell advertising space on the perimeter of the toilet structure.

Essentially, in this case, what we are doing is leveraging real estate value as a tool to subsidize or pay the capital expenditure of creating a modern toilet that lends itself to a much higher level of hygiene and upkeep than a municipal toilet would. It would, in that sense, be comparable to a toilet in a fine mall in the city and, therefore, attract users willing to pay a premium for its use.

Consider This

A structure with a spacious, state-of-the-art public toilet on the ground level with a prominent, clean entrance in the front, manned by a smart attendant who collects money and lets you in. Flanking the toilet at one end is an ice-cream parlour and on the other a florist or gift-card vendor. A broad staircase outside the building leads to a sprawling coffee shop on the upper level. The coffee shop maintains the premises and is geared to making sure that the toilet is scrupulously clean, hygienic and odourless, failing which it runs the risk of losing patrons and business.

While there is a strong case for the Sulabh model for a certain section of the population without access to toilets at the household level, who cannot afford to pay more than Rs 2 or Rs 5 to use a public toilet, there are an equally large number of people willing to pay Rs 10, Rs 20 or even Rs 50, provided there is a clean, hygienic and odourless loo.

In the absence of a clean public toilet, people will often go into a restaurant and order something just because they want to use the bathroom, spending an average of Rs 100 to Rs 200 in the process. The argument is that people started by paying Rs 5 for parking, graduating to Rs 10 and Rs 20, and are now willing to pay Rs 50 for a safe place to park their cars. Therefore, it is only a matter of availability of a certain value – eventually when people are in a situation where they need to use the facilities and public toilets of a certain standard are available, they will get around to paying whatever it costs to use them.

It maybe said, therefore, that the public toilet-cum-coffee shop effectively generates a robust revenue model around the business of the public toilet, leveraging real estate value to subsidize capital expenditure, utilizing a pay-per-use model to cover operational expenses and wiring the success of the coffee shop to the hygiene of the public toilet, thus creating a sustainable mechanism to ensure its operational goodness.

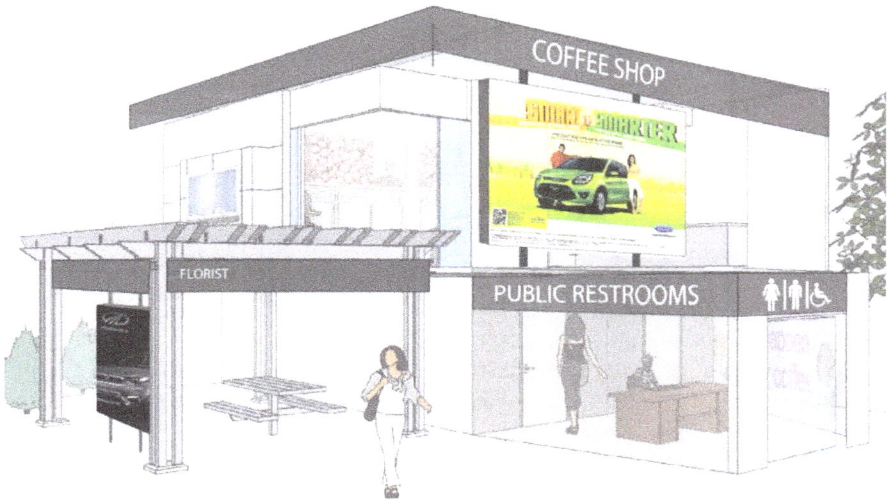

Some Might Argue

Coffee shops and other retailers may not want to share premises with a public toilet, and that this may potentially act to negatively incentivize franchises, or corporations from bidding for coffee shops in public toilet structures. The response to this is that modern technology makes it possible to build the public toilet in a way that doesn't intrude on the retailer's space and ensure that it remains clean, hygienic and odourless, provided that it is maintained properly. In the past, toilets were built outside the home, as far as possible from the bedrooms. Now, it is of the greatest value for any residential accommodation to have attached bathrooms – they have gone from being toilets to washrooms to glamour rooms. Even when malls are designed, the largest toilets are placed next to the food court. In fact, when the idea for the public toilet-cum-coffee shop was first suggested by the author (Goonmeet Chauhan) to the MCD, prior to the 2010 Commonwealth Games, it found great traction from both the government and potential licensees.

Inverting the Problem into an Opportunity

Assuming that the total area available on each floor of the toilet structure is 1,250 sq. ft, 250 sq. ft on the ground floor is given over to a staircase and lift – the model envisages a disabled-friendly situation, while the toilet itself is 800 square feet with an additional 100 sq. ft on either side for an ice cream parlour, florist or gift shop. Therefore, the coffee shop receives a concession, which is equivalent to 1,250 sq. ft on the first floor and an additional 200 sq. ft on the ground floor, which can be leased to other retail businesses under the terms of the license.

Let us assume that the coffee shop spends Rs 50,00,000 on acquiring a license for the public toilet and another Rs 50,00,000 on building the structure (at an approximate rate of Rs 2,000 per sq. ft). Considering a typical license of 15 years, if the coffee shop were to lease out a similar premises for the same period, it would pay (at the rate of Rs 150 per sq. ft) a rent of Rs 2,17,500 per month, amounting to approximately Rs 4 crore for the entire 15-year period. Effectively then, the coffee shop spends just one-fourth of what it would normally pay to acquire the same premises in the rental market and it gets the premises fitted out to its specifications – in the case of a rental, the coffee shop would be required to spend extra money on the interiors.

Consider any major marketplace in Delhi – South Extension or Greater Kailash – which attracts between 50,000 to 1,00,000 visitors every day. Of these, if 1,000 people were to use the public toilet in a single day, at Rs 10 per use, it would generate Rs 10,000 a day and Rs 3,00,000 a month, which is certainly enough to equip and illuminate the toilet, hire appropriate staff to keep it clean and even install a mini sewage-treatment plant and solar-lighting panel to make it a green facility.

In addition to revenues from the coffee shop and the public toilet, the concessionaire stands to earn between Rs 50,000 and Rs 70,000 per month (at the rate of Rs 250 to Rs 350 per sq. ft) from sub-leasing the space on either side of the toilet, for which it can typically realize a much higher rate per square foot. The concessionaire also generates between Rs 1,00,000 and Rs 6,00,000 from selling prime advertising space on the perimeter of the toilet structure, at the rate of Rs 50,000 to Rs 1,00,000 per hoarding per month, depending on the location of the toilet.

Suddenly, the public toilet becomes sensible business and the city municipal authorities find themselves flooded with applications from people who want to construct public loos. Twenty years ago, who could have imagined that people would be willing to pay for bottled water? Now, you have multinational companies, run by top-notch business graduates, which manage clean water – so why not clean loos?

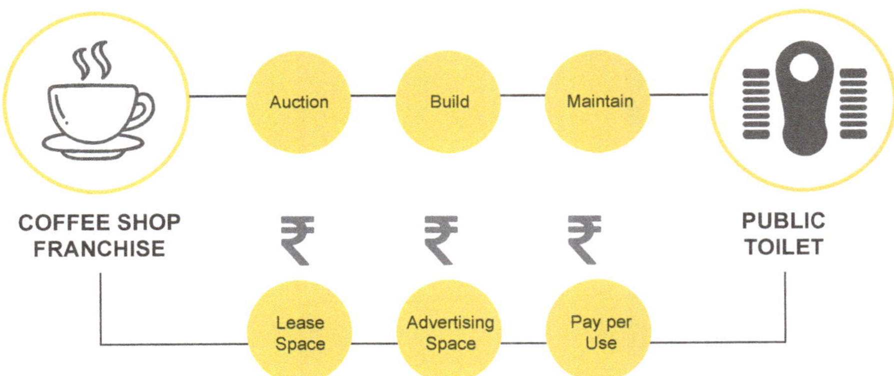

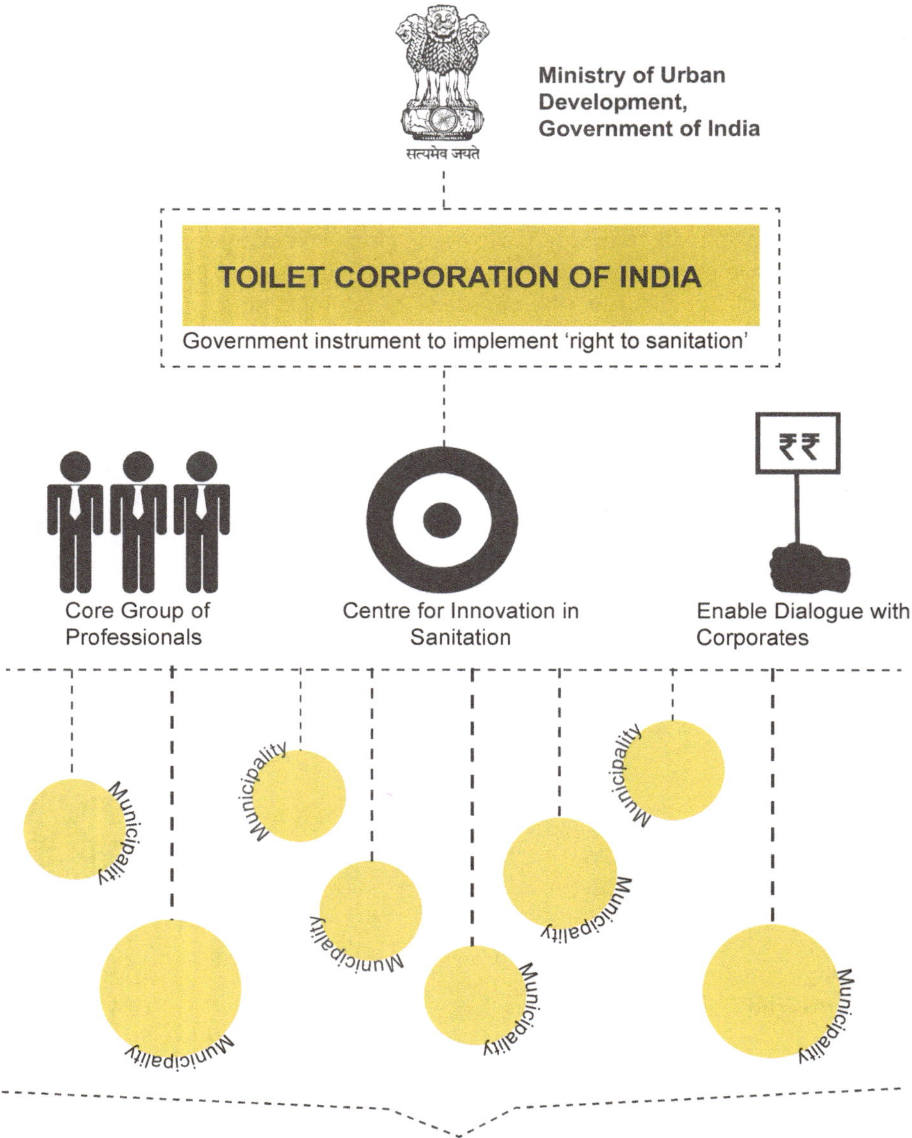

LARGEST RETAIL SPACE RESOURCE OF INDIA

'with cumulative leasable retail space of 15 crore sq. ft'

The Way Forward

Toilets Corporation of India (TCI)

The government's involvement in the sanitation sector is one of the most important factors behind sustainable and large-scale sanitation outcomes. Under the leadership of Narender Modi, the initiative for universal access to sanitation has been given a renewed push. What started in 1999 as a Total Sanitation Campaign (TSC) for Comprehensive Rural Sanitation, was subsequently recast as Swachh Bharat Abhiyan (Clean India Mission), which aims to eradicate open defecation across India. It covers 4,041 cities and towns.

In rural India, 12 crore toilets are to be built at a cost of Rs 1.96 lakh crore. Of these, 8.6 crore have been built already. A special fund called Swachh Bharat Kosh has been created for this mission. While multiple agencies are pushing the construction of new toilets at urban and rural sectors, and in the private and public domains, the management of these facilities continues to face the same challenges of poor maintenance and neglect.

Taking the model forward, the first step, therefore, is for the government, in consultation with the Ministry of Urban Development, to set up an autonomous authority called the Toilets Corporation of India (TCI), which, working in collaboration with municipalities across the country, fulfills its mandate to provide safe, clean and hygienic public toilets to the citizens of India, as well as manage and maintain them through an innovative model. What this will do is create a core group of professionals with domain expertise in public sanitation and bring in a far more nuanced approach to the issue of toilets as opposed to local councilors or municipalities attempting to map the learning curve in each city. The TCI will bring in a certain level of predictability and a professional, structured methodology to the issue of sanitation, similar to other nationalized bodies such as the National Highway Authority of India (NHAI) or the Airports Authority of India (AAI), where the government has taken the mandate in a more centralized way rather than leaving it to individual cities to create their own infrastructure. It will also powerfully demonstrate the government's intent to execute and affect the fundamental right of every citizen to sanitation.

As an apex body, it will be possible for the TCI to enter into dialogue with corporations and other entities at a far more senior level and to bring in collaborations that can only be possible at a certain scale. If the Coca Cola Company were to introduce a new soft drink, for instance, and were looking to launch an integrated advertising campaign across major cities in the country, it could, in principle, approach the TCI directly for advertising space on public toilet structures pan-India instead of having to deal with individual municipalities overseeing single public toilets. For Coca Cola to deal with the CEO of the TCI where the municipality is only one of the partners but not the sole driver would be far easier than to deal directly with the Brihanmumbai Municipal Corporation or a corporator from Chennai.

The TCI could also leverage its centralized position to engage or partner with large manufacturers to drive innovations in public sanitation. Let us assume that India needs 1,00,000 well-made and well-maintained public toilets in the next four years, which means it needs 10,000 toilets a year and approximately 1,000 toilets a month. At these numbers it would be possible for the TCI to mandate, say, Mahindra and Mahindra to develop an assembly line for low-cost, pre-fabricated toilets and sewage-treatment plants with shorter installation times to replace regular brick-and-mortar structures. So instead of the MCD giving a notice in the *Times of India* for a contractor to build a single toilet complex, suddenly there is a step-up in the entire level of operations with larger corporations vying to participate in the resulting economies of volume and scale.

The result is that the loo ecosystem is energized and when Mahindra and Mahindra actually develops the Rs 10,00,000 toilet block which can be erected in a week, the TCI becomes the centre of a technology revolution around sanitation – supplying toilet blocks to Africa, South East Asia and the rest of the world

Taking the TCI to Rural India

Consistent with its mandate to affect the right to sanitation to every citizen of India, the TCI may choose to use the money generated from auctioning licenses to the public toilet-cum-coffee shop and its pay-per-use model to build toilets in rural areas – in effect transferring the subsidy from city to village and fulfilling its obligation to the rural citizen. Assuming that one-half from the proceeds of the auction was to go to the municipality while the other half was to accrue to the TCI as a levy. The TCI would have available, a fund in excess of Rs 25,000 crore (at the rate of Rs 25,00,000 per toilet times 1,00,000 toilets) supplemented by a one-third share of revenue from the pay-per-use model from each public toilet, amounting to an additional Rs 12,000 crore per year (at the rate of Rs 12,00,000 per toilet per year for 1,00,000 toilets). At a construction cost of Rs 20,00,000 per toilet and an average of 2 public toilets per village for 6,50,000 villages, the investment required for rural sanitation would be in the region of Rs 2,60,000 crore, which sum could easily be made available from the fund over a period of 5 to 10 years, making it possible to bring about a dramatic transformation in the rural public sanitation landscape in India within a decade.

Consider This

At an average of 1,000 toilets per city across 100 cities (1,00,000 toilets) and 1,450 sq. ft per toilet, the TCI effectively becomes the owner of 14.5 crore square feet of prime retail space, which is more than 38 times the size of the Mega Mall in Dubai, considered the single largest retail space in the world.[127]

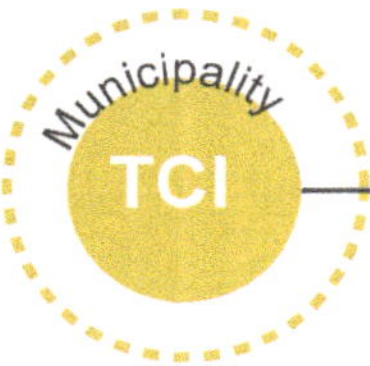

CELLULAR MAPPING

Municipality authority conducts cellular mapping excercise in each city to identify potential market-places for the construction of the public toilet-cum-coffee shop to divide them into cell.

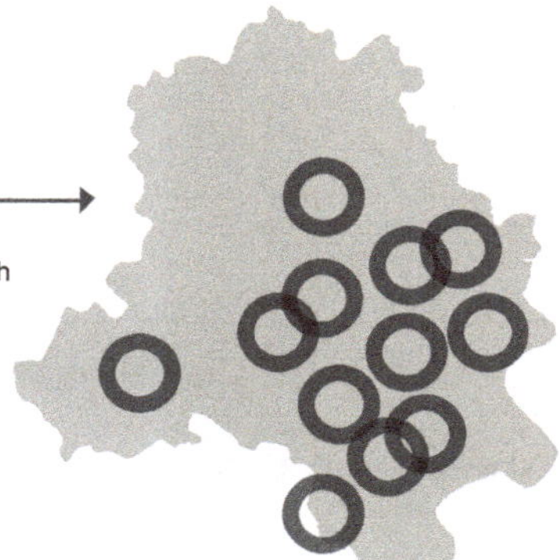

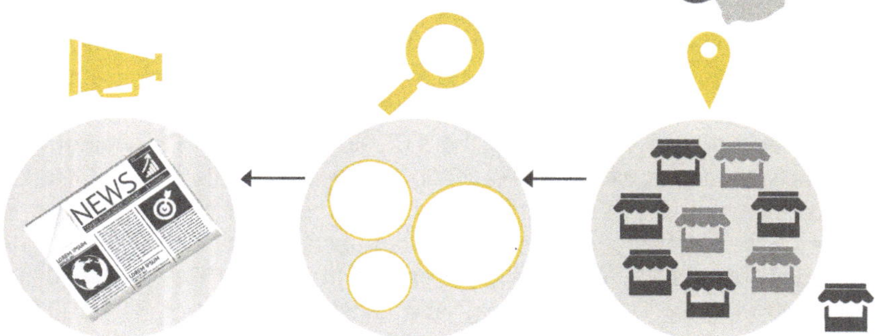

Each consisting of a cluster of 10 to 15 markets, for ease of administration.

Assessment of the value of land, availability of retail space and toilet requirement in each market-place. Classify each location on the basis of project size–small, medium and large.

The final step would be to place prominent advertisements in daily newspapers to inform prospective licenses and subsequently to auction separate BOOT licenses for each cell.

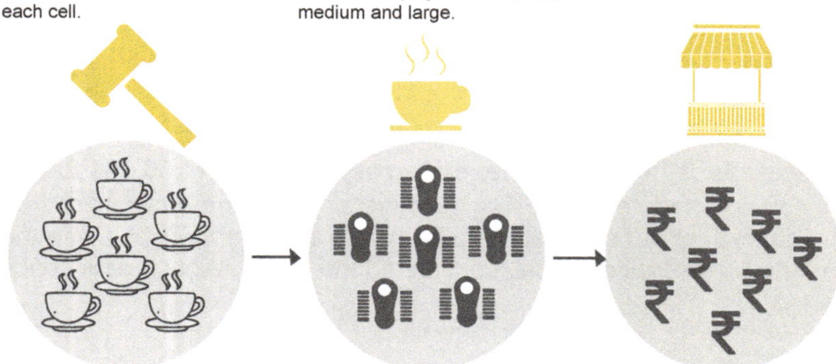

Create a robust competitive market with multiple players across each city, vying to provide clean, hygienic public-toilet faciliitites and to attract bigger players and multinational corporations to the business of the public toilet.

A coffee shop franchise or corporation gets licenses to operate coffee shops at 10 premium locations by winning a single auction.

For a smaller retailer – a gift shop, a florist or an ice-cream seller, for instance, looking to establish a presence in Delhi, the public toilet-cum-coffee shop becomes a valuable source of premium retail space and a great vehicle for expanding or establishing a presence in prime locations across the city.

Cellular Licensing

The next step is for the municipal authority, under the aegis of the TCI, to conduct a cellular-mapping exercise in each city to identify potential marketplaces for the construction of the public toilet-cum-coffee shop and create separate cells, each consisting of a cluster of 10 to 15 markets, for ease of administration. The municipal authority must follow up the cellular mapping with an assessment of the value of land, availability of retail space and toilet requirement in each marketplace and based on the assessment, classify each location on the basis of project size (small, medium and large) and accordingly recommend the value at which the auction of the license should commence.

The final step would be to place prominent advertisements in daily newspapers to inform prospective licensees and subsequently, to auction separate BOOT licenses for each cell. What cellular licensing will do is enable the creation of a robust competitive market with multiple players across each city, vying to provide clean, hygienic public-toilet facilities and attract bigger players and multinational corporations to the business of the public toilet. Assuming, for instance, that the city of Delhi is mapped for 1,000 public toilets-cum-coffee shops divided into 100 cells of 10 toilets each. In the case of South Delhi, locations at East of Kailash, Kailash Colony, M-Block Greater Kailash I, N-Block Greater Kailash I, M-Block Greater Kailash II, Alaknanda, Chittranjan Park, Nehru Place and Kalkaji could be auctioned together to one licensee. The idea is that it would be easier for the licensee to develop and maintain a single, integrated infrastructure of maintenance for the 10 public toilets within his cell and to drive sustained improvements in quality and efficiency, which a small player with a license for a single toilet may not be able to achieve. For instance, if each toilet requires 2 janitors, the licensee may choose to build in some level of redundancy by hiring 22 janitors instead of 20 – he has two substitutes floating around in case of absentees in any of the 10 markets in his cell. For a larger player – a coffee shop franchise or corporation, cellular licensing offers the opportunity for corporate traction. If it can get licenses to operate coffee shops at 10 premium locations by winning a single auction, it saves time and negates the hassle of negotiating with 10 individual vendors or landlords. Similarly for the smaller retailer – a gift shop, florist or a an ice-ream seller – looking to establish a presence in Delhi, the public toilet-cum-coffee shop becomes a valuable source of premium retail space and a great vehicle for expanding or establishing a presence in prime locations across the city.

Welfare Association

Concurrently with the auction of cellular licenses, what the municipal authority could do is set up a series of oversight committees that would take in as stakeholders the welfare associations of each market as well as local councilors from the area to help the government oversee the auctions and ensure that the public toilets are maintained and not subsequently shut down. As an additional incentive, the model could allow for a significant portion of the proceeds collected from the operation of the public toilet to be directed to the welfare association as stakeholder and partner. Assuming that of the Rs 3,00,000 generated by the toilet every month, 1,00,000 would go directly into the coffers of the welfare association – which is typically a substantial sum for any association – it could be used for security, illumination, maintenance, horticulture and a general renewal of the market space, putting into motion a very positive trend towards the rejuvenation of marketplaces across Indian cities.

Some Might Argue

The welfare association might object to the construction of the public toilet structure or otherwise find reason to hinder its operation and continued success. To this we submit that the public toilet-cum-coffee shop model allows for a portion of the money generated by the public toilet to be directed to the welfare association of each market, creating a financial incentive and wiring the association as stakeholder and partner to its continued success. Now even if the coffee shop chooses not to maintain the toilet or fails to repair it, it is in the interest of the welfare association to ensure its operational goodness, and it may choose to assume a supervisory role pushing for the maintenance of the toilet structure.

Informal Retail Sector

In addition to the small retailer and the advertising agency, it may also be in the interest of the concessionaire to engage the informal retail sector in a regulated manner to create business activity at the entrance to the toilet premises so that it becomes a safe and animated place, conducive to women entering the toilet at any hour. What is lacking in India is that the moment you exit from a premises – a shop, restaurant or home – the space immediately outside is never regulated, creating an interface which is knee-jerk. So you may have a clean home, but the road outside is filthy and comes as an unpleasant shock every time you step out. Since we are typically going to be creating public toilet-cum-coffee shops in existing parking lots or at the side of parks, it is very important to consider what the open space around it will be used for.

Currently a majority of the informal retail sector, consisting of small vendors, carts and vans, operates below and beyond the law and while the government is aware of its existence, it cannot possibly stifle it due to its very critical role in terms of job creation. The result is that we have an informal sector which operates with the police as the *mai–baap*, with each vendor paying the local police to operate from a specific section of the sidewalk or road.[128] Although in the specific case of the public toilet-cum-coffee shop, the revenue from the informal sector is likely to be insignificant – typically each vendor would be able to pay between Rs 2,000 to Rs 5,000 a month, so far as the coffee shop is concerned, if it doesn't regulate who uses the area outside its entrance, chances are someone will occupy the space anyway, littering the area and paving the way for a steady deterioration of the immediate surroundings.

Therefore, if a couple of women vendors are sitting and selling something outside the toilet premises, not only is the space kept clean, it creates a level of comfort and safety for women wishing to enter the toilet. Here, the informal sector not only provides a dynamic element but also fills the gap in the shopping experience by providing things which are not expensive enough to be stacked by a shopkeeper.

A space could also be created for roadside artists and musicians that would further animate and add a new dimension to the area outside the public toilet, offering them legitimacy so that they are not harassed by the police and acknowledging to them that the city values their presence. There could be a caricaturist or a musician sitting outside or different artists at different times of the day. It could become a speaker's corner with college students using it as a forum for debate and some steps or seating around it could naturally spring up or be part of the design for people to sit and enjoy the performances.

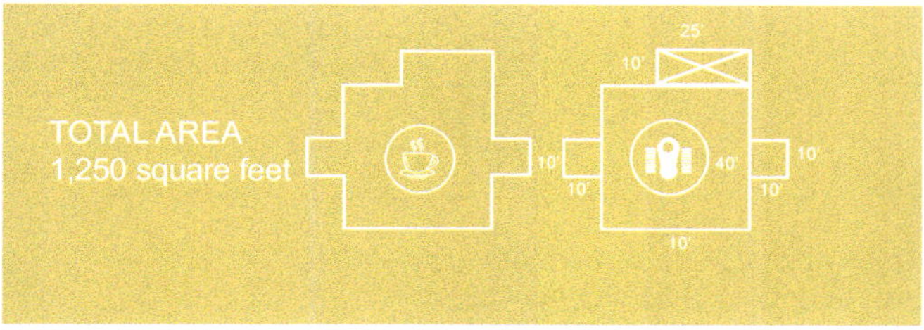

EXPENSES
Borne by coffee franchise (assuming coffee franchise leases the public toilet for 15 years)

Auction	₹ 50,00,000	▼
Build	₹50,00,000	▼

RETURNS
earned due to public toilets
(Rs 5.5 lakh-Rs 11.5 lakh) per month

Advt Space	₹100,000–₹600,000 per month	▲
Lease Space	₹150,000–₹250,000 per month	▲
Pay per Use (₹ 10)	₹ 300,000	▲

1/3rd Concessionaire
use it for operational expenses of the toilet in the cell

1/3rd Welfare Association of Markets
use it for upkeep of the market

1/3rd Toilet Corporation of India
use it for operation of non remunerative loos in rural India

1000 (No. of people in a day) x **10** (Cost per use) x **30** (Days in a month) = ₹ 300,000

~ ₹100,000 = **upkeep** of the market

Sustenance Model

TCI has a self-sustaining model that can create 1 lakh toilets in urban and rural India – All new and all for **free**.

AUCTION

TCI charges each concessionaire approximately Rs 50 lakh per cell to build and maintain toilets for a certain number of years in urban area.

Assuming 1,000 toilet cells are auctioned across a spread of 100 cities all over India

1,000 x 100 = 1 lakh toilet cells
Money from auctioning toilet cells = 1×10^6 x 50 lakh

= ₹50,000 CRORE

50%

~ Rs 25,000 cr
is raised by TCI in auctioning toilets for 1st fifteen years

50%

~ Rs 25,000 cr
is given to the municipality for the welfare and upkeep of municiple area

~ Rs 12,000 cr
is raised in every year by TCI from pay per use model in urban areas

Well-equiped Facility

Cleanliness and Hygiene Maintaned

Sewage Treatment Plant

Green Facility

In India, there is a need for atleast 2 public toilet blocks for every village. Considering there are atleast

~ 6,45,000 villages

13,00,000

Toilets need to be made to provide for 6,45,000 villages

~₹2,60,000 CR

is the cost needed to make 13 lakh toilets, which is more than the 2019 defence budget of India

TCI has ₹25,000 crore (10% of the needed sum) from auctioning Toilet Cells, added to which is an yearly earning of ₹12,000 crore.

It is now possible to effectively reach the target of creating 13 lakh toilets.

Mahindra...a pre-fabricated toilet manufacturer?

Size of Automobile Market is Rs **5,00,000 crore** by 2020

If large automobile players like Telco/Mahindra can set up a production line for pre-fabricated toilets, being manufacturing and R&D giants, manufacturing and distributing pre-fabricated 13 lakh toilets will seem like a great opportunity for the automobile industry.

It would enhance the size of the market by 30–50%.
India could start exporting pre-fabricated toilets to the world.
It would effectively add significantly to the GDP, and generate substantial employment!

Stakeholders

The public toilet-cum-coffee shop model brings together an integrated system of stakeholders, all of whom are wired to the success and the continuing operational goodness of the public toilet. The government as cause and change agent has a fundamental obligation to provide clean, hygienic and safe public toilets to every citizen of the country. In acknowledgement of this obligation, it creates a corporation which acts as an enabler to bring in private enterprise as the operating agent. The operating agent, in accordance with its mandate, engages the small retailer, the advertising agency and the informal sector as interested parties and the welfare association as beneficiary and oversight agent.

The idea is that the larger the number of stakeholders embedded in the toilet's success, the better the chances of its sustained operational goodness.

As the primary stakeholder, the government becomes positively correlated to the success of the public toilet. It not only earns from the auction of the public toilet structure, it also saves money and governance time that it would have otherwise spent on building the public toilet itself. It fulfills its obligation to the citizen, gains great mileage from the creation of retail space and jobs and sets in motion a revenue-generation mechanism for the rejuvenation of existing marketplaces.

As the operating agent, the coffee shop corporation takes on the mandate of investing in, building and operating the public-toilet structure and in the process benefits from access to prime retail space at a much cheaper rate. The operating agent brings in the small retailer and the advertising agency, creating for itself, the opportunity to earn substantial revenues from selling advertising space and sub-leasing extra area in the public-toilet structure. For the small retailer and the advertising agency in turn, the public toilet-cum-coffee shop becomes a valuable opportunity to gain access to prime locations across the city.

The operating agent also engages the informal sector to animate and lend safety to the toilet interface; in return the informal sector as a beneficiary gains legitimacy and an inclusive space to operate without harassment.

Since it shares premises with it, the coffee shop is geared to making sure that the toilet is meticulously clean and hygienic. There could, however, be a strong tendency on the part of the coffee shop to have a dysfunctional loo or to close it down altogether because that would be the easiest way of creating hygiene. To counter this possibility the public toilet-cum-coffee shop model creates a financial incentive for and wires the welfare association of each market to its continued success. Now even if the coffee shop chooses not to maintain the toilet or fails to repair it, it is in the interest of the welfare association to ensure its operational goodness and it may choose to assume a supervisory role in pushing for the maintenance of the toilet structure.

The people's rights are, thus, addressed and the citizens as ultimate beneficiaries and must overcome their inhibitions, accept the public toilet system and rise to the occasion by using the public toilet in a sensible and evolved with civil manner.

The Public Toilet/Coffee Shop

Agent of Urban Renewal and Change

In conclusion, the public toilet-cum-coffee shop has the potential to become an urban renewal agent in marketplaces across Indian cities. It marks the breakdown of a negative spiral – 'nothing can improve' – and sets in motion a positive conversation by creating an opportunity to develop the marketplace and its open spaces to create an urban identity that's contiguous, contemporary and progressive. The public toilet-cum-coffee shop thus becomes a new gravitational point around which all change happens – a visible symbol of change and rejuvenation.

Thus, India 2025 gets 14,00,000 clean, safe and hygienic toilets – all new, all for free!!

A LETTER THAT CREATED HISTORY

Date: 02 - 07 - 1909

Divisional Railway Officer, Sahibgunj,

Respected Sirs,
I am arrive by passenger train Ahmedpur station and my belly is too much swelling with jackfruit. I am therefore went to privy. Just I doing the nuisance that guard making whistle blow or train to go off and I am running with lotaah in one hand and dhoti in the next when I am fall over and expose all my shocking to man and female women on platform. I am got leaved at Ahmedpur station. This too much bad, if passenger go to make dung that dam guard not wait train five minutes for him. I am therefore pray your honour to make big fine on that guard for public sake. Otherwise I am making big report to papers. (ORIGINAL LETTER)

Your faithful Servant, Okhil Chandra Sen

Okhil Babu wrote this letter to the Sahibganj divisional railway officer in 1909. It is on display at the Railway Museum in New Delhi. It was also reproduced under the caption Travellers Tales in the *Far Eastern Economic Review*.

Any idea why this letter has historic value?
That's right – It led to the installation of toilets in trains in India!

TCI

सत्यमेव जयते

'MY RIGHT TO SANITATION'

Central/national body driven by a unified goal – to provide safe, clean and hygienic public toilets

Chapter 7

QUEST FOR EQUITY

Equality is equal distribution of resources, while equity is distribution of resources such that everyone gets equal opportunity.

- Simar Pratap Singh Chauhan

Source: Graphics designed by author's graphic team

Introduction

Historical Narrative

One of the key values of modern society is the notion that 'all are equal'.

'Equality' has been held sacred by most modern nations for a few decades now, more particularly since the demise of the colonial empires. In the Western world, the French Revolution could be credited with celebrating the value of equality, with its motto of liberté, egalité, fraternité. In 1865, the United States abolished slavery through the 13th amendment during the presidency of Abraham Lincoln. In 1868 through the 14th amendment, the word 'equality' formally found its way into the United States Constitution. Another historic moment in the struggle for equality occurred in 1993, with the end of Apartheid in South Africa and the birth of a new democracy under the leadership of Nelson Mandela.

In ancient India during the Vedic period, equality as a value was enshrined in the Vedas and the Upanishads. The Rig Veda clearly states that wife and husband are equal halves of matrimony and are equal in all respects. The Upanishads clearly state that we individual souls are all equal and neither male or female. Women wore the sacred thread and were taught the holy mantras of the Vedas. Some were Brahmavadinis, that is, women who devoted their lives to study the scriptures. Kshatriya (warrior) women were also taught martial arts and use of arms. The caste system was not hereditary, nor was it rigid. As time progressed, however, the values of equality diminished greatly and the society got fragmented along caste lines, the caste system became rigid and hereditary, the lower castes were treated as untouchables and exploited. Both social equity and gender equity suffered as the aggressive feudal mindset gripped society.

Many spiritual and social reformers have espoused the cause of equality like Buddha, who gave up worldly riches to lead the life of an ascetic, preaching the philosophy of 'Dharma' and love for all beings, or Shankaracharya who rejected the hereditary caste system and said 'all are born brahmin' or Guru Nanak who gave the most inclusive message of 'there is no hindu, no mussalman – all are children of the same god' – 'ik onkar' or Raja Ram Mohan Roy who became a champion of women's empowerment and empowerment of landless farmers.

The methods of Ram Mohan Roy were more attuned to the working of a modern state and he used his scholarship and knowledge of state craft to push through legislations for the abolition of 'Sati', a dreadful custom in which young widows were burnt alive on their husband's funeral pyres.

Ram Mohan Roy was the Father of Indian Journalism and he believed in the freedom of the press. He edited a newspaper called *Sampled Kaumudi* in Bengali. He expressed his views powerfully in English and through his editorals, he impacted public consciousness and raised important political, social and economic issues. Rabindranath Tagore said this of him: 'Ram Mohan was the only person of his time to realize completely the significance of the modern age. He knew the ideal of human civilization does not lie in the isolation of Independence, but in the brotherhood of interdependence of individuals and nations.'[129] Much after his death, beginning in 1930s, the Brahmo Samaj became a vehicle to carry forward his social and religious reforms. It became very clear through the example set forth by Raja Ram Mohan Roy that legislation was the most powerful tool for social emancipation and to push gender equity.

Mahatma Gandhi took the issue of social equity as seriously as he did the issue of Independence. Gandhi got the Congress in the Karachi session in 1931 to commit to the twin issues of Independence and eradication of untouchability, and at his behest a resolution was adopted, which declared, 'all the citizens are equal before law irrespective of caste, creed or sex'. In 1938, the removal of the Civil Disabilities Act was passed by the Madras legislature which provided that no 'Harijan' shall be disabled from any social or public amenity. In the same year, it also passed the Malabar Temple Entry Act which threw open the temples in Malabar. Gandhi also took up the cause of the untouchables, the dalits, christening them with name 'Harijans' meaning 'Children of God'. He worked with the Harijans to ensure they had equal access to drinking water and education.

It was at his behest that Dr B.R. Ambedkar, leader of the depressed classes, was asked to join the Central Cabinet and to be the chief architect of the Indian Constitution. In the very Preamble of the Indian Constitution, this value is enshrined beautifully.

PREAMBLE TO THE CONSTITUTION OF INDIA

WE, THE PEOPLE OF INDIA, having solemnly resolved to constitute India into a SOVEREIGN DEMOCRATIC
REPUBLIC and to secure to all its citizens:
JUSTICE, social, economic and political;
LIBERTY, of thought, expression, belief, faith and worship;
EQUALITY of status and of opportunity; and to promote among them all
FRATERNITY assuring the dignity of the individual and the unity of the Nation;
IN OUR CONSTITUENT ASSEMBLY this twenty-sixth day of November, 1949, DO HEREBY ADOPT, ENACT AND GIVE TO OURSELVES THIS CONSTITUTION.

While much has been achieved in terms of empowerment of backward classes through the instrument of reservation, which provides for a separate preferential quota for economically weak and socially backward castes and tribes for admission into educational institutions and government jobs, state legislature and even the parliament, much more needs to be done. Much progress has also been made towards empowerment of women over the last seven decades since Independence. We are currently ranked 131 among 188 countries across the globe on the basis of Gender Inequality Index, published by UN.

Today in India, women participate in education, industry, politics, media, sports, engineering and healthcare. The overall labor force participation is more than 25%. Despite the progress, the patriarchal mindset of traditional Indian society continues to inflict injustice on women and the girl child and a lot more needs to be done towards transforming attitudes. We need to replace 'Patriarchy with Parity!' We must also recognize that all new policies that are designed to fulfill the objectives of equity be apolitical in nature and be aligned to promotion of meritocracy and fair play.[130]

India - A Welfare State

The Constitution of India envisages India to be a 'socialist republic'. Socialism in India is not to be understood in the Russian context where all resources are owned by the state and the state secures welfare for all. Socialism, as envisioned in the Indian Constitution, aims at elimination of inequality in income, status and standards of life. The 'Directive Principles of State Policy' in part four of the Constitution clearly encapsulates the long-term goals of Indian governments at the centre and the state and directs them to act as welfare states.

A welfare state is the concept of a government where the state plays a key role in the protection and promotion of the economic and social well-being of its citizens. It is based on the principles of equality of opportunity, equitable distribution of wealth and public responsibility for those unable to avail themselves of the minimal provisions of a good life.

Two extremes exist within the notion of welfare states. In one model, the state seeks to provide basic access to education, health, livelihood to the people 'most in need' by taxing the 'haves'. This model creates a basic divide between 'us' and 'them' and many people, especially 'haves', don't like the idea, because they don't gain anything.

It also requires intense bureaucratic intervention to determine who is 'needy'. This model is prevalent in the U.S. in a very successful manner. The other model distributes welfare with as little bureaucratic intervention as possible to all people who fulfill easily established criteria. This requires high taxing, of which almost everything is channeled back to tax payers with minimum expenses for bureaucratic personnel. The intended result is a broader support for the system since most people receive at least something. This model is prevalent in the Scandinavian countries.

Despite all efforts by states to alleviate the sufferings of the 'have nots', inequities persist. The rich become richer and the poor, poorer. No wonder, social and economic inequity has become the central theme for all the elections held in recent times and the verdict is very clear. 'Much more needs to be done'. Unless governments are able to decode this and implement solutions that 'empower' as opposed to 'doles', we shall continue to see disruptions and social unrest and while development indices shall improve and the extent of inequitable distribution will grow.

What Governments in India Are Doing?

This piece chronicles some recent examples of successful government schemes which have had a meaningful impact. They would help in understanding how the ideas shared later in this chapter are relevant to promotion of equity. It's a small minuscule slice of many well-intentioned endeavours under three broad heads:

1) **Gender equity**
2) **Economic equity**
3) **Social equity**

We cannot all succeed when half of us are held back.

- MalalaYousafzai

There is no tool for development more effective than empowerment of women.

- Kofi Annan

Initiatives towards equity by various govts. in India

GENDER EQUITY

- LEGISLATIONS FOR WOMEN EMPOWERMENT
- GOVERNMENT SCHEMES
  - BETI BACHAO BETI PADHAO
  - MUKHYA MANTRI BALIKA CYCLE YOJNA
  - KANYA SHREE PRAKALP PROGRAM

ECONOMIC EQUITY

- GANDHI NATIONAL RURAL EMPLOYMENT GUARANTEE (ACT)
- PRADHAN MANTRI JAN DHAN YOJANA
- MINIMUM SUPPORT PRICE
  - DIRECT INCOME TRANSFER
  - LOAN WAIVERS
  - CORPORATE SOCIAL RESPONSIBILITY

SOCIAL EQUITY

- MOHALLA CLINICS
- EDUCATION– GOVT SCHOOLS, I.I.T.S, N.I.T.S, A.I.I.M.S
- EMPLOYEES STATE INSURANCE CORPORATION
- PRADHAN MANTRI JAN AROGYA YOJANA

Gender Equity

Legislation

There have been some significant legislation that have meaningfully impacted the lives of women in our country. Article 14 of the Constitution guarantees all Indian women equality before law, Article 39 (d) guards the economic rights and ensures equal pay for equal work, Article 42 allows provisions to be made by the state for securing just and humane conditions of work and maternity relief for women. In fact the Maternity Benefit Act 2017 provides for a full 26 weeks, paid leave as against 12 weeks in the 1968 Act. This shall benefit close to 1.8 million women annually and make India one of the top three in duration of maternity leaves.

Acts like the Dowry Prohibition Act 1961 and Protection of Women Domestic Violence Act 2005 have also provided much relief. To protect women at the workplace, the Sexual Harassment of Women at Work Place (Prevention, Prohibition and Redressal) Act 2013 provides for stringent punishment.

The Panchayati Raj system was formalized in India in 1992 and it was a big step in 'Gram Swaraj', a concept first proposed by Mahatma Gandhi. In August 2009, the Union Cabinet of India approved a 33% reservation for women in Panchayati Raj Institutions at the village, block and zila levels. A village in Kerala, Kodassery, has had 100% of its elected members as women. Some states are also providing 50% reservation in Panchayati Raj Institutions.

The Women's Reservation Bill which sought to provide 33% reservation for elected representatives in parliament was passed in the Rajya Sabha, which was no small victory in itself as earlier attempts had been assiduously defeated in the lower house by a still, largely male-dominated parliament. Later it lapsed because it could not be put to vote in the Lok Sabha – the lower house of the Indian parliament.

India has a skewed sex ratio and pre-natal sex determination and related female foeticide has been a matter of grave concern. The Pre-Conception and Pre-Natal Diagnostic Techniques Act 1994 – which – prohibits sex selection after conception and has been a fairly successful intervention in urban India.

During the lengthy and historical debates in the Constituent Assembly, there arose the most fundamental question of all – whether or not to provide universal adult franchise. Its seeds had been sown much earlier. The leaders of the freedom movement had been committed to this since 1928. On 19 May 1928, the Report of the All Parties Conference chaired by Motilal Nehru (with stalwarts such as Subhas Chandra Bose, Sir Tej Bahadur Sapru, Sir Ali Imam and M.R. Jayakar as members) stated that the conference was opposed to any artificial restrictions on the right to vote and pressed for universal adult franchise as well as equal rights for women. On 23 October 1928, B.R. Ambedkar – brilliant jurist, politician, Dalit leader and social reformer, who campaigned against social discrimination of India's depressed classes – too supported this in his deposition before the Simon Commission. The 1931 Karachi session of the Indian National Congress adopted a resolution that encapsulated this.

Government schemes

The Ministry of Women and Child Development was created as a separate ministry in 2006; earlier, since 1985, it was a mere department placed under the Ministry of Human Resources Development. The ministry now more purposefully addresses gaps in state action for women and children by promoting inter-ministerial and inter-sectoral convergence to create gender-equitable and child-centred legislation, policies and programmes.

The National Commission for Women (NCW), the Rashtriya Mahila Kosh and four other autonomous organizations also work under this ministry to implement programmes directed towards women's empowerment and gender equity.

THE BETI BACHAO BETI PADHAO SCHEME

The Beti Bachao Beti Padhao scheme was introduced in October 2014 to address the issue of declining Child Sex Ratio (C.S.R.). It is a tri-ministerial effort comprising the Ministries of Women and Child Development, Health and Family Welfare and Human Resources Development. The overall goal is to celebrate the arrival of the girl child and enable her education. Around 100 districts with poor C.S.R. were the first to benefit from the 100 crore outlay that was provided for in the budget. In March 2018, the Beti Bachao Beti Padhao Yojana scheme was expanded into a pan-India scheme covering all 640 districts.

The prime objectives of Beti Bachao Beti Padhao are:

- Prevent gender-based sex-selective elimination
- Ensure survival and protection of the girl child
- Ensure education of the girl child

It is a well-intentioned scheme at bringing across social awareness, measuring the declining child sex ratio and sharing the same with community and stakeholders. Some financial incentives have also been rolled out under Sukanya Samridhi Yojna where higher interest rates are accorded to bank accounts in the name of the girl child and money can only be withdrawn for health, education or marriage from these accounts.

In Bihar, the Mukhya Mantri Balika Cycle Yojna, where free cycles were distributed to school-going girls, had multiple other benefits like empowering girls with confidence and incentivizing them to attend school. The Poshak Yojan of free uniforms and Mukhya Mantri Akshar Anchal Yojna of Rs 10,000 scholarship for girls securing 60% and more also increased enrollment in schools.

In West Bengal, the Kanya Shree Prakalp Program, which is providing a monthly financial assistance of up to Rs 750 per girl child, is touching 5 million girls and is a very successful programme. Kanya Shree Prakalp's central objective is to impact the high incidence of child marriage and high incidence of school drop-outs in adolescence, especially in the case of the girl child. West Bengal's indicators were far worse than the national average. The scheme costs the exchequer approximately Rs 1,200 crore annually. It has currently over 50 lakh beneficiaries. All beneficiaries receive an additional annual scholarship of Rs 500 in their bank accounts and a lump-sum of Rs 25,000 if they get married after the age of 18 and are still pursuing education at that age.

It has become a very successful scheme. Later in this chapter, we shall present an even more powerful scheme which builds on Beti Bachao Beti Padhao Yojana and the Kanya Shree Prakalp. It could be a model to be implemented across all states, possibly with some extra support from the centre in terms of funds and expertise.

Economic Equity

MAHATMA GANDHI NATIONAL RURAL EMPLOYMENT GUARANTEE ACT (MGNREGA)

The Mahatma Gandhi National Rural Employment Guarantee (Act) Scheme is a flagship programme of the Indian government aimed at providing a social safety to scores of rural masses battling poverty.

The World Bank has called it the world's largest public works programme with approximately 182 million beneficiaries, costing the exchequer approx 8 billion dollars annually and touching about 15% of India's population.

It aims to provide at least 100 days of wage employment in a financial year to every household whose adults volunteer.

It was first proposed as an act by Prime Minister P.V. Narasimha Rao in 1991 and finally enacted in 2006 by the Manmohan Singh government.

The current government led by Prime Minister Narendra Modi has further strengthened the implementation, with a focus on transparency and accountability in implementation. For districts adversely affected by floods and other calamities, provisions have been made to increase allocation from 100 wage days per household to 150 wage days.

Apart from providing economic security, this scheme has led to empowerment of women in villages and mitigating rural-urban migration, and has also enhanced wage-levels in both rural and urban India. It has been indisputably one of the most powerful and effective poverty-alleviation programmes in post-Independence India.

PRADHAN MANTRI JAN DHAN YOJANA

The National Mission for Financial Inclusion, also called Pradhan Mantri Jan Dhan Yojana, is a programme for financial inclusion for the poorest of poor. The central idea is to provide a zero-balance bank account to every adult in every household. This scheme was launched by Prime Minister Narendra Modi in August 2014. Over 34 crore bank accounts have since been opened including 18 crore accounts in the name of women. Over Rs 90,000 crore, or $13 billion, have been deposited in these accounts.

These accounts are being used for direct benefit transfer wherein government subsidies are directly transferred to the beneficiary, thereby curbing corruption and avoiding delays. These accounts also provide for a limited overdraft facility ranging from Rs 2,000 to Rs 10,000 and an accidental insurance cover of Rs 2,00,000 and life cover of Rs 30,000.

Biometric technology has also been used to include illiterate persons into the fold. In order to facilitate opening and operating of bank accounts in remote rural areas, banks have been allowed to use business correspondents to assist in outreach of the banking facility. A RuPay debit card facility has also been added, which is a free facility for up to four remittances per month.

It has been in many ways a meaningful step towards financial inclusion – it makes us ready as a nation for a less-cash economy with the poor sections of the society finally getting a chance to access cheaper credit, receive governments financial benefits in their own accounts without dealing with intermediaries, and eventually developing a culture of savings and using modern banking to empower themselves financially.

While there are real challenges to effective usage of these facilities and almost 48% of the accounts are inactive, it is still a progression from where it began: 52% or 15 crore accounts are active and like all transformative moves, the adaptation is slow in the early years and eventually the critical mass shall be achieved.

PRADHAN MANTRI JAN DHAN YOJANA is definitely a powerful step in the right direction.

MINIMUM SUPPORT PRICE

The economic condition of the Indian farmers is extremely distressing. The vagaries of weather and unpredictability of the agricultural product markets play havoc on the farmer's income potential. To bring in a certain degree of financial stability, the union government offers to buy agricultural produce at a minimum support price, through a cost-plus-profit based mechanism. This helps safeguard the farmer's interest when the open markets fall below the cost of the produce. The government announces minimum support price on 24 agricultural commodities two times every year.

In the current budget, the intent has been to offer a return of 50% as profits to the farmer over and above their input costs including tenancy charges on the land.

In principle minimum support price is a good method to support the poor farmers. There are several issues, however, which remain unaddressed.

Two chief issues are:

The computation method for ascertaining input costs for various crops is often out of sync with reality.

The poorest farmers mostly lease the land from the wealthier landlords and the tenancy costs and interests paid on the input costs are way higher than the assumed costs in minimum support price computation and so a poor farmer still finds himself struggling to make ends meet.

A large number of farmers take debt to pay for their input costs and when they are unable to pay back their interest, they are forced to pledge their lands and raise more debt. This leads them to a debt trap with many choosing to end their lives in the face of insurmountable odds.

FARM LOAN WAIVERS

To counter this genuine problem and take these hardworking farmers out of their financial woes, many state government have announced and implemented in some measure farm loan waivers. These farm loan waivers have cost the exchequer close to Rs 1,00,000 crore in the last year alone. While the relief brought to farmers is in itself inequitable and those who have raised debt from informal channels do not benefit, it does bring some degree of relief to the marginalized farmers. The modalities of implementation, however, are ill-thought, opaque and liable to corrupt practices. The modalities need a hard relook with solid guidelines formulated that future loan waiver schemes could follow.

DIRECT INCOME TRANSFER

In order to address the issue of helping the poorest of poor farmers and non-farming village folk, the union government as well as the various state governments have envisioned a universal basic income scheme affected through direct transfers into the bank accounts of marginalized families.

Telangana's R.B.S. (Rythu Bandhu Scheme) and Orissa government's KALIA (Krushak Assistance for livelihood) are two of the most recently implemented direct transfer schemes providing approximately Rs 8,000 to Rs 12,000 per acre to medium, small and marginalized farmers.

The landless farmers still get left out of these schemes. Future direct income transfer schemes must learn lessons from the existing schemes and create a robust mechanism for a more inclusive and equitable transfer of funds, where the most vulnerable don't get left out.

CORPORATE SOCIAL RESPONSIBILITY

While governments play their role as vanguards of equality in welfare states, India has a unique distinction of having a legislation that requires private enterprise to also contribute their bit to the upliftment of society.

In April 2014, through an amendment in the Companies Act 2013, India became the first country in the world to have a mandatory statute for corporate social responsibility. Vide this amendment in the Companies Act, all companies with net worth greater than Rs 500 crore or companies with a turnover of Rs 1,000 crore or a net profit of greater than Rs 5 crore annually shall be mandated to spend at least 2% of their net profit towards CSR. This mandatory clause was preceded with a CSR clause in the draft Companies Bill, 2009, which introduced CSR as a voluntary initiative; however it required companies to disclose their CSR expenditure to its shareholders.

While corporates in India have been actively pursuing social upliftment initiatives from the pre-Independence era, this formal transparent methodology has created a funding ecosystem where donors have focused experts to evaluate between effective and ineffective contributions and equally organizations in need of funds have a more reliable pipeline of CSR funds and can therefore attract better talent and also implement meaningful social and environmental programmes in a planned manner.

The total CSR expenditure pan India since 2014 has exceeded Rs 30,000 crore and the figures for 2018–19 is approximately Rs 8,500 crore. CSR is truly a transformative step towards promoting equity.

Social Equity

Access to healthcare, shelter and clean food are key determinants of social equity. Many governments at the state and central level have focused on these three objectives over the last decade.

MOHALLA CLINICS

The Delhi government in 2015 initiated this simple and novel idea of bringing primary healthcare centres to the high density–low income colonies of Delhi, thereby making it convenient and accessible.

The typical lower middle class person who would have to take a medical leave from office or a daily wager who would otherwise loose his whole day's wages, were he to visit a conventional government hospital because of the long queues and travel time to the hospital, can now access basic health services like medicines for a cold, cough, fever, stomach infection and also get blood tests done near his home or on the way to the bus stop/metro stations.

This decentralized convenience store–type solution to primary healthcare centres has proved to be a successful model. This model does add to the challenges of the health professionals in terms of logistics of ensuring availability of doctors and trained paramedics on each port of call. There are also challenges of inadequate supervision through senior doctors.

All these challenges notwithstanding, the model has succeeded in making healthcare services more accessible and, therefore, the pains needed to surmount the logistic challenges will be well worth it. The city currently has 105 mohalla clinics and the government plans to take the tally to 200 in the near future.

THE EMPLOYEES STATE INSURANCE CORPORATION (ESIC)

ESIC is created as an autonomous corporation consequent to the passing of the ESI act in 1948. It functions under the aegis of the Ministry of Labour and Employment, Government of India.

While initially this scheme was intended to safeguard factory workers as a health insurance scheme, its ambit has grown manifold over the last seven decades.

The ESI Act requires all organization with more than 10 employees with a salary of less than Rs 21,000 per month to be registered with ESI and contribute towards this health insurance scheme.

In the event of temporary disability injury, absence due to maternity or any loss of wages, the incumbent is compensated by ESIC through their collective funds.

Over the years, in collaboration with various state governments, ESIC has also set up hospitals to provide free medical services to all persons registered with the ESI.

Around 8 crore citizens of India are current beneficiaries. In case of death during work or permanent disability, the ESIC also provides for cash compensation and for family pension. Under the revised norms for ESIC, even poor families registered under the Rashtriya Swastha Bima Yojna are covered under the ESI and can avail of the vast network of facilities. Currently there are 150 ESI hospitals, with a total of close to 20,000 beds, 1,400 ESI dispensaries and 800 ESI centres to avail of cash benefits.

The impact of this health scheme across urban and semi-urban India is very significant in promoting social equity.

AYUSHMAN BHARAT YOJNA/PRADHAN MANTRI JAN AROGYA YOJANA OR NATIONAL HEALTH PROTECTION SCHEME

To bring free and quality healthcare to the poor and vulnerable, Pradhan Mantri Jan Arogya Yojana was launched in 2018 as a nation-wide health initiative. Under Pradhan Mantri Jan Arogya Yojana, an insurance cover of up to Rs 5 lakh is provided per family for secondary and tertiary hospitalization wherein cashless healthcare can be availed at private empanelled hospitals by all those who are deemed eligible as per the Social–Economic Caste Census (SECC) data. About 10 crore rural and urban poor families are likely to benefit from this scheme. People holding a valid Rashtriya Swastha Bima Yojna Card (RSBY) are also eligible for the benefit.

At this juncture around 16,000 hospitals are already empanelled across 26 states, around 18 lakh people have received secondary and tertiary healthcare and around 3 crore E-cards have been issued to vulnerable families. Pradhan Mantri Jan Arogya Yojana is still an evolving scheme; however, it holds great promise as a safely net around vulnerable families.

Education: The Elixir of the Disempowered!

Contrary to popular narrative, the various governments since Independence, both at the center and the state, have done a whole lot towards providing funds for education. The following table 'Statement Indicating the Public Expenditure on Education' gives a good idea of the large sums of money invested over the years into educational infrastructures and the institutions that govern it. While education is a state subject, the center too funds centres of excellence such as the IITs, IIMs, AIIMS, Kendriya Vidyalaya, and different prime ministers have in their respective budgets prioritized funding on education, while some do maintain status-quo. The chart has been classified prime minister–wise and years have also been earmarked. Two budgetary indicators are key to seeing how the impetus to education has fared across the last seven decades. They are:

Total Education Budget as a percentage of the total government budget

Total Education Expenditure as a percentage of the country's GDP

While successive governments have improved their budgetary allocations, year on year, as a percentage of government's own budgets, it started with 8% and rose significantly to almost 12% during the first prime minister Jawaharlal Nehru's premiership; thereafter, it remained within 9% to 11% through the years of Lal Bahadur Shastri and Indira Gandhi. During the latter half of her first 10 years, the absolute number did see a significant growth, from a little under Rs 500 crore in 1966 to over Rs 2,000 crore in 1976 – so four-fold in 10 years. Prime Minister Rajiv Gandhi's premiership saw a two-fold increase during his tenure and percentage to budget increased to around 12% to 13%. Under Prime Ministers V.P. Singh and Chandra Shekhar, the incremental momentum continued. Under Prime Minister Narsimha Rao's premiership, the percentage improved marginally to over 13.3% but on a significantly higher base, his tenure also saw a two-fold increase in outlay over 4 years.

Under Prime Minister Atal Bihari Vajpayee, the percentage rose significantly and touched a new high of 14.6% and an education budget-to-GDP rate of 4%, both of which were new highs. His premiership also saw a two-fold increase over 5 years. Under Prime Minister Manmohan Singh, education expenditure rose steadily and became over four and half times in 10 years. While percentage to GDP remained around 4%, the percentage of education budget to overall budget reached a new high of 15.76%, the highest so far. His premiership also saw some significant impetus to setting up of 6 new AIIMS, 4 new IITs and 30 new NITs, essentially 1 for each state. New IIMs, NIFTs (National Institutes of Fashion Technology) and NLU (National Law University) were also approved across India.

Another very significant intervention was the promulgation of Right to Education RTE Act in 2009. Education for children between 6 and 14 became a fundamental right and the government had to be providing it free. To implement this plan, a public–private schools' partnership was envisaged, wherein private schools have to set aside 25% seats for children from economically weaker sections. The government would reimburse the schools for this inclusion.

The most significant part of this scheme is the inclusive integration of underprivileged ones with privileged ones, with both growing up together as equals. It creates the basic foundation for a equitable society and both children get a real taste of the importance of individual merit before social privilege since they all compete in sports and studies at a level-playing field. The act also created additional capacity at a fairly rapid pace.

Under the premiership of Narendra Modi, the education budget continued to grow at a steady rate. The previous government's initiatives of adding new IITs, IIMs and AIIMS were furthered and now each state has been earmarked to have one each, so broadly 30 IITs, 30 IIMs and 30 AIIMS have been sanctioned. Work has begun on many while some are under land-acquisition phase. The impetus for 30 NITs has also been strengthened, and the focus and pace of implementation is praiseworthy.

The Ministry of Human Resource Development also constituted a committee to create a New Education Policy. This committee, chaired by former cabinet Secretary T.S.R. Subramanian, presented a draft report of 200 pages. The three salient features being liberalization of the education industry, greater autonomy for the central and state educational institutions and increase in government expenditure to 6% of GDP to really fulfill the untapped potential for our large young population. While autonomy to central universities has significantly increased in the current dispensation, the overall outlay is woefully short of the government's own target. It's essentially in the vicinity of 3% against the targeted 6% of GDP. Hopefully, this and the successive governments shall build on the momentum of new centres of education which are being established and also find the courage and will to double up the education ministry's budgetary outlay.

While the various governments at centre and state levels are doing much to further the cause of equality, I have captured in the following pages some seminal ideas that further and accelerate the cause of equality.

Statement indicating the Public Expenditure on Education

Name of the PM	Year	G D P at current prices (at factor cost) (Rs. in crore)	Total Expenditure by All Sectors (Rs. in crore)	Expenditure on Education by Education Department (Rs. in crore)	Expenditure on Education by Education and Other Deptts. (Rs. in crore)	Expenditure on Education by Education and Other Deptts. as % age Public Exp.	Expenditure on Education by Education Department as % age GDP	Expenditure on Education by Education & other Deptts as %age GDP
Jawaharlal Nehru	1951-52	10080.00	814.14	64.46	64.46	7.92	0.64	0.64
	1952-53	9941.00	857.67	72.26	72.26	8.43	0.73	0.73
	1953-54	10824.00	908.20	80.06	80.06	8.82	0.74	0.74
	1954-55	10168.00	973.74	95.82	95.82	9.84	0.94	0.94
	1955-56	10332.00	1111.26	118.39	118.39	10.65	1.15	1.15
	1956-57	12334.00	1158.01	132.88	132.88	11.47	1.08	1.08
	1957-58	12610.00	1416.62	150.26	150.26	10.61	1.19	1.19
	1958-59	14106.00	1594.36	173.78	173.78	10.90	1.23	1.23
	1959-60	14816.00	1770.06	207.59	207.59	11.73	1.40	1.40
	1960-61	16220.00	1997.93	239.55	239.55	11.99	1.48	1.48
	1961-62	17116.00	2225.40	260.30	260.30	11.70	1.52	1.52
	1962-63	18302.00	2942.67	278.76	278.76	9.47	1.52	1.52
	1963-64	20916.00	3488.97	313.93	313.93	9.00	1.50	1.50
Gulzarilal Nanda Lal Bahadur Shastri	1964-65	24436.00	3844.91	369.29	369.29	9.60	1.51	1.51
	1965-66	25586.00	4404.82	432.61	432.61	9.82	1.69	1.69
Indira Gandhi	1966-67	29123.00	5100.24	487.83	487.83	9.56	1.68	1.68
	1967-68	34225.00	5619.77	593.14	593.14	10.55	1.73	1.73
	1968-69	36092.00	6922.07	649.13	649.13	9.38	1.80	1.80
	1969-70	39691.00	7908.07	760.23	760.23	9.61	1.92	1.92
	1970-71	42222.00	8787.12	892.36	892.36	10.16	2.11	2.11
	1971-72	44923.00	10610.89	994.82	1011.07	9.53	2.21	2.25
	1972-73	49415.00	11863.56	1128.80	1150.43	9.70	2.28	2.33
	1973-74	60560.00	12884.48	1274.29	1300.72	10.10	2.10	2.15
	1974-75	71283.00	14625.03	1539.98	1570.67	10.74	2.16	2.20
	1975-76	75709.00	17958.99	1809.11	1849.47	10.30	2.39	2.44
	1976-77	81381.00	20482.83	1987.44	2039.09	9.96	2.44	2.51

Statement indicating the Public Expenditure on Education

Name of the PM	Year	G D P at current prices (at factor cost) (Rs. in crore)	Total Expenditure by All Sectors (Rs. in crore)	Expenditure on Education by Education Department (Rs. in crore)	Expenditure on Education by Education and Other Department (Rs. in crore)	Expenditure on Education by Education and Other Deptts. as % age Public Exp.	Expenditure on Education by Education Department as % age GDP	Expenditure on Education by Education & other Deptts. as %age GDP
Morarji Desai	1977-78	92881.00	22666.31	2256.17	2630.60	11.61	2.43	2.83
	1978-79	99823.00	26134.84	2561.08	2994.69	11.46	2.57	3.00
Charan Singh	1979-80	108927.00	30915.39	2868.92	3347.57	10.83	2.63	3.07
	1980-81	130178.00	36398.39	3374.33	3884.20	10.67	2.59	2.98
Indira Gandhi	1981-82	152056.00	41715.71	3790.15	4298.29	10.30	2.49	2.83
	1982-83	169525.00	49768.76	4761.79	5509.17	11.07	2.81	3.25
	1983-84	198630.00	61889.25	5454.48	6229.53	10.07	2.75	3.14
	1984-85	222705.00	69025.45	6432.77	7455.88	10.80	2.89	3.35
	1985-86	249547.00	67091.41	7456.97	8713.02	12.99	2.99	3.49
Rajiv Gandhi	1986-87	278258.00	80454.66	8450.32	9479.13	11.78	3.04	3.41
	1987-88	315993.00	92518.38	10430.19	11798.35	12.75	3.30	3.73
	1988-89	378491.00	107543.75	12408.72	14069.82	13.08	3.28	3.72
V.P. Singh	1989-90	438020.00	126045.99	15044.21	17192.50	13.64	3.43	3.93
Chandra Shekhar	1990-91	510954.00	146711.52	17193.66	19615.85	13.37	3.37	3.84
	1991-92	589086.00	170370.38	18757.61	22393.69	13.14	3.18	3.80
	1992-93	673221.00	190327.49	20952.97	25030.30	13.15	3.11	3.72
P.V. Narasimha Rao	1993-94	781345.00	218535.15	23413.10	28279.69	12.94	3.00	3.62
	1994-95	917058.00	251691.92	27232.15	32606.22	12.95	2.97	3.56
	1995-96	1073271.00	286194.55	31516.59	38178.09	13.34	2.94	3.56
H.D. Deve Gowda	1996-97	1243546.00	329389.92	36371.64	43896.48	13.33	2.92	3.53
I. K. Gujral	1997-98	1390148.00	370838.48	41109.32	48552.14	13.09	2.96	3.49
	1998-99	1598127.00	439768.12	51225.26	61578.91	14.00	3.21	3.85
	1999-00	1786526.00	512519.33	61281.46	74816.09	14.60	3.43	4.19
Atal Bihari Vajpayee	2000-01	1925017.00	572160.14	62498.09	82486.48	14.42	3.25	4.28
	2001-02	2097726.00	619713.14	64847.70	79865.70	12.89	3.09	3.81
	2002-03	2261415.00	678548.31	68561.54	85507.34	12.60	3.03	3.78
	2003-04	2538170.00	743668.96	73044.93	89079.25	11.98	2.88	3.51
Manmohan Singh	2004-05	2971464.00	797345.74	81280.85	96694.10	12.13	2.74	3.25
	2005-06	3390503.00	889713.96	94483.70	113228.71	12.73	2.79	3.34

Statement indicating the Public Expenditure on Education

Manmohan Singh

Year	G D P at current prices (at factor cost) (Rs. in crore)		Total Expenditure by All Sectors (Rs. in crore)		Expenditure on Education by Education Department (Rs. in crore)		Expenditure on Education by Education and Other Department (Rs. in crore)		Expenditure on Education by Education and Other Deptts. as % age Public Exp.	Expenditure on Education by Education Department as % age GDP	Expenditure on Education by Education & other Deptts. as %age GDP
2006-07	3953276.00		1033872.60		110340.36		137383.99		13.29	2.79	3.48
2007-08	4582086.00		1191514.68		125379.63		155797.27		13.08	2.74	3.40
2008-09	5303567.00		1495733.62		152822.40		189068.84		12.64	2.88	3.56
2009-10	6108903.00		1734074.75		190136.08		241256.02		13.91	3.11	3.95
2010-11	7248860.00		1997801.29		233510.11		293478.23		14.69	3.22	4.05
2011-12	8736039.00	p	2249526.46		270091.78		333930.38		14.84	3.09	3.82
2012-13	9951344.00	q	2619814.66	(RE)	321754.18	(RE)	408421.71	(RE)	15.59	3.23	4.10
2013-14	11272764.00	a	2951873.31	(BE)	365965.23	(BE)	465142.80	(BE)	15.76	3.25	4.13

p= provisional estimates RE= Revised Estimates

q= quick estimates BE= Budget Estimates

a= advance estimates

Note:- G D P Figures for the years from 1979-80 to 1998-99 are on the base year 1993-94 series , from 1999-00 to 2003-04 are on the base year 1999-00 series. from 2004-05 to 2010-2011 are on the base year 2004-05 series and 2011-12 onwards are on the base year 2011-12 series.

Source : - (1) GDP figures are taken from National Accounts Statistics published by C S O.

(2) Expenditure on Education Figures are taken from Budgeted Expenditure on Education published by D/o Higher Education.

The Solution

REWARD FOR TAXES PROGRAMME – THE KAR-SHREE PROGRAMME

India is a nation with a very small taxpaying population. Out of 125 crore (1.25 billion) citizens, there are only 4 crore (40 million) tax assessees. Out of these only about 40 lakh people declare an annual income of over Rs 10 lakh (Rs 1 million or $15,000 p.a.). In reality, many times more number of people earn higher sums than that. Tax avoidance, evasion and under-reporting are rampant and blantant.

There are many reasons for this, including understaffed taxation offices, corrupt officials and an ecosystem of chartered accountants that thrives on tax-evasion advisory. Often times, even those of us who pay taxes honestly worry because there is no sense of acknowledgement. One also worries about misuse of the exchequer for foreign jaunts of ministers and their wasteful security paraphernalia. Even among tax officials, the unsaid rule is to milk the already compliant. The previous governments had also understood this and so they introduced a slew of indirect taxes, more specifically, the service tax which significantly enhanced the tax collections.

The current government has also shown keen intent to increase tax compliance and the demonetization of old currency notes was a bold attempt at curbing this menace. The efficacy of that measure in the short term is open to judgement; perhaps, hard data in the long term would help in arriving at a fair conclusion. There is clear sense of fear, however, in hoarding cash and a clear push towards a cheque economy.

What is quite clear however is the aversion of the citizens at large to paying taxes honestly.

The key questions are:
'Hum ko kya mila?' (How do I gain?)
'*Babu log apne tax dete hain?*' (Do these bureaucrats and politicians pay taxes on their slush money?)
'Mera woh dost tax nahi deta – aish kar raha hai!' (Lots of friends don't pay – they are flourishing!)

What if we can flip this argument around and instead create an ecosystem where people want to pay their taxes voluntarily and happily because it now affects their status in society and offers social and financial privileges like, say, the Frequent Fliers Programme of airlines.

The Kar-Shree Programme could accomplish this by awarding titles based on income tax paid for 3–10 years. A five-level Kar-Shree Programme shall take into account geographical territory, nature of business and gender while running comparative assessments of all tax assesses.

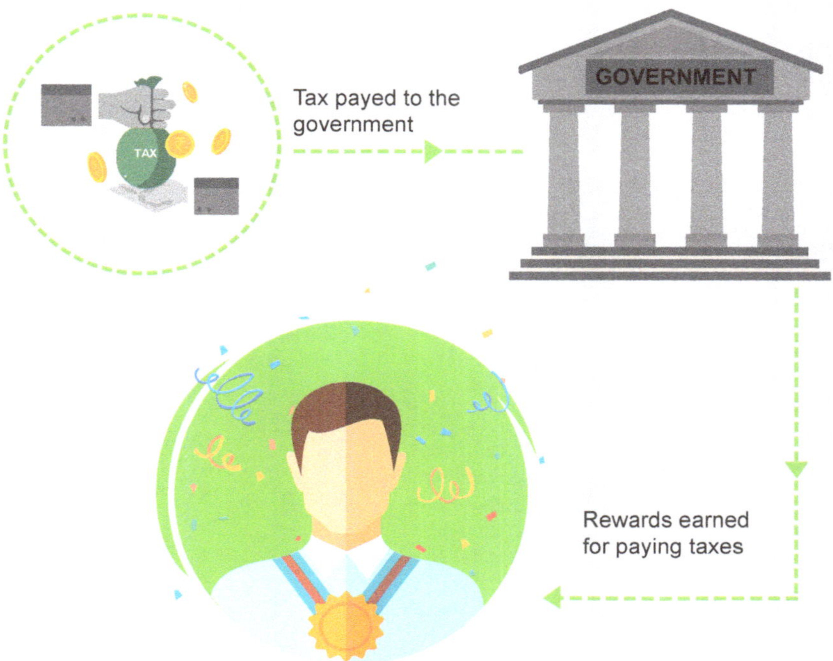

NAME OF THE AWARDS	NATURE OF BUSINESS	GEOGRAPHY	GENDER (MALE)	GENDER (FEMALE)
PARAM SHREE NARAYAN MURTHY	TOP 1% X 10 YEARS INDUSTRIALIST	TOP 1% X 10 YEARS (NATION) INDIA	1% 10 YEARS	1% 10 YEARS
MAHA SHREE R.K. SINGH JI	TOP 5% X 5 YEARS LAWYER	TOP 5% X 5 YEARS (STATE) BIHAR	5% 5 YEARS	5% 5 YEARS
SWARN SHREE B.K. GUPTA	TOP 10% X 5 YEARS CHEMIST	TOP 10% X 5 YEARS (CITY) JODHPUR	10%	10%
KARM SHREEMATI VYAYA GUPTA JI	TOP 10% X 3 YEARS STRUCTURE CONSULTANT	TOP 10% X 3 YEARS (CITY) PUNE	10%	10%
DHAN SHREE SATPAL KAPOOR	TOP 20% X 3 YEARS PROPERTY AGENT	TOP 20% (CITY) (NATION) AMBALA	20%	20%

It shall be a simple, yet dynamic, ranking system that shall soon become aspirational because of the incumbent privileges. None of the privileges would violate the dignity of those who are not well endowed, nor would it give any legal immunity of any sort. Essentially it's about gamifying the whole ecosystem of taxpaying by offering an incentive that is more valuable than money – state honour.

Both the corporate and government worlds have used the gamification of titles successfully. It must offer additional physical and financial privileges and a digital biometric photo card like a credit card with an expiry date for the incumbent.

Consider This

Tatkal (priority) services for Shree assignees at all banks, airports, hospitals and government offices.

Receive personal invitations to all relevant government/important events.

Append and use title as a mark of respect accorded by nation during the live currency of the title. Paramshree and Maha Shree being lifelong titles like 'Sir' or 'Rai Bahadur'.

Get priority listing in all club memberships nationally as well as access to all central and state government clubs and guest houses like an officer.

Shree assignees to get privileges in banks like priority banking, privileged credit cards, like lower interest rates on loans.

Shree assignees to be included in citizen-oversight committees of central and state governments depending on level. This way then they can also be responsible for taxpayers' money being utilized.

Once this programmes is notified and run for a few years, it would create a society that will begin to look up to its taxpayers and especially the ones who make significantly more contribution relative to their peers in the same nature of business, geography or gender.

So whether a person owns a large tech company or is a teacher who declares their extra income officially or a neighbourhood chemist in a small city, such a person would acquire the status of a good taxpayer and a good citizen along with an official title. The state would not have to use punitive means for tax recovery. As an example, the first ecosystem to latch onto this will be the marriage industry. Instead of advertisements announcing high six-figure salary, advertisements might well begin to read, D/O a Swarn Shree from city of Ambala. The Shree assignees would become the new social elite instead of the ubiquitous potbellied businessman with a gold chain and a prominent photograph with a random local politician.

The Shree assignees would gradually gain esteem and become the new elite, the new 'Barons who's who'.

And the cool thing is that there's no way of bribing your way into the Kar-Shree Program. It's pure mathematics and therefore leaves no scope for discretion.

The Kar-Shree Program would usher in an era of inspired tax paying citizenship .

Equity Foundation of India

The Equity Foundation of India (EFI) is imagined as an autonomous empowered body that shall become the Vanguard of Equity for the citizens of India. It shall function as an adviser, regulator, advocacy institution and most importantly, as a funding agency to work towards effecting social, economic and gender equity. In order to make its working effective across the country, its board would be chaired ex-officio by the prime minister and the vice chair would be the executive head of the institution. It would also have executive heads at union ministry levels and at the level of states for supporting various ministries and states with expertise, implementation horsepower and funds.

Principally, the EFI would engage in three distinct ways:

Expert Group and Advocacy Body

For creating the vision and action plan along with various union and state ministries and bring global expertise on social, gender and economic equity onboard.

Equity Foundation of India – Index of Equity

The index of equity (IOE) would be simple self-assessment list of acts that would allow an entity to score itself on a 0–100 scale. The IOE would be mandatory for filing tax incentives/dis-incentives.

It would apply to:

- Individuals
- Small and medium enterprise
- Corporates and institutions

The Equity Foundation of India Fund

The EFI would derive significant funds under a new inheritance regulation, the EFI savings bonds with tax-free yield, some tax incentives for donations to EFI fund, the EFI's first claim to all unclaimed assets and monies act, the new CSR regulations, among others. The EFI fund, which could have an annual outlay of $5 billion to $10 billion, could become a significant catalyst and change agent in effecting social, gender and economic equity.

For ease of understanding, this chapter is assembled into three parts:

How the Equity Foundation of India would derive its funds

- Grants
- Inheritance tax
- Unclaimed Assets and Monies Act
- Index of Equity (IOE) Incentive Programme
- Augmented CSR
- Capital Gains tax reduced if donation made to EFI
- EFI - Bonds
- The EFI - Daan Shree Title program and donations

Some Implementable Ideas Equity Foundation of India shall fund and Advocacy Initiatives

- WISE Academies (World Initiative for Service and Education – EFI shall pay per child fee for education in free residential schools for underprivileged children)
- Karam Shree Program: A volunteer programme funded by EFI
- BBBP card: Nanhi Laxmi Card
- Women Inheritance Rights Act
- Registry – Women to get deep discounted pricing on registry and home loans
- Teachers Monetary Awards
- Rural Teachers Fund
- Women's Healthcare: 30% discount across all healthcare industry through legislation
- First-House Registration – 1% registration fee (3-year lock-in)

Equity Foundation of India – Index of Equity: Measuring our performance as a citizen in relation to equality. A guiding light in the form of a checklist, that would enable an individual, small enterprise, large enterprise or institution to rate its own performance, and subsequently vetted from accredited equity consultants.

This score would be incentivized by the government and corporate institutions to foster an ecosystem-based approach towards the pursuit of equity.

How the Equity Foundation of India Would Derive Its Funds

Equity Foundation of India Fund – To power the various initiatives of the Equity Foundation of India, a fund called Equity Foundation of India Fund shall be created with an outlay running into few thousand crores annually. This Equity Foundation of India Fund shall derive funds in the following way:

Grants

From government and non-government institutions towards signature projects of Equity Foundation of India.

Inheritance Tax

Inheritance tax levied on individuals as a mild yet effective instrument to redistribute the inequitable distribution of wealth at the important juncture of 'inheritance', mankind's most potent instrument of inequity (discussed later in the chapter).

Equity Foundation of India's – Right to Unclaimed Assets and Monies Act

The Equity Foundation of India–Unclaimed Assets and Monies Act (UAMA) could bring in large amounts of monies languishing unclaimed in banks and various deposit schemes which can be put to productive use. Also many assets which suffer on account of a clear title or have no clear inheritor could be subsumed into the assets of Equity Foundation of India and auctioned in the open market to unclock their value. These monies would power the Equity Foundation of India Fund.

Index of Equity Incentive Programme

The Index of Equity (IOE) would become a good barometer of efforts towards Equity – made for an individual, enterprise or institution. To encourage them, an incentive programme could be effected which would offer tax incentives or be linked to the title rewards programme of the Kar-Shree Programme.

Augmented Corporate Social Responsibility

Most large corporates choose avenues for implementing their CSR initiatives in a professional and scientific manner and employ internal CSR officers to over-see the effective implementation of the same.

Many medium and small corporates, however, don't have the wherewithal to manage their CSR. They could use Equity Foundation of India initiatives for this. Additional provisions to earmark at least 25% of CSR funds for Equity Foundation of India could also be added in the Companies Act to strengthen Equity Foundation of India.

Equity Foundation of India Bonds (Tax-free bonds like NHAI)

Equity Foundation of India shall also create assets to help the underprivileged in their quest for empowerment. Assets like Equity Foundation of India youth hostels for young students and new entrants to the working class. These hostels would provide inexpensive yet dignified accommodations and run on tight profit-and-loss statements.

Equity Foundation of India shall also provide secured education loans and micro-enterprise loans at concessional rates to underprivileged candidates in addition to scholarships given through Equity Foundation of India Fund.

To fund such concessional secured loans and social empowerment assets, the Equity Foundation of India shall issue Equity Foundation of India bonds backed by the governments. The interest proceeds on these long-term bonds of say 3 to 6 years shall be tax free and match the returns of savings accounts, thereby making these an attractive and safe investment.

The funds from grants, augmented CSR, inheritance tax and EFI UAMA will flow to the Equity Foundation of India fund. These monies shall fund and back the initiatives of EFI like WISE and Nanhi Laxmi.

Equity Foundation of India – Daan Shree Title Program

Much like the Kar-Shree Title Program which would incentivize and reward honest taxpayers with titles and some democratically acceptable privileges, the Daan Shree Title Program shall incentivize and reward donations by individuals to the Equity Foundation of India Fund.

The three level Daan Shree Title Program would be as follows:
Param Daan Veer Top 1% Donations to EFI – Fund in any state
Maha Daan Veer Top 10% Donations to EFI – Fund in any state
Daan Veer Top 30% Donations to EFI – Fund in any state

So Mr Malhotra from Bhatinda could become Param Daan Veer S.K. Malhotra. People love being credited for their charitable acts, here they would get to flaunt their titles which shall be awarded every year and the incumbent shall be table to hold the title for, say, 3 years.

It would be displayed on the Equity Foundation of India website, backed by a title – I-card to get mild privileges at railway stations, airports, and police stations, for example. Credible social acknowledgement would be quite gratifying and serve the cause of Equity Foundation of India fund generation quite meaningfully.

Some Implementable Ideas

World Initiative for Service and Education (WISE) Academies

The WISE programme envisages setting up of a residential school chain with a capacity of one million children. It would cater to children from impoverished backgrounds where little ones have to often contend with unhygienic living conditions, unstable and violent homes, improper nutrition and basically sub-human conditions that deny these children the opportunity of fulfilling childhoods, of healthy living conditions and growing up with fun and learning.

An egalitarian, casteless society is only possible if all children have access to safe, clean homes and high-quality education. The reality is far from this. In fact the current capitalist construct of society has created a new class divide wherein the instrument of inheritance and individuals' greed for acquisition of assets and privileges seriously prejudices the flight of a child born into a less-privileged environment. Education, however, is the elixir that arms an individual to navigate the complex maze of this capitalist society and empowers in a manner where knowledge, industry and intent together can help surmount all walls and allow every child to fulfill his or her flight to a better life.

The WISE programme would ensure every child gets a chance to fly. Once we have succeeded in empowering the child with worldly education, we must offer a moral compass that would guide and embolden the ideals of rational enquiry, brotherhood of human kind, egalitarism, concern for women and, in general, an ability to lead a truthful life, free of vices that can only come from the study of scriptures and service to community.

At WISE, every child shall get an opportunity to become a world citizen with modern education, spiritual education and an opportunity to experience the community-service programme that each WISE Academy would run in its neighbouring communities. The WISE programme envisages 300 centres across India of 3,500 children each. Essentially 30 states shall have ten centres at an average with 3,500 children, totalling one million children.

Each WISE Academy shall comprise:

A residential district with well-appointed hostels for girls and boys aged 4 to 18, resident mothers and staff who would be caregivers to these children, staff quarters and resident teachers' accommodation.

An educational district with classrooms, laboratories, library, administration areas, and sports zones for indoor and outdoor sports up to state-level games standard, cultural activities facilities and so on.

Community-empowerment centre where all community outreach programmes shall be conducted.

Each WISE Academy shall be set up in a rural / semi-urban setting and be built on approximately 20 to 30 acre campuses. The funding for these academies shall be done entirely by the EFI Fund and shall use two models.

Model 1

Private – EFI Partnership: On a WISE campus owned by an accredited private educational trust. In this model, the capital investment in terms of cost of land and building is borne by a private educational trust and the EFI shall pay annual charges on a per student basis. This asset-light model would allow EFI to scale up to 300 centres or more at a faster pace. It would also be far more cost effective since the private educational trust would be able to acquire land and build at a more cost-effective manner than their government counterparts.

Model 2

EFI sets up 30 pilots: WISE Academies in each of the 30 states. These academies would set the gold standard for other academies to be set up in those states in collaboration with private educational trusts. All the facilities and their technical specifications areas per child would get defined through these pilot academies.

W.I.S.E. FOUNDATIO

WORLD INITIATIVE FOR SERVICE & EDUCATIO

Prepare **'citizens of the world'**
Who embody the qualities of a **saint-soldier**
and pursue **integrity & excellence**

MPOWER

)ne million families

communities around our sanctuaries

W.I.S.E
FOUNDATION

At W.I.S.E. foundation, we commit ourselves to ensure every child gets a school education because every child deserves a chance to fly. *"Soora so pehchaniye, Jo ladhe deen kehet....* (declares Guru Gobind Singh). He alone is brave who can fight for the Supreme cause – the cause of the poor, the downtrodden.

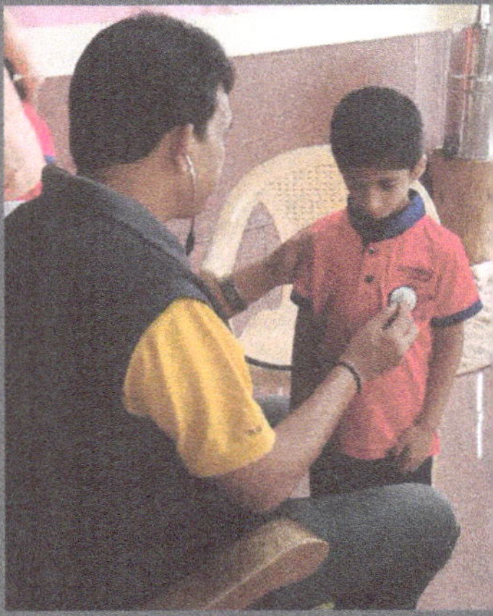

The WISE Programme Decoded

The World Initiative for Service and Education, in short WISE, would aspire to do the following:

Put a million poor kids in a residential school: Children without a desirable present would now have a beautiful present and a promising future. Every year put 100,000 beautifully minted world citizens out there in stratified world. These children, having received fulfilling childhoods of love, affection and having experienced the lessons of community service while still in school, would go on to blossom as individual citizens and pay back by engaging with global issues as responsible and proactive citizens.

Transform the lives of a million families that live around the WISE academies. The WISE community-service programme would carry forward the mandate of EFI and the union and state government towards social, financial and gender empowerment in communities around them.

Each academy would be headed by a director called a param guru and the community service programme shall be run by a dedicated team, which in turn shall be supported by visiting volunteers and students of the WISE Academy. This jugalbandi of school education coupled with real-time problem-solving in communities shall help accomplish the true objective of creating inspired, confident citizens who would lead fulfilling lives dedicated to collective good as opposed to self-serving educated denizens of world masquerading as citizens.

Once these children complete their education and join the global/Indian work-force, they would also take their own families out of the miseries of poverty and empower them socially and economically. Within a span of 20–25 years, this initiative would directly impact 3–4 million children and along with their families some 20 million individuals. For most of them the transformation from the impoverished fringes to mainstream would otherwise be unthinkable even in a hundred years.

Financial Model

Capital Cost

Assuming, the built-up area per child for a school from kindergarden to class 12 to be approximately 100–120 sq. ft per child, and a strength of 3,500 children, we are looking at approximately 3.5 lakh to 4 lakh sq. ft built-up area per academy which would cost approximately Rs 80 to 100 crore including semi-urban or rural land. Assuming a 50 year lifespan on investment and an average 2% on maintenance plus upgrades, it works out to approximately 2 lakh per child as capital cost assuming 3.500 x 4 = 14,000, children would study in the 50 years span.

No. of students using one campus in 50 years		Total cost incurred, including initial investment plus maintenance and routine upgrade.
3500 x 4	14000	$100 \text{ Cr} \times (1.02)^{50} = 280 \text{ Cr}$

Therefore, cost per child over 12–14 years = $\frac{280 \times 10^7}{140 \times 10^2}$ = 2Lacs per child

Operational Cost

Based on the study of sainik schools, and some other private residential schools that provide proper facilities, the cost per child per annum is approximately Rs 1 lakh to Rs 1.25 lakh.

This cost includes all costs applicable on the child for boarding, lodging, food, uniform, casual wear and wardens. It also includes cost of teachers, admin staff, laboratories and utilities and all sundry expenses for running an institution. So for a campus of 3,500 kids, approximately Rs 35 to 45 crore per annum.

So for Model 1 to work successfully, a reasonably philanthropic but financially prudent private educational trust would like to receive the full cost of operational cost plus a normal opportunity cost of the capital investment in the land and construction.

Consider This

The EFI mandates a graded payment be made of WISE academies on the basis of the performance of the children basis a certain objective assessment using some online and offline assessment tools.

Say, Top 20% students across the country receive Rs 2.0 lakh p.a.
Next 20% students across the country receive Rs 1.8 lakh p.a.
Rest 40% students across the country receive Rs 1.5 lakh p.a.
Bottom 20% students across the country receive Rs 1.25 lakh p.a.

Assuming an average WISE Academy receives say Rs 1.65 lakh p.a. averaged over for all the kids.

It would receive approximately 3,500 x 1.65 = Rs 57.75 crore
So, inflow = Rs 57.75 crore
OP EX = Rs 43.75 crore (3,500 x 1.25 lakh per child per annum)
Remainder = Rs 14 crore
Therefore, Rs 14 crore is return of the capital invested

Which is 14% on the investments of Rs 100 crore. Even if it dips to 8–10%, it would still be financially viable for private philanthropic/education trust.

This model would allow many dysfunctional engineering and medical colleges to remodel themselves and reconstitute themselves as WISE academies. This would be win-win situation for the private educational trusts, for EFI and for the children who will be able to benefit from this idea at a sooner date than would be possible if EFI were to build 300 centres from scratch.

The total cost of funding a million kids would be approximately 1.6 lakh x 10^6 i.e. 1.6 x 10^5 x Rs 106 = 16,000 crore per annum, that is, Rs 500 crore per state. Considering we spend Rs 40,000 crore on MGNREGA, Delhi spends Rs 1,800 crore on electricity subsidy. It is an amount that can be easily expended by EFI with union and state government support and using other sources of money.

BBBP Card

Nanhi Laxmi Scheme

In keeping with the government's impetus to address female infanticide, foeticides and incumbent unfavourable child sex ratio, the Beti Bachao Beti Padhao Yojana seeks to alter the context wherein a girl child's birth becomes a cause for celebration.

While the campaign began with focus on 100 worst-affected districts, it was eventually launched as a national-level programme with three ministries collaborating for the same: Ministry of Women and Child Development, Ministry of Health and Family Welfare and Ministry of Human Resource Development.

Currently under this initiative, campaigns like: #Selfiewithdaughter were used to create a public discourse on the subject of love within the family-fold for the girl child. It's really ironical that the very culture that deified Sita, Parvati, Laxmi, Durga and Saraswati should seek to eliminate the girl child in the womb.

The real reason for this prejudice stems from the system of dowry wherein the girl's father has to part with unreasonable sums of money while giving his daughter's hand in marriage to an eligible bachelor. The more coveted the groom, higher is the dowry payable for the alliance.

Even after marriage, the practice of grooms seeking financial assistance for bride's family continues. Maternity expenses and other significant expenses like investments in a new business or a home are also events where girl's father or brother are expected to chip in.

The patriarchal construct of society also ensures that girls don't receive the same treatment in their own homes in terms of access to healthier food, new clothes, play time.

The brothers typically receive preferential treatment over their sisters and in time they also begin to consider themselves superior and start to assert their rights.

The malice is so deep rooted that even highly educated families with economists, doctors, engineers and lawyers who have received modern education and are conversant with the values of equality and women empowerment engage in the malice of dowry and also deny their sisters their rightful share in ancestral property or assets.

In light of this, only a three-pronged strategy can really transform the situation:

Public discourse be encouraged and vigorously pursued to end the practice of dowry and ensure girls get their rights within their own families and then in their in-laws' house.

To this end, an act – Protection of Women's Inheritance Rights and Prevention of Prejudiced Acts – by Parents and In-Laws needs to be implemented.

Also while defining inheritance tax (discussed later in this chapter), denial of rightful inheritance to the girl child must result in higher tax whether in the form of inheritance tax in case of sale of asset or in form of extra municipal levy, wherein the differential goes into the coffers of EFI.

The Protection of Women's Inheritance Rights and Prevention of Prejudiced Acts by Parents and In-Laws would function by levying financial penalties on the accused rather than following penal provisions like jail terms since one must guard against frivolous misuse.

The final penalties however should be severe to act as a sufficient deterrent for delinquents.

So, when applying for school admissions, parents would have to declare where the girl child's siblings are studying; likewise when applying for a passport, any bank loan among others. More on this is explained under the heading 'inheritance tax', later in the chapter.

Lineage – Middle Name and Surname

Another reason why a girl child is seen as unequal to a boy child is because the boy becomes the torch-bearer of the family name. He is the 'scion', rich or poor. Subconsciously, every man wants his surname to propagate and his progeny to be known by the same name. Historically, Indians were able to handle this issue better than Westerners.

So Robert Bruce S/O Robert Bruce S/O David Bruce was the trend in some Western societies. In India, however, while the lineage was established by the father's surname which became the family name, the child was known by his or her mother's name.

So Ram was Kaushalya-putra. Ram was a Raghuvanshi where 'vansh' refers to lineage.

Krishna was born to Vasudev (father) and Devaki (mother) and brought up by his foster parents Nanda (father) and Yashoda (mother).

Among his many names were Devakinandan and Yashodanandan, so mother's name was a key part of a child's name.

Karan, the great warrior in Mahabharat, was known as Kuntiputra Karan.

So if all forms hereinafter ask the mother's name in lieu of father's name the patriarchal monopoly on the naming syntax can be dented.

And if the mother's surname can become the middle name of the progeny, then the whole premise of continued lineage would get positively transformed.

This third part of the three-pronged strategies would be a key change agent for the relatively impoverished sections of urban and rural India.

Every girl child born to a family with an income below a threshold of say Rs 2 lakh per annum would qualify to receive a BBBP card. It would be like a secure credit card in its physical form and allow the following benefits for the girl's well-being Rs 10,000 shall be credited every year to the card from the year of birth till the girl gets married or turns 21.

This card would be useable to buy anything like a credit card subject to a maximum of Rs 1,000 per month. Think of it as an allowance of Rs 833 p.m. from the government, effected through the EFI coffers, so the girl child is not a financial burden on the family.

For any educational or health-related expenses, the monthly limit may be enhanced to say Rs 5,000 per month or 30% of the total amount in the card at that time.

Once the child is 15, the limit on redemption could be removed, to allow for payment of college tuition fees and/or marriage. For a girl child who pursues college education, the annual allowance would be trebled to Rs 30,000 per annum for a period of 3 years, to encourage girls to pursue education beyond schooling and simultaneously provide for a sustenance allowance.

All girl children who marry post 18 years would receive their marriage gift of Rs 25,000 from EFI to alleviate the financial burden of marriage which often pushes the impoverished familys to seeking expensive debt. A lot of families may use this card as a monthly savings scheme for the girl child, to be redeemed for exigencies or marriage. To encourage this, the card would function as a normal savings account.

The BBBP card–Nanhi Laxmi Scheme would once again re-establish the girl child as the harbinger of wealth for the family – a true Nanhi Laxmi.

Inheritance Tax

Inheritance and inequity are two sides of the same coin. Remove inheritance from society and all inequities imposed by virtue of birth would also diminish with time.

When two teams compete in a sporting arena, there are equal rules and equal tools which ensure that the best performing team or individual wins. So Roger Federer v/s a young talented player would be an interesting match if the rules of inheritance allowed Roger to use a superior racket, serve using a better ball, have more liberal rules or choose a more convenient turf while his young opponent would have to play with a broken racket and similar such handicaps, all this because Roger would have inherited rights and privileges through the previous titles he has won.

And to make matters more interesting, Roger's son would inherit these privileges! What would be nature of tennis that would get played out!

The passage of all rights and titles from one generation to the next generation was a notion that evolved as human settlements moved into the agricultural age. It ensured some sense of continuity, stability and permanence. A son could be expected to pay his father's debt and equally receive all liens. As settlements grew, the feudal age set in, where the power of the feudal lords vis-à-vis their subjects grew with every generation to a point where inheritance of estates' finances and military might created a divided society.

The oppressor and the oppressed. This was the point where it was no longer a level-playing field. Inequality as an accepted social reality had established its ugly hold on our social consciousness.

While inheritance of privileges ensured permanence and continuity, it severely dented meritocracy and fair play. The social and financial ecosystem became an impediment in an individual's ability to accomplish their full potential through life. The feudal ages saw many revolutions when the oppressed communities rose together to dismantle the social and financial ecosystem. Alongside these social revolutions, the world saw changes in political systems, evolution of monetary systems, industrial revolution, rise of modern science and eventually the birth of modern nation states where most of the world's citizens live within institutional frameworks that guarantee a certain degree of equality and dignity to all individuals. Also, the legal framework began to see all individuals as equals in the eyes of law.

In any journey of transformation of values in a society, it starts with a few thought leaders espousing a progressive value that furthers the self-expression of an individual in society, then the legal framework gets altered through legislation, then the popular narrative begins to change and eventually the slow wheels of mainstream social change begin churning.

It's taken us a century or so to accept women folk into the mainstream of the working-class population. Equal pay for equal work is a right that is still in the last quartile of the transformative journey in advanced economies. In many countries, the journey hasn't even begun.

The concept of 'inheritance' per se assumes permanent lien on a piece of land or a legal financial entity which in the larger scheme of things belongs to the whole community or perhaps to no one for posterity. It must be understood that each of us are, at best, custodians of wealth and not owners in posterity.

So within the capitalist construct of nations, social consciousness has to rekindle and embrace the notion of custodianship over ownership. Sharing in measured doses is the only answer to addressing inequitable distribution of wealth and privileges. Eventually measured dose of sharing emboldens the ecosystem by providing meritocracy and fair play a better footing, by providing access to education, shelter and health to the weaker sections.

In the relay of wealth transfer, each generation shall reaffirm its commitment to sharing by paying the taxes on inheritance to the EFI which, in turn, shall fund various interventions in providing equity as delineated in the chapter.

How the tax shall be affected (levied) to ensure two objectives:

- Monies paid to EFI
- Rights of girl child / sibling are honoured

Monies Paid to EFI

To ensure wider compliance to inheritance tax, the percentage must be moderate at say 5%. This too should be levied on the circle rate in the case of immovableassets, their official value and in case of financial instruments, on the date of effect of the inheritance. In case of assets held as jewellery, art, heirloom, similar tax shall be levied based on fair value on date of effect of inheritance.

In case of immovable assets where assets are simply being transferred to the inheritors and not being sold to a third party, there could be liquidity issues. To address this, levies surcharges could be added to the municipal taxes or utility bills to compensate for payment of the inheritance tax for those who may not be income tax assessors. These surcharges would be routed to the EFI. Some reasonable time of say 3 years may be accorded to fully settle the dues.

For income tax assesses, it would be a part of their tax returns and non-payment could lead severe penal charges in terms of interest of say 18% or other prudent measures. All income tax departments would need to have an EFI desk that would function in an advisory role as well as executive role to manage inflows into the EFI. In effect, the inheritance tax would be as powerful as CSR has been in funding charitable projects in India.

Protect Inheritance Rights of the Girl Child / Sibling

One of the most troublesome pieces of the gender-inequality narrative is the treatment meted out to sisters and daughters at the time of inheritance. Even educated families with highly distinguished male inheritors suddenly dorn this feudal concept and deny their sisters the rightful shares in inheritance. While social consciousness now looks down on 'dowry' and there are enough legal safeguards to check this malice, the denial of inheritance to the girl child is still socially acceptable, even considered morally right. While the incumbent girl looses financially and the corresponding empowerment it brings socially, she also experiences loss of love and bonding within the family. There are only a few who raise disapproval, however, most adorn the sacrificial mask and accept it as the social norm. What it does is that it cements the notion within families that women can be subjugated. It perpetuates patriarchy in the most fundamental way.

Attacking this would mean, destroying the citadel of patriarchy.

Under the new inheritance law, there would be financial incentives and disincentives to steer social behaviour. So in case of equitable distribution of inheritance, the tax would be 5%, however, in case of inequitable distribution of wealth, the portion which is inequitable or whole could attract an inheritance tax of 25% or similar surcharge on municipal levies, utility bills, income tax and wealth tax to provide a serious disincentive and also deny perpetrators the option of hiding behind some legal obfuscation. In the interim period of legal obfuscation, the additional levies would continue to be in force in case any inequities are affected.

In case where siblings are asked to relinquish their share in favour of one or more siblings, again of the deemed share of the relinquishing party, 25% would be transferred to the EFI.

The nuts and bolts of the act would certainly need to be fleshed out. It would have to be mild, effective, practically executable, and legally tenable, and above all something that would find social acceptance and support. This act and the monies that would flow into the EFI would be potent catalysts in the quest for greater equity.

The Kar-Shree Program incentivizes the payment of taxes through the Title for Tax Rewards programme.

The Equity Foundation of India emerges as the vanguard of equity, and using various sources like the EFI–Bonds, access to unclaimed monies, Daan-Shree EFI donations, effect equity through Nanhi Laxmi Scheme, WISE academies and such schemes.

The Inheritance Tax and Prevention of Prejudiced Acts by Parents and In-Laws would effect social and gender equity meaningfully.

Chapter 8

OFFICE OF BHARAT

COUNTRY	POPULATION (2012)	OLYMPIC MEDALS[131]
USA	313.9 million	2,684
SWEDEN	9.6 million	627
SOUTH KOREA	50 million	296
BULGARIA	7.3 million	220
ETHIOPIA	91.73 million	45
INDIA	1.23 billion	26

Scale
= 10 million

A BILLION CAPABLE PEOPLE YET JUST 26 OLYMPIC MEDALS?

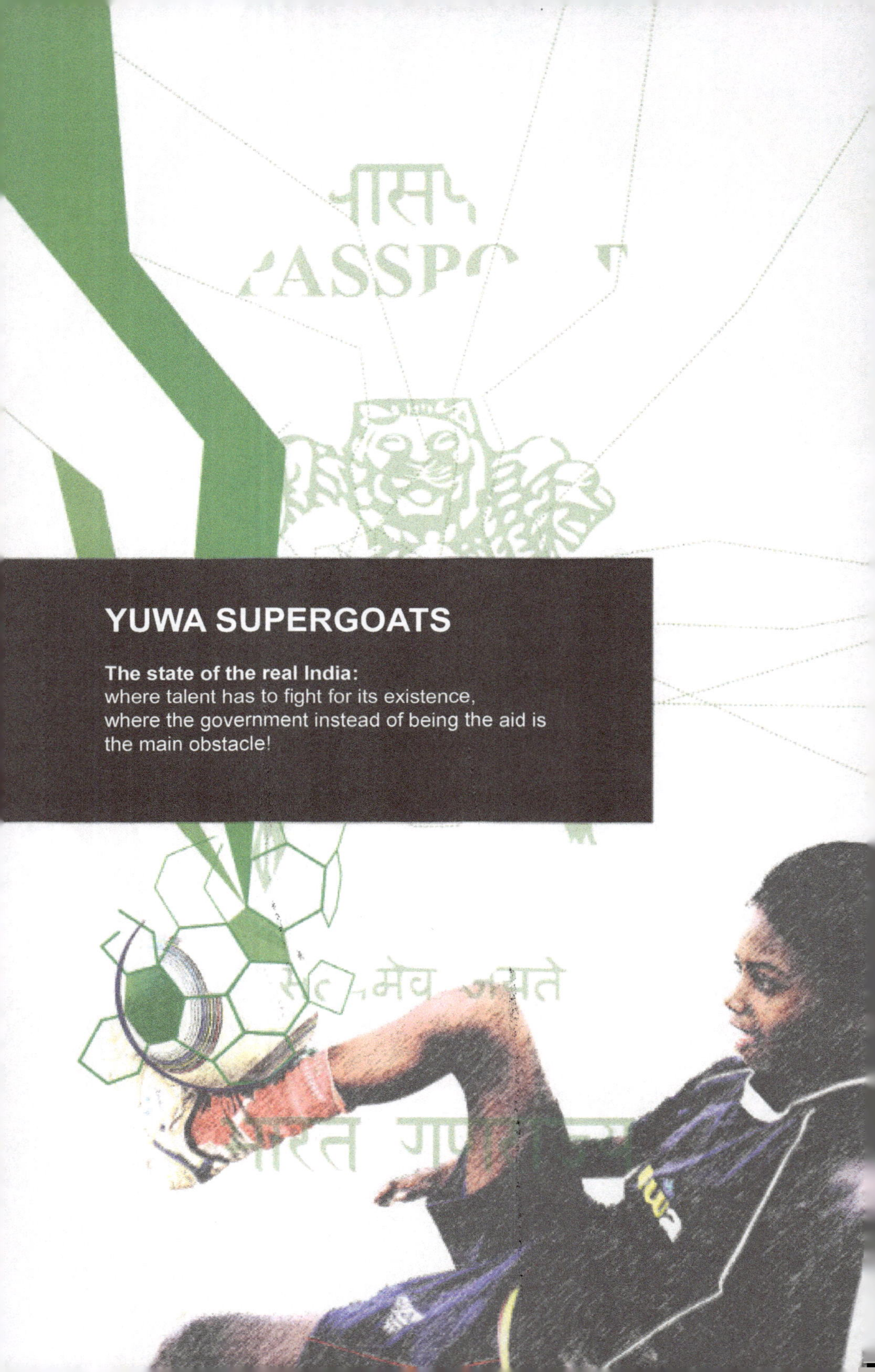

YUWA SUPERGOATS

The state of the real India:
where talent has to fight for its existence,
where the government instead of being the aid is
the main obstacle!

Introduction

The state of government dysfunction in rural India is well captured in the story of the Yuwa Supergoats. It begins in the village of Ormanjhi, 25 kms outside Ranchi, in Jharkhand. Here, 7 years ago, a young expatriate, Harvard graduate named Franz Gastler, decided to give up his well-paid corporate life in New Delhi to set up a football-training academy for girls to encourage them to participate in sports.

Over the years, this group of girls gradually improved in their skills and confidence. Gastler managed to get them invited to a major youth football tournament in Spain. Here, they could try their luck against some of the top youth teams from around the world. There was just one small problem standing in their way: none of Gastler's Supergoats had passports. In fact, most didn't even have a birth certificate in hand, which would be required to make a passport. With only a little bit of time left before the tournament began, the girls began doing the rounds of the local block office near their village to obtain their birth certificates. Only then would they be able to apply for a passport, before applying for the visas.

For 4 years, the girls had battled skeptical – even hostile – parents in order to play the game they loved. Now, with an exciting and once-in-a-lifetime opportunity to see the world, their parents had finally turned around. The same could not be said about the local block development officer.[132]

When the girls approached him for their birth certificates, he first slapped and verbally abused some of them. Even though access to their birth records was a right, the officer demanded bribes and forced them to sweep his office. This humiliating abuse lasted 3 weeks before the girls plucked up the courage to tell Gastler and his colleague Rose Thompson about the real reason for the delay in paperwork. With a timely intervention from his contacts at the Ministry of External Affairs in New Delhi, Gastler finally managed to obtain the birth certificates, passports and visas just in time for the girls to head to the tournament.

THE PROBLEM

1. Growing Governance Deficit

1. Dysfunctional public infrastructure and inadequate amenities.
2. Government's administrative apathy
3. Feudal self-serving social structure
4. Hapless existence

2. Failing Rural Economy

1. Agriculture is a very high-risk low-gain enterprise forcing people away from the villages.
2. Lack of real-time pricing information for farmer.
3. Lack of granaries and cold-storage facilities forcing the farmers to sell cheap.
4. Absence of a mature food processing Industry.

3. Skills, Education and Sports Neglect

1. Inadequate and poor quality of vocational training programmes.
2. Absence of skill upgradation and skill-enhancement programmes at rural level
3. Inadequate and poor quality of Educational Infrastructure; confused government policy towards educational industry.
4. Inadequate physical sports infrastructure; poor government policy on management of sports.

4. Disconnect between Bharat, India and Desi

1. Agriculture is a very high-risk low-gain enterprise forcing people away from the villages.
2. Lack of real-time pricing information for farmer.
3. Lack of granaries and cold-storage facilities forcing the farmers to sell cheap.
4. Absence of a mature food processing industry.

The experience of playing on a proper, grassy football pitch, in front of a large crowd and against competitors who were physically much larger would have overwhelmed any ordinary team. The tenacity and grit of the Supergoats, however, helped them not only reach the quarter finals of their first ever international tournament, they even won bronze in a second tournament they participated in on that same trip.

As is typical, the stumbling blocks the Supergoats faced in Ormanjhi were only resolved after their success story made it to the press. It began with the suspension of the block development officer who had physically and verbally abused the girls. This was followed by a promise from the state and centre to contribute towards a new team bus and stadium. Amazingly, several Supergoats have now graduated to play for both the state team and even the national squad. It just goes to show how far people can go if they are given access to the right platform and opportunities.

But why should it take stories in the press to deliver basic government services to India's citizens? Indeed, why can't government services simply 'work'?

The story of the Supergoats would seem harsh, draconian even, in any civilized part of the world. In India, it is commonplace. But is there anything that can be done about it? The answer is yes, but to get to it, we must first understand the myriad problems plaguing rural India ... or as some call it, Bharat. We've categorized these under four heads.

A Growing Governance Deficit

Life in India's villages is Spartan. There are few amenities and public infrastructure is often little more than a dirt road and barely adequate electricity (if there are no power cuts). It can take hours to reach a decent hospital, and the police only show up if something really serious has gone wrong.

Most problems are left to the panchayat. In short, we suffer from a desperate inadequacy of government services in rural areas. In fact, many villages are totally devoid of any government presence whatsoever. Like the Supergoats in our story, millions of rural residents struggle to get access to even basic government services. If it's not the administration, it's the school headmasters who remain absent. If the headmasters are doing their jobs, it is the cops who act exploitatively. No matter what government service a villager needs, be it rations or education or even his MGNREGS job, government officials ensure he has to struggle to get it.

In nearly a third of all districts in India, insurgents such as the Maoists wield considerable authority over rural life. This is a problem for two reasons. One, there is little economic and human security, thanks to the constant violence. Often villagers are caught in the cross-fire as police and rebel forces fight. So, if it's not government apathy that kills, it is the so-called 'enemies of the state' who take matters in their own hands. Either way, our villagers lead a fairly hapless existence.

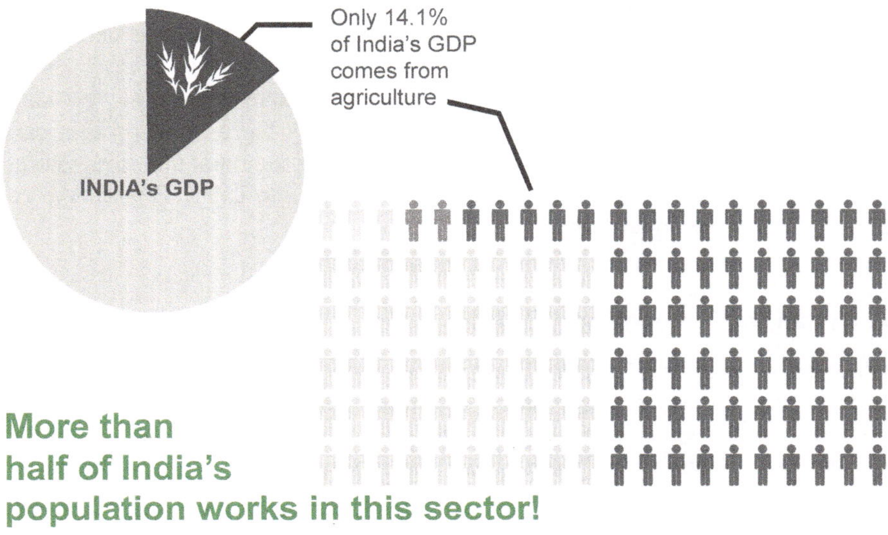

The Failing Rural Economy

While agriculture and its allied activities contribute only 14.1% to India's GDP, at least 58.2% of all Indians work in this sector.[133] Almost all of them are based in rural India. Therefore, it's hardly an exaggeration to say that our villages survive or die based on this one sector. Unfortunately, at the moment, it's failing. Agricultural growth averaged just 3.6% over the Eleventh Five Year Plan period. The target it fell short of was an equally abysmal 4%. This is not even enough to keep up with inflation.

At the heart of its failure is a simple equation: Where a kilogram of fruit is sold for Rs 50 in our cities, the farmer who produced it gets paid only Rs 5. The rest is eaten up by the many middlemen who take a huge cut off the farmer's hard work.

There are many reasons for this, chief among them a lack of real-time pricing information for farmers. This allows middlemen to cheat farmers of a fair price. And since their produce is perishable, they have a very small window within which they can bargain or hold out for a better price.

A lack of granaries and cold-storage facilities at the village level further compounds the problem of perishability. Forty percent of India's food produce goes to waste every year – this is worth roughly Rs 50,000 crore.[134] This is not because Indians waste food. It's because it either rots away in granaries or is eaten up by pests. The Food Corporation of India is partly to blame. By paying warehouse owners a fixed price per square metre to store grain, its model incentivizes storage quantity, not quality.

Of course there are more complex reasons as well. For example, India's average yield per hectare is abysmal when compared even with other third-world countries.

Take onions, for instance. Onion prices affect every household, given the pervasiveness of this vegetable in Indian cuisine. In 2008, Indian farms yielded 10.1 tons/hectare. On the other hand, Pakistani farms yielded 13.1 tons of onions/hectare, Chinese farms yielded 20.79 tons/hectare, Egyptian yielded 32 tons/hectare; in Niger, onion farmers yielded 35.5 tons/hectare. The world average for 2008 was 17.9 tons of onions/hectare.[135]

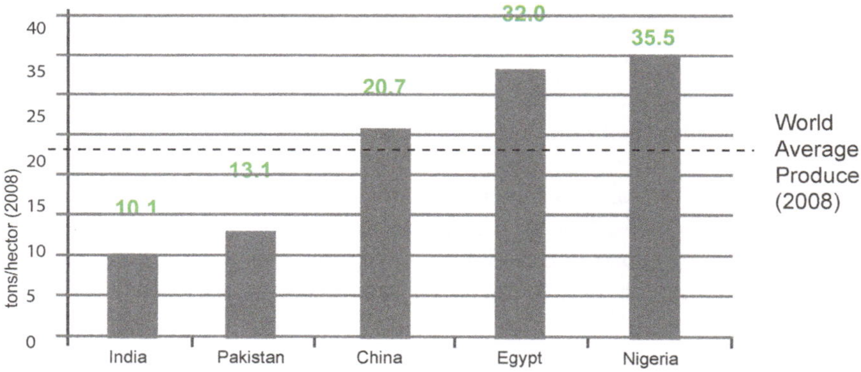

Yields are an accurate measure of the productivity of rural agriculture, and, consequently, the larger rural economy. The higher the yield, the more money a farmer will earn by tending to the same plot of land. This figure is affected by everything from farming techniques to water availability, soil fertility, weather patterns, pests and seed varieties. In Nigeria, one of the world's poorest nations, onion farmers got 350% more yield on the same area of land than Indian farmers. The disparity is staggering.

Another reason is farmers' input costs. These include labour, seeds, fertilizer and other resources. Let's say these cost him Rs 4 per kg. In case of a drought or a flood or a premature or late monsoon, he goes into a loss. A farmer's access to funds is typically at a very high interest because of such uncertainties. Therefore, he is stuck in a perpetual debt trap and could end up resorting to suicide. On top of that, it is becoming increasingly difficult to find an adequate workforce because most young people want to move to the city, rather than stay tied to the village.

If we were to summarize these problems, we'd put them in three broad categories.

a. **Absence of granaries / cold storage**
Farmers have no place to store produce. So there is a very strict deadline to sell their product. The first buyer who offers a decent price gets his goods. Middlemen take advantage of this desperation.

b. **No access to information**
Small-scale farming, as we explained earlier, is an economically unviable profession in India. Farmers know this but have few options. It is not that they aren't smart enough to do other things. For example, farmers are instinctive meteorologists. They can forecast tomorrow's weather for you based on which way the wind is blowing. All of them are also experts at veterinary sciences to take care of their livestock and working animals. Many have an innate knowledge of botany, as they are able to diagnose crop diseases and apply the right medicines or remedies to save their crop. They also find time to develop irrigation and chemist skills to manage their farms better.

In other words, farmers as not simple people who lack the capacity to understand complex subjects. Far from it. The real problem for them is they do not get access to information on how much their produce is really worth in the market.

c. **Lack of food processing**
Currently, a farmer's customers are restricted to how far he can deliver his produce without it getting spoilt. But what if the farmers could immediately convert at least some of their produce into jams, jellies, pickles and other ready-to-eat foods, almost the day they took it off their farms?

Without these basic facilities, it's not surprising that agriculture is a fairly poor professional option. The person who is responsible for putting every single meal on our tables is, today, the worst off in the country.

Skills, Education and Sport

India's oft-talked about demographic dividend could just as easily become our ticking time-bomb. Basic education is failing in many places. In 2012, students from 73 countries, including India, participated in the Program for International Students Assessments test. The results were shocking – Indian students get placed 72nd in the competition.[136] Only students from Kyrgyzstan fared worse on average.

India ranks
72nd / 73rd
In Program for
International
Student Assessment
test in 2012

According to the assessors, the average Indian student was 200 points behind the global topper. The Indian students who participated came from Tamil Nadu and Himachal Pradesh, two states with reputedly healthy education systems. As many as 89% of Himachali students were found to have a reading proficiency below the required standard.

Another issue is that rural teachers often don't show up for work. This is not the rule, but it is common enough to be regarded as a serious problem. As a result, the students end up dropping out of school and working on their parents' farms, despite the offers of a mid-day meal. In fact, in 2009 alone, UNICEF reported that 80 lakh children between the ages of 6 and 14 were out of school.[137] Given the poor rates of higher education, most companies are hard-pressed when it comes to finding talent. The few who are available aren't necessarily 'natural fits'. Skills and vocational training is negligible. This forces many companies to invest scarce and expensive capital on re-training employees, something that should have happened in high schools or colleges. While the adult literacy rate has improved to 74%, it is still far behind the global average of 84%.[138] Most of India's illiterate adults live in villages. Not only do they lack access to government services, but thanks to their inability to read or write, they do not possess the tools either, to engage with and benefit from the wider economy.

Vocational training for adults is another black hole. One of the reasons our bridges seem crooked, and even newly laid roads feel bumpy, is because the labourers involved rarely get much training to do their job. This is the same reason we often see gaps in door frames or faulty electrical wiring in houses and offices. This lack of skills doesn't just affect the lifestyles of rich city dwellers, it also degrades the income potential of labourers. In some cases, unskilled labourers earn as much as 20% less than skilled ones.[139]

Let's examine another problem. We are the second largest population in the world but we fare so poorly in sports. Why is that? Some people say it is because there is no scope for professional sports in India. This is not entirely true. Virtually every government public sector unit and department and many companies have a sports quota. These provide ample employment opportunities for talented sportsmen. The real problem is there are very few quality sporting facilities and coaches available to help children hone their skills to a professional level. Even when the government invests in high-quality sports infrastructure and coaches, somehow the lure of money and power brings political appointees into the management ecosystem, and they invariably compromise the selection process, or simply mismanage the governance of these sports bodies.

The absence of such facilities means that children play their sports on streets or swim in ponds and canals. No wonder cricket does well in India; all you need is a single bat and ball and a little open space. Tennis, squash, swimming, track-and-field and shooting all require considerable investment in facilities and equipment. The absence of a viable business model for sporting academies in India can be directly tied to the poor performance of our sportsmen and women at international events.

The Disconnect between Bharat, India and Desi

One of the other major problems for citizens in our villages is the glaring disconnect between their aspirations and the opportunities available to them. This Bharat–India disconnect is not just a source of great resentment due to unfulfilled aspirations, it is also widening the socio-economic gap on everything from health and education to incomes and quality of life.

Another unfortunate result of the disconnect is that when 'Bharat' shows up in 'India', it is confronted by a totally alien operating environment. That's when crimes like rapes and thefts occur, thanks to the confusion about appropriate norms, behaviours and values.

That's not to say that the problems are only one way. Urban Indians are just as guilty of heinous, exploitative crimes against those who arrive from the villages to try their luck. There have been several cases of abuse of domestic help, including locking maids in the house for days, starving them for not performing tasks well or even physical torture such as beatings and branding with hot iron.

While the extreme cases are worth noting, there is also lower key mistreatment of domestic help that either goes under the radar, or is even implicitly condoned. This includes low wages, general disrespect, employing child labour and allowing minimal social interaction and few holidays. Even the simple denial of a weekly off to a housemaid is exploitation of 'Bharat'.

In fact, segregation is against the notions of inclusion and social equity. At the posh Delhi Gymkhana, there are explicit signs banning 'maids and pets' from certain areas. These behaviours are not always intentional, and many are the result of a lack of sensitivity. Either way, they are a source of friction and need to be fixed.

This is certainly not the future that tens of millions of young rural Indians are hungry for. Unfortunately for them, they are often surrounded by poor infrastructure and resources, which limit their ability to improve their lot. After all, a substandard education or substandard schools will not create a world-class workforce. Many of the ills can be solved if these young people had the opportunity to speak to knowledgeable professionals who can not only coach them to better professional standards but also give them something to aspire to.

What is needed is to build bonds of connectedness. Inclusion and sensitivity are a natural progression from connectedness and the only antidote to the 'evil of otherisation'.

There are tens of millions of city dwellers today who would want to give back to their home towns in some way. And let's not forget about the millions of Indians who live abroad in places such as London or Singapore or Hong Kong or the San Francisco Bay Area. Unfortunately, there is no established route for them to 'give back', unless they personally visit their villages and supervise a project. This is possible perhaps once a year. The distances and time involved means that this too could become tedious and logistically impossible. But what if there was a way for these young software engineers, doctors, lawyers, fashion designers, journalists and businessmen in the US, UK, Singapore, Hong Kong, and so on, to mentor young people who want to take up similar professions back home?

Imagine how many millions of future Indian professionals can benefit from such a mentorship programme. Imagine the benefits this would bring to the economy if we had so many well-trained individuals showing up in the workforce – our GDP growth would soar.

Author's Hypothesis on How Live Ecosystems Evolve

CENTRE and PERIPHERY: Three Stages of Equilibrium and Evolution of Ecosystem

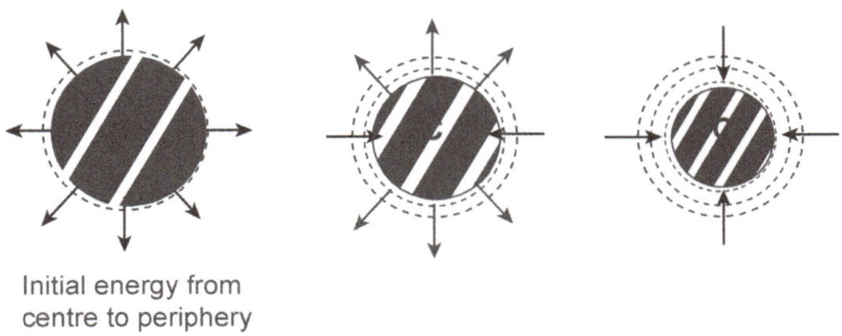

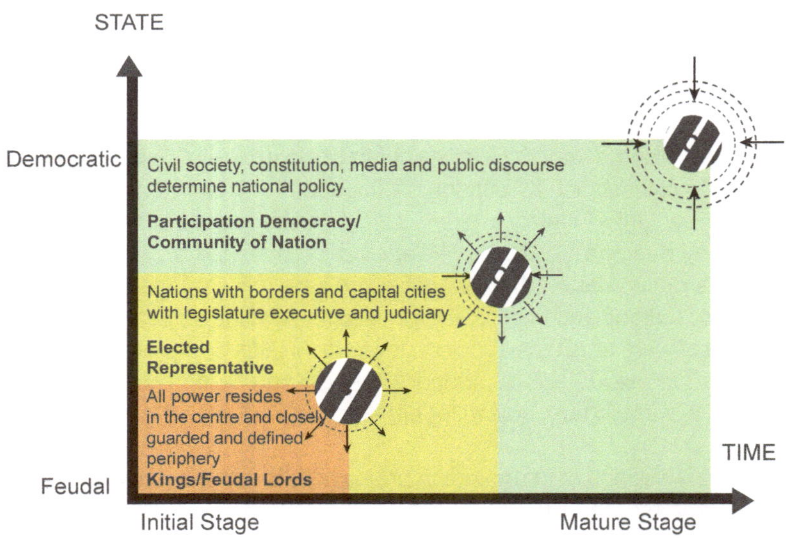

A Prelude to the Solution

Virtually everything in nature is built around a strong core. The tiny atom and the largest galaxy alike have strong central cores that enable other objects such as electrons or stars to inhabit their periphery. The core keeps its peripheral constituents in order by giving them something to gravitate around, else there would be chaos.

The centre is what gives the initial energy to the periphery. Then, over time, the periphery itself shores up the centre.

Similarly, human institutions have evolved around a similar concept. Initially, kings and feudal lords single-handedly wielded all power, building societies around their writ. Over time, the societies themselves evolved and strengthened, demanding more rights and freedoms and ultimately establishing modern democratic governments. Still, even democratic governments have a head of state as the central decision-making authority.

Now, in the context of 'Bharat', to transform cultural and traditional habits that have built up over history, such as the caste system and bureaucratic red-tapism, you need a big, bold, powerful idea that can be executed quickly and forcefully. The pace and quantum of change should be powerful enough to disrupt the inertia in the system, especially that which would seek to maintain the status quo. Citizens need to be able to recognize the new idea as something that will be genuinely beneficial to their way of life and livelihoods.

That is what the Office of Bharat aspires to be ... the change agent, the cause agent; a formidable centre for rural transformation and evolution ... a rural hub.

Habitat Drivers

Historically, human settlements have flourished around four major habitat 'drivers' – political power centres, economics and trade centres, education centres and transport hubs. Rome, Brasilia, Delhi, Moscow and Beijing are all cities that rose thanks to their place as political capitals. Mumbai, New York, Shanghai and Hong Kong all centred around economic and trade activities. Boston, Pune, Oxford, Cambridge, and Takshashila and Nalanda of yore are examples of cities that were built around education. Atlanta, Singapore, Dubai and more recently, Brussels, have flourished as transport hubs.

HABITAT DRIVERS

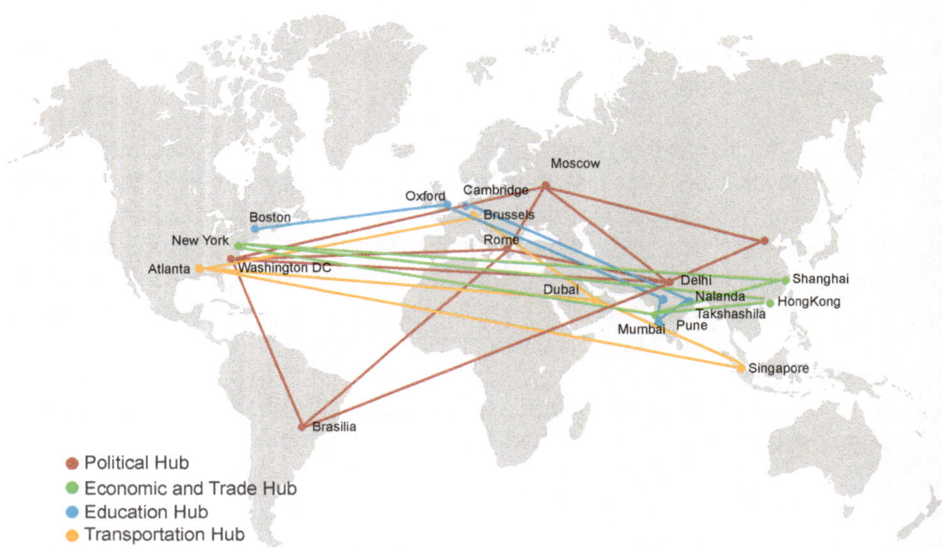

The Solution

If you wanted to start a business today, one of the first things you would do is find yourself an office space. This could be something as basic as converting a spare room in your home or renting a space in an office block. Either way, whether you are a government institution, factory, company or one-man consultancy, you need a dedicated work space – an office.

In India, the government has several levels of local administration beginning with the state, then the district, the tehsil, block and village panchayat. The physical institutions that administer these various offices are typically scattered around the region and most are in a decrepit state. That's why the government works in such a disjointed manner, making service delivery inefficient.

Crime and sluggishness thrive in anonymity. So if you know that nobody is watching, if you know that you won't get caught, all kinds of devious designs and thoughts are going to occur and reflect in your actions. Similarly, if you work in an organization which is not under the scanner, you are likely to be a little more sluggish, as opposed to working at the headquarters where your performance is noticed.

Most offices the world over have shifted from cabins and rooms to an open plan. One of the main reasons for that was physical transparency. It brings in a certain sense of equity in that everybody knows that they are more or less equal. Of course, the very senior officers still enjoy private spaces for important or sensitive meetings.

The important thing, however, is that with such high visibility and transparency, work is more efficient. Lots of teams sit in the same place, enabling a higher degree of collaboration due to physical proximity. If a file moves from one team to another, the receivers cannot say, 'I did not receive it.' So it's fairly easy to map who is doing what and conduct follow-ups.

THE OFFICE OF BHARAT

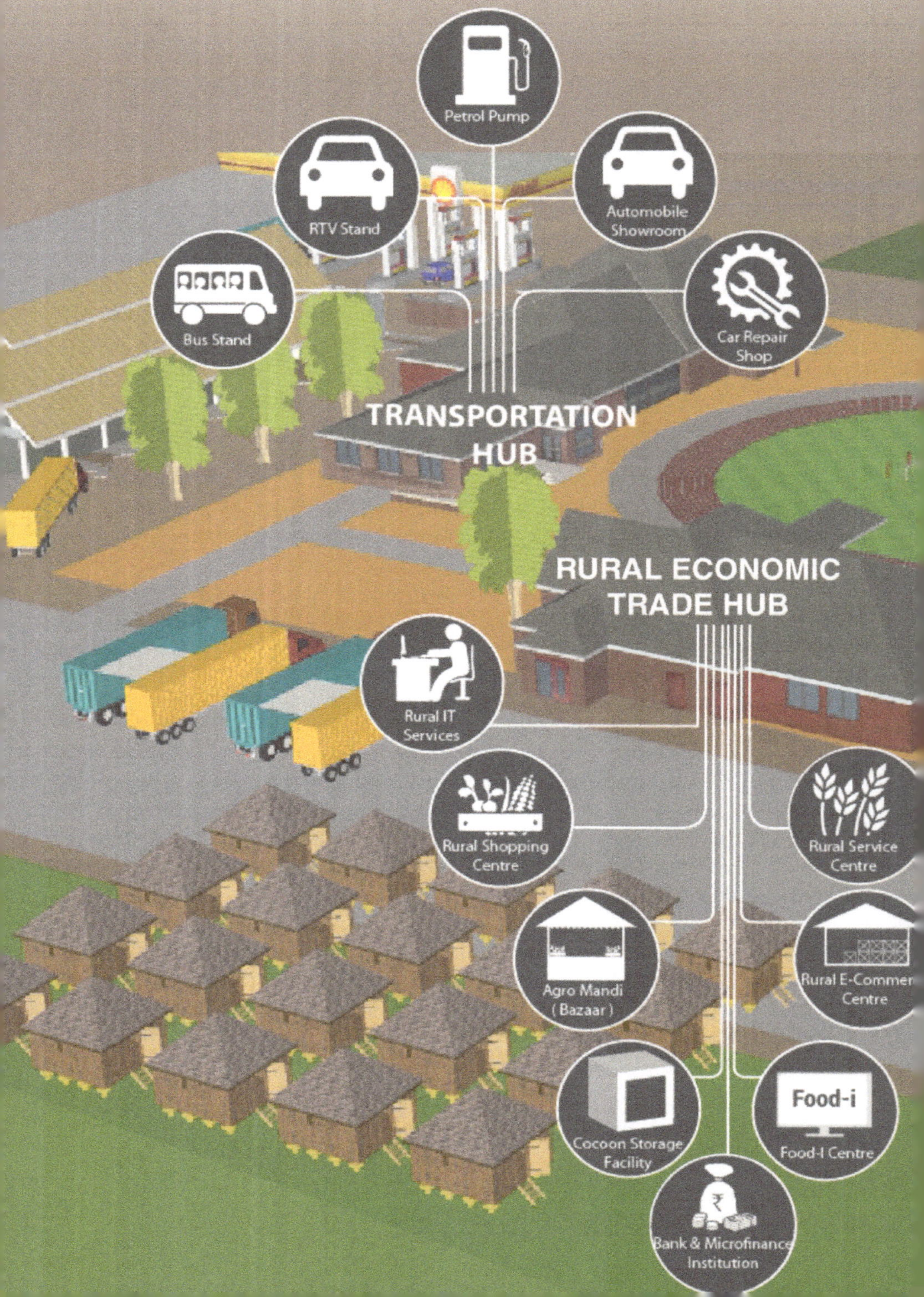

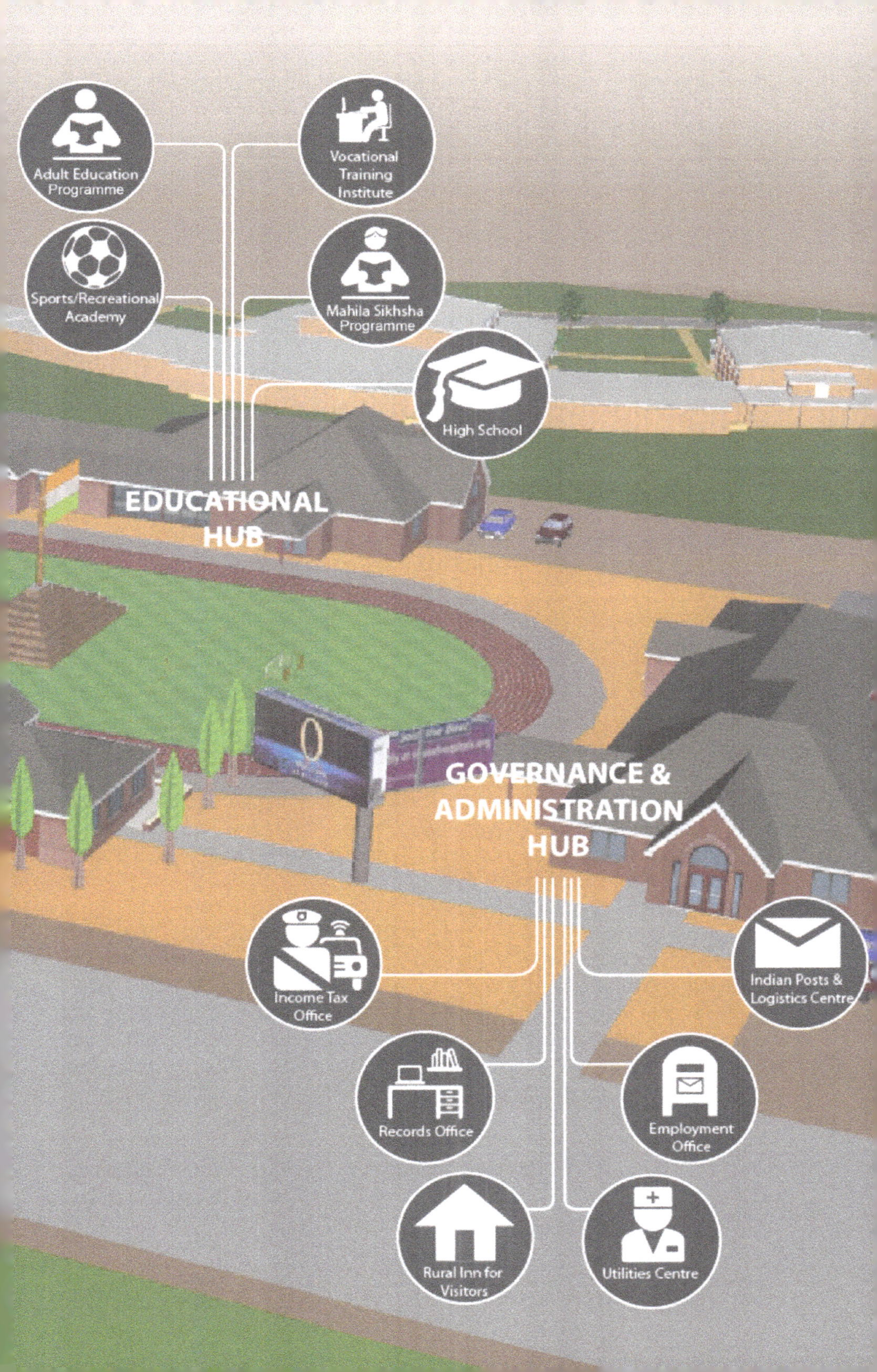

Adult Education Programme
Vocational Training Institute
Sports/Recreational Academy
Mahila Sikhsha Programme
High School
EDUCATIONAL HUB
GOVERNANCE & ADMINISTRATION HUB
Income Tax Office
Indian Posts & Logistics Centre
Records Office
Employment Office
Rural Inn for Visitors
Utilities Centre

The Office of Bharat

What if we could create a single campus for every rural block in the country, which would combine all four of these habitat 'drivers' namely: administrative power, economics and trade, education and transport.

Imagine a rural 'Office of Bharat' – a single, 50-acre campus; one for each of India's 4,000-odd blocks that would address the four problem areas we identified earlier; the governance deficit, the failing rural economy, poor education and skills development and the Bharat–India disconnect.

For governance and administration, it would house the local block officer, a police station, a records office, a post office and a primary health centre.

For education, it would have a middle and high school, a mahila shiksha programme, and a vocational training and adult literacy institute, and even a sports and recreation academy.

To boost the rural economy, it would house a state-of-the-art agricultural commodities market, supplies and agricultural commodities stores, a modern, insulated, module-based granary and cold storage (explained later), retail shops, restaurants, banks, and so on.

The centre would also house the transport hub for the block, with a bus stand for long-distance travel, an RTV stand for shorter distances to nearby villages, petrol pumps, a vehicle service and repair shop and perhaps even a car dealer. The entire campus would be spread out around a central quadrangle. At one end would be a giant screen on which local authorities could broadcast everything from important government announcements and notices to the prices of grains and vegetables, movies, cricket matches and even political speeches during the elections.

To hasten the creation of 'Office of Bharat' they could be situated on railway land wherever possible. It would do away with the complications of land acquisition. It would also strengthen its position as a transport hub.

The Office of Bharat would have seven distinct features:

CENTRALIZED

Every conceivable government and private service in one place.

This would make it a convenient place for rural Indians to access government services as well as engage with the larger Indian economy, education system and society. The co-location of so many government services would improve collaboration, reduce overlaps and ensure oversight of erring government officials. With a centralized office space, the school headmaster and the police adhikari and the post office adhikari would all keep a watchful eye on each other, making sure they're all doing their jobs. What's more, since the offices are centralized, it would be much easier for district magistrates or district collectors to visit and monitor officials who work under them and keep a check on their performance. With a centralized office, the government can even think about installing a biometric attendance system where everyone – from the policemen to school teachers, health-centre paramedics, block officers and postal workers – can reliably log in their attendance. The centralization of government services will make it easier for villagers in the same block to get multiple tasks done in one trip.

NEW

It would create new equity, opportunity, capacity and quality.

Rural Indians would now have access to government and economic services on par with their urban cousins. This would create new opportunities for them to participate in the economy. It would create new capacity to grow the rural economy. And all this would happen at a level of quality previously unavailable to rural India. Farmers can sell of their vegetables, attend a short workshop on a new seed programme, and get minor health concerns attended to at the primary health centre, all in the same day. In the evening, they could all settle in the quadrangle and catch the latest day–night cricket match and build a sense of community and connectedness.

The farmer's wife could bring her children to the school, she herself could then go to her job within the same complex making agro-based processed foods or working as a midwife in the clinic and perhaps even post a few letters to relatives in other places. Those who do not work on farms, such as cobblers, blacksmiths and tailors, would also benefit from the centralization of government services. What's more, hardware retail stores would ensure all their supplies were reliably available.

FREE

It would be built for free and run privately on a BOOT model.

What if all this new infrastructure could be built without any public money being spent? In fact, what if private organizations readily invested in not just building this infrastructure but in maintaining it as well? All the government would have to do is provide the land for the development, award the leases to private companies and staff it with relevant government officials. The entire construction would not cost the exchequer a single paisa, but be borne by private companies looking to engage with and profit from a revitalized rural economy. We will explain this in greater detail later in this chapter. Since the Office of Bharat itself will be run on a profit-and-loss model, it will ensure 100% return on investment. As a result, the centre will thrive.

MARKET FORCES

The unleashing of market forces as a privately, for profit set-up.

With the Office of Bharat running on a for-profit basis, market forces will ensure that rural entrepreneurs thrive. This isn't just about farmers who innovate with their produce. Secondary and tertiary sectors such as food processing or farm equipment manufacturing, as well as general services, will also thrive in rural India, as incomes rise.

END OF FEUDALISM

It will disrupt rural India's feudal and caste-based narrative.

Even in modern times, a quasi-feudal system heavily dominates rural India. However, market forces do not recognize caste or tribes. They reward the entrepreneur. By providing rural Indians with universal access to government services and economic platform and opportunities, India's centuries-old restrictive rural society will disappear in a matter of a decade.

POWERFUL

It would co-locate the four habitat drivers in one place.

Earlier, we discussed the energy and transformative effect that even one habitat driver can bring to a community. Now imagine all four habitat drivers co-located in one building, and then replicate this model four thousand times across the entire country. These hubs will eventually become the mini transport hubs for the area. Rickshaws and 'jugaad' taxis will begin to ply to and from the hub to its surrounding villages, making transport easier.

A WINDOW

It would be a window to connect Bharat with the rest of India.

The Office of Bharat will help rural Indians connect with businesses as well as urban and semi-urban Indian society. It will be their platform to sell their goods to India and receive goods and services in return. It will flatten the roadblocks that currently stand in the way of social connectedness across the urban–rural divide.

SAFETY

With all services in one location, it reduces the need to visit far-flung offices.

As a centralized office providing all government services at the block level, villagers will no longer be required to travel to far-off places to get their dues. The transport hub would ensure regular connectivity to every village in the block. Also, with police and the block officer always on hand, few other government officials would try to exploit villagers.

OVERSIGHT AND COLLABORATION

Rapid solutions and accountability.

With all block-level government servants in one place, there will be more rapid and closely monitored implementation of rural programmes. Government servants will no longer be able to make excuses about delays when the office they need the proverbial 'file' from is right next door.

Consider This

The Office of Bharat would become a window to 600 million rural consumers. This market has largely been ignored except for novel attempts such as Re 1 shampoo sachets or Rs 5 Cola bottles. The main reason has always been access; it is incredibly difficult to reach them. The existence of a transport hub at the Office of Bharat changes that. Now, you have a centralized hub not just for rural citizens to come and access government programmes but to also access private goods and services. The market opportunity is literally unprecedented.

THE SYSTEM IN ACTION

Let's see how the Office of Bharat addresses the four major problem areas we identified earlier.

Governance – the smart village *ishtyle*

With a 50-acre campus, the Office of Bharat would house the following:

The main office of the block development officer, an official who wields much authority in rural India. From here, villagers can access land records, birth and death records, and even revenue records.

A primary health centre, equipped with trained medical staff, paramedics and midwives. Thanks to its central location, this PHC can easily refer patients with complicated illnesses to major hospitals in the district or the bigger cities. It would become a centre for implementing rural health programmes and monitoring and containing outbreaks of diseases. The main police station for the block will also be located here to attend to local law-and-order needs.

Hubs that are located in natural disaster-prone zones can be equipped to double as emergency shelters. For example, they could house people during cyclones or following earthquakes or floods. The complex itself would be built to withstand earthquakes and floods. It could even become a refuge spot during riots as policemen and medical facilities would be nearby. A helipad atop the administrative or medical block would enable rapid mobilization of not just medical care, but also security personnel.

If you look at America, if there is any major national issue, the president himself would address the people on television. Even we sitting in India know what the US president is saying. Indian leaders tend to give only one or two public speeches each year and most of them repeat the same points over and over again. This is not to suggest that the prime minister has to come and speak publicly on every issue, but the government must create spaces where it can address citizens more directly. It needs to have a face that people can relate to.

This is where the big screen in the quadrangle comes into play. Politicians will not have to waste time hiring helicopters to shuttle from one place to another. During election time, political parties can buy air time on each of the big screens to air their views to the citizens.

During national emergencies, such as calamities or war, the big screens can relay crucial details like emergency phone numbers or public safety information and become a trusted source.

When such events are not taking place, corporates can pay for their ads to run in the central quadrangle. In the evenings, film distributors can air movies or TV shows. The money earned from political and corporate revenues can go straight towards the upkeep and maintenance of the hub.

The Rural Economy

Each hub would house a sabzi mandi where farmers can sell their wares. Each sale will be weighed and checked for quality. These measures will be recorded electronically and uploaded to a centralized database. The reason for doing so will be explored later in this chapter.

The hub will also have a granary and cold storage to store perishable items before they're shipped off to the market.

Finally, local entrepreneurs can run food-processing units at the hub to turn fresh, raw produce from the farms into foods such as jams, juices or pickles.

Rural artisans and handicraft experts would be able to sell their wares to the market and also have a platform to distribute their products nationally and globally.

The hub will provide a few guest rooms for visitors from outside the area, such as government officials, people visiting families in the area, or salespersons who are on market visits to local retail shops. These rooms can become an additional source of revenue for the hub to maintain itself.

In addition, there will be retail shops and restaurants for consumers, as well as hardware and supplies stores for farmers, blacksmiths, tailors, and so on.

Finally, banks and money-transfer facilities would go a big way in connecting the rural economy to the mainline economy.

Lack of access to market information is a key aspect that is hurting India's farmers. One of the main components of the hub will be the 'Big Screen'. This will constantly display the latest food prices through a centralized feed. This way farmers no longer have to rely on the middleman for information. They will know the fair price for their grain and also be able to demand it from buyers.

The real revolution for India will only happen if villages are thriving economies and great habitats to live in. This will ensure that people will not have a push out of the village and head to the city for opportunities. Now, if we have created these hubs, a great school, sporting infrastructure and retail shops, great policing, a post office, bank branches – everything that you need in terms of convenience – our villages will be wired to the world.

The engine of the rural economy is agriculture. To create a great agriculture revolution, we need to understand what it is plaguing agriculture today.

New-Age Granaries and Cold Storage

As we mentioned earlier, when a farmer brings in his produce, it will be checked for quality, weighed and then immediately stored in a 10 × 10 × 10 feet, RFID-encrypted container called the cocoon. This cocoon would be specially designed to be airtight, watertight, dust-proof, rodent-proof and made of food-grade materials. The cocoon will also be marked for its quality and identified by the farmer who produced it. This container will then be entered into a National Food Inventory called the Food-I (pronounced 'foodie').

For more details on why this system is superior to the current PDS and how it will work, please refer to the further section on Dematerializing Agriculture.

Real-Time Information

Small-scale farming, as we explained earlier, is an economically unviable profession in India. The problem is they do not have real-time information with which to make a decision to sell. The buyer, in this case the middleman, has an incentive to hide real market prices from the farmer so that he makes a higher profit when he sells the produce in the cities. So, the same fruit which sells at Rs 50 in the city was bought from the farmer at just Rs 10 per kg. None of that extra value percolates down to the farmer. There are two solutions to this. First, the dematerialization of agriculture, which has been discussed below; and second, flashing live market prices for all locally produced foods on the big screen in the quadrangle during market hours. Farmers can check the latest prices before selling their goods to the sellers, thus ensuring a fairer price for themselves.

The WOWBharat.org Portal

India's villages have a wealth of rural handicrafts from art work to textiles, pottery and furniture. Every state has its own unique styles and designs. The trouble is rural artisans have suffered largely because they are unable to sell their wares to the market and get a fair price for it. Some organizations such as FabIndia have developed a model, but this is just one such company.

Imagine if every rural artisan could sell his or her wares through a single website – the Window of the World Bharat or WOWBharat.org. The site would display handicrafts from every state and have information about the artist producing it. The products would be searchable by category (saris, textiles, painting, sculpture) or by state. Visitors could buy straight from the site and the artist would begin producing a custom-made piece of artwork for the buyer. Bespoke artwork would ensure a healthy price for the artist.

What's more, the buyer would be assured that the artisan is fairly paid because the billing system would be programmed to split profits evenly. Fifty percent would go straight to the artisan's bank account, which is now accessible to him at the rural hub. Forty percent would go into local projects and charities. A final 10% would go towards profits and maintenance of the WOWBharat portal.

This would revive India's dying handicraft traditions by ensuring a fair wage for the artist and access to his or her products for a global market.

Once the artwork is produced, the artist has to go to the local post office at the rural hub and ship it off to the buyer. The money would already be waiting for him in his bank account. From there, he can also collect new orders from other buyers.

Food-Processing Units

Food-processing units based at the hub could directly procure produce from the farmers to turn them into a variety of products such as jams, jellies, pickles and other ready-to-eat foods. This not only adds value to the produce, ensuring higher prices for farmers, it also increases the shelf-life of the goods.

FOOD-I COCOON

REGULAR COCOON

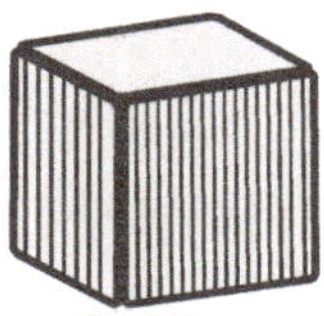

For Rice

AIR CONDITIONED COCOON

For Mangoes

COLD STORAGE COCOON

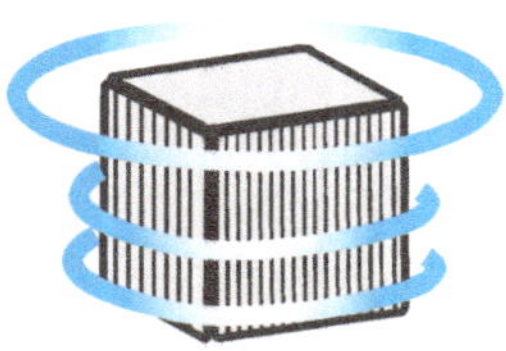

For Cherries

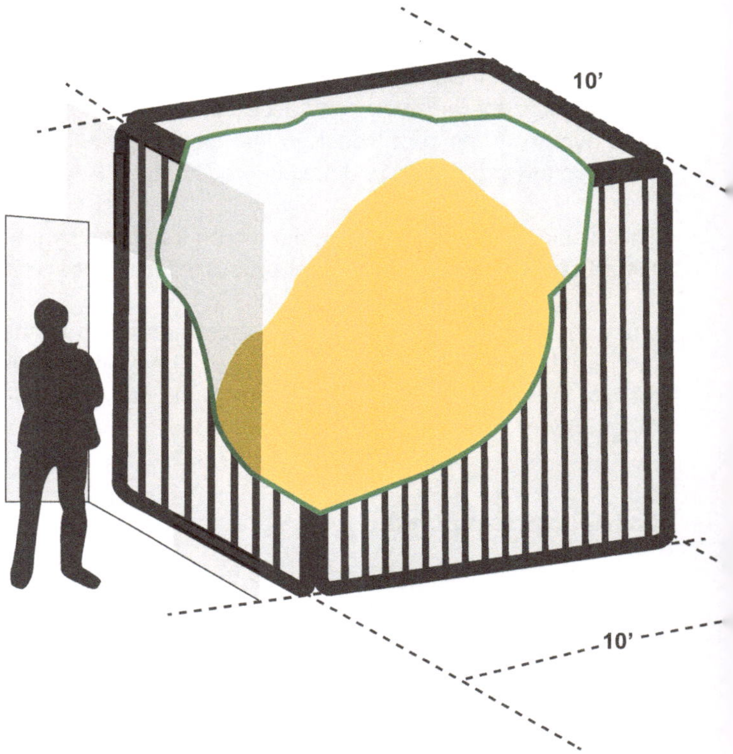

Air-Tight **Water-Tight** **Dust-Proof**

The National Food Inventory Corporation shall own the cocoons and offer them on lease to farmers for a percentage of the sale proceeds of the produce stored in the cocoons, much like a mall owner leasing out space on revenue-share basis.

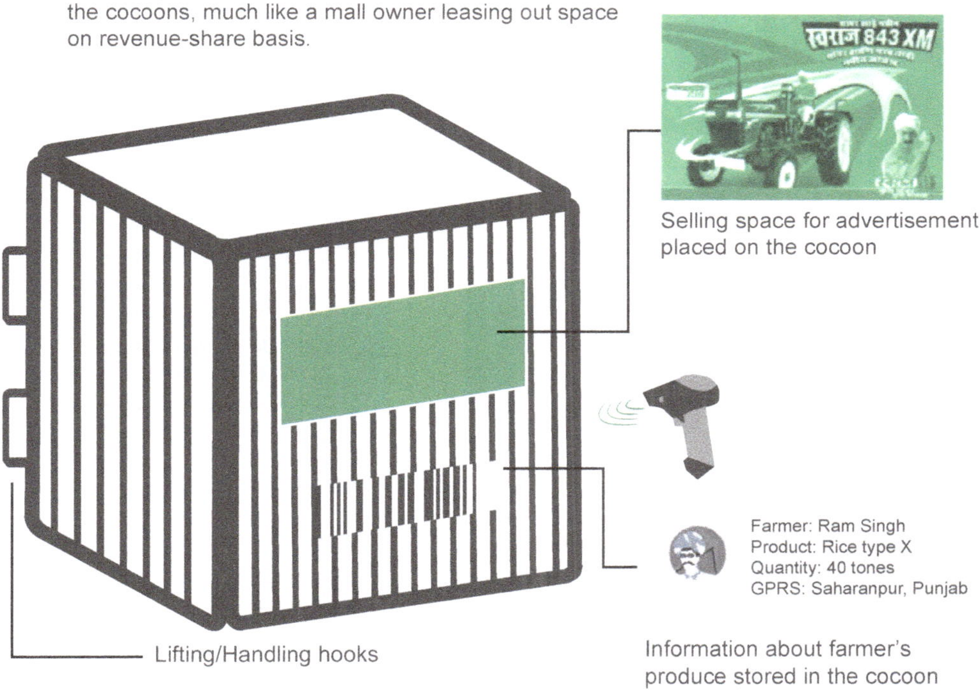

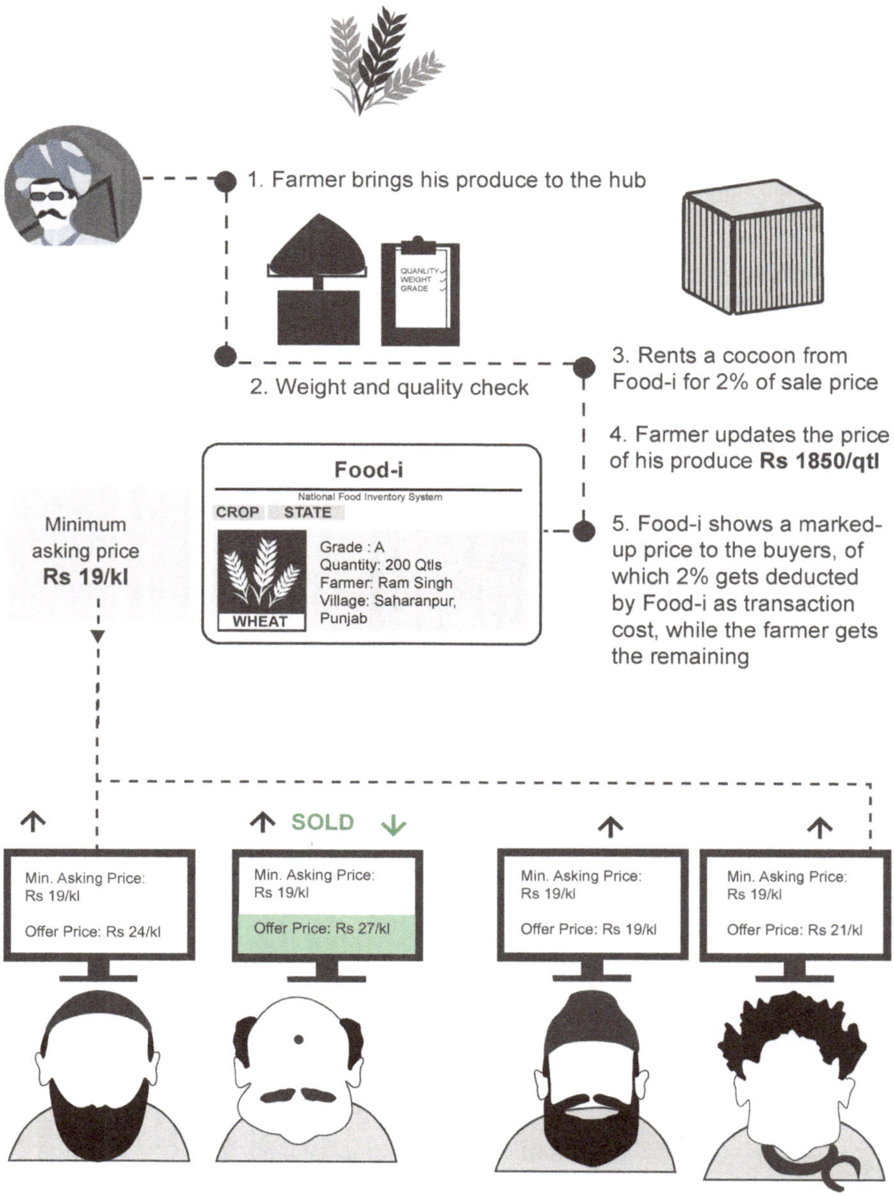
1. Farmer brings his produce to the hub
QUANLITY
WEIGHT
GRADE
2. Weight and quality check
3. Rents a cocoon from Food-i for 2% of sale price
4. Farmer updates the price of his produce **Rs 1850/qtl**
5. Food-i shows a marked-up price to the buyers, of which 2% gets deducted by Food-i as transaction cost, while the farmer gets the remaining
Food-i
National Food Inventory System
CROP STATE
WHEAT
Grade : A
Quantity: 200 Qtls
Farmer: Ram Singh
Village: Saharanpur, Punjab
Minimum asking price **Rs 19/kl**
SOLD
Min. Asking Price: Rs 19/kl
Offer Price: Rs 24/kl
Min. Asking Price: Rs 19/kl
Offer Price: Rs 27/kl
Min. Asking Price: Rs 19/kl
Offer Price: Rs 19/kl
Min. Asking Price: Rs 19/kl
Offer Price: Rs 21/kl

Dematerializing Agriculture

This is a powerful concept because anything that gets dematerialized becomes highly efficient as it becomes a part of the frictionless economy. The first thing that human beings dematerialized were words. They enabled us to communicate quickly and unambiguously. That's why languages and words and ideas were so powerful, because they were an effortless means of communicating our thoughts.

In fact, to extend the argument, letters and books dematerialized people. You no longer had to be present at the place where your interlocutor was to convey a message. Emails took this concept one step further by eliminating time as a factor in communication.

The next thing to get dematerialized was money. In the barter system, the only way economics could work was if you exchanged apples for oranges. Suddenly you had a currency that denoted a value and you could carry it around with you easily.

Even shares, once dematerialized, dramatically increased the volume of stock market trading. No longer did traders have to wait for each individual share to be logged into the system each time they were bought and sold. Automated, dematerialized shares could now be traded at the click of a button, making the process faster and more efficient by several orders of magnitude.

If you come to more recent times, the moment we created computer software, it dematerialized products themselves. You could make copies quickly, or transport at the speed of light.

Similarly, imagine a situation where you have some farmers who have 20 cocoons of wheat in Maharashtra and some with 20 cocoons in West Bengal and some with 20 cocoons in Punjab. These cocoons, as we mentioned, are tested for quality and given ratings. Then the containers are recorded in a computerized National Food Inventory or Food-I, and available for trading on an open and transparent online system. The moment you do this, the level of transactions with go up dramatically.

A new ecosystem that empowers farmers and consumers, upscales quality through measurement, brings down prices by removing middlemen and eliminates hoarding by bringing in all real-time data on a transparent universal platform.

Say, I'm a buyer in Delhi. I don't know where or how many A-grade quality containers of wheat are available. With this new system, I place an order on the Food-I for 20 cocoons of wheat at Rs 20 a kg. The system will be able to efficiently cater to my order from the nearest available consignment in Punjab. This might take maybe one day to reach me, instead of ordering it from West Bengal, which would take 4 days. This will revolutionize the selling and buying of agricultural produce.

This system could also be designed to work like the stock market, whereby buyers can bid electronically on prices for each cocoon of food produce. The highest bidder wins the shipment. Farmers can directly benefit from such competition because it ensures them of a higher price for their goods and helps in making the market more transparent. They also do not have to worry about being cheated of their hard-earned money as all transactions would be electronically recorded and the proceeds from the sales would automatically be credited into the farmers' bank accounts, which are also located at the hub.

And this system would begin at the rural hubs itself. A team can take in the agricultural produce from the farmer at the sabzi mandi, check it for quality, weigh it, pack it for shipment in a standard-size container and get it ready for a buyer. All these parameters – including weight, quality and the identity of the farmer – can be recorded digitally so you know exactly what kind of produce and how much of it came from which farmer.

Third parties can be engaged to set standards for A-grade or B-grade wheat so that both buyers and farmers know exactly what standards are expected from each other. This way, prices can also be set more fairly and transparently.

Cocoon's mobility

- Farmer putting produce in the cocoon 'at the farm'

- Cocoon gets taken to village collection point/office of bharat depot

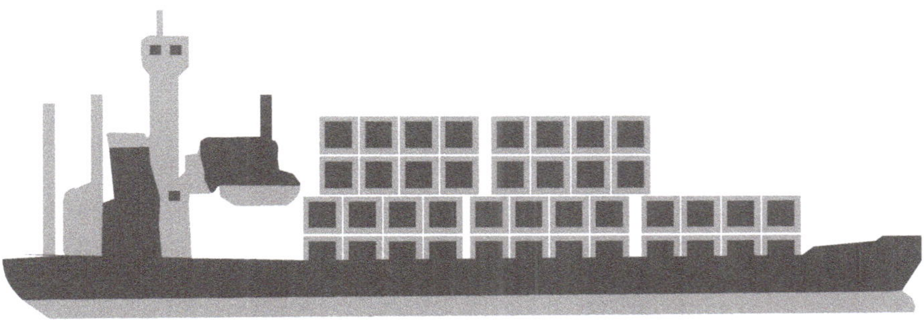

- Cocoon can be taken to other states by different modes of transports – train and ships

Once you start dematerializing food produce into electronic records, you can bring in much more efficiency. For example, the payments can all be settled via electronic bank transfers, which will be linked straight to the farmer and buyer's bank accounts. And the food itself can be transported via the Indian postal service's new logistics wing, which will also have cold-storage transport facilities, should the need arise.

Imagine the day when a farmer sells his entire harvest at the Food-I godown. Then, by the time he's walked over to the car showroom, on the other side of the hub, the money from the sales has already been deposited into his account and he's ready to buy a brand new car for his family!

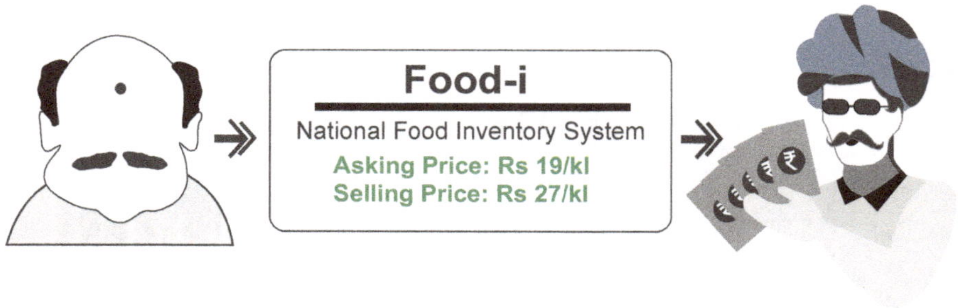

The farmer's Food-I statement would also inform him that he has received 20.5% more than his minimum quoted price because now there is competition among buyers for his produce. This would be an instant feedback mechanism for the farmer to understand how the new system is immensely beneficial to him.

EDUCATION, SKILLS AND SPORT

The hub would include a middle or senior school for local students.
The schools will be equipped with a sports academy and playgrounds to practice games such as cricket, hockey, football or track and field, swimming and so on. Each school would have well-stocked science and computer labs.
A separate facility for polytechnic and vocational skills training for adults. Here, adults can upgrade existing skills or learn new ones. There can also be an adult literacy programme that teaches rural citizens to read and write, not just in the local language, but perhaps also in English.

Today, teachers don't want to work in rural India because the facilities are poor. Now imagine this beautiful infrastructure in which they can teach, which also houses other facilities to make their lives easier. There can be a proper dormitory for teachers and even a smart home for headmasters. They can enjoy a decent lifestyle in a relaxed and well-equipped atmosphere. In addition, the design phase could address another problem rural students face – the absence of a clean toilet.

Volunteerism would also rise with students from urban areas spending a few weeks each year teaching rural students through programmes such as Teach For India.

There is an added benefit. Many teachers in rural India play truant at the moment because there is no one to supervise their attendance. If all the facilities are centralized at the rural hub and attendance of government officials is taken using biometric means, errant teachers will not be able to skip classes. This has a direct benefit on the outcomes of the children in class.

Adult skills would be another major focus. Companies are desperately looking for skilled labourers but simply do not find enough of them. By providing facilities for polytechnic and vocational schools, private companies can invest in designing and running the training. Each year, they train as many workers as they require and hire them straight out of these schools, reducing the headache of having to hunt for workers.

Adult workers could gain immediate benefits by upskilling themselves. Farmers in particular can learn new seed techniques, new irrigation methods, better crop management, new sales and marketing techniques, which will bring immediate returns to their incomes. Rural women can learn new skills to earn supplemental incomes for their homes from traditional handicrafts to skills that could place them in marketing or customer-facing roles or even operating plant machinery.

Adult literacy is another low-hanging fruit. By improving literacy rates, we will enable greater participation by rural folk in our democracy and economy, strengthening both immeasurably. This will have tremendous spin-off benefits.

When it comes to sports, we have the second-largest population in the world but still fail to get respectable results at the international level. At the rural hubs, one could include a self-contained sports academy with a cricket practice pitch, swimming pool, track-and-field facilities, volleyball, basketball, kabaddi multipurpose court.

These sports academies can be privately run by rural entrepreneurs. They can charge students nominal fees for professional coaching and equipment, while using that to maintain the facilities. This way, the government does not need to be involved in upkeep and maintenance.

Millions of young children dream of a career in sport but have no facilities to learn. If you want India to do better at the international level and develop a viable sports industry, then we need more kids playing sports. The rural hub will have enough space to house these facilities and will operate on a pay-and-play basis. Teams or individuals can rent out the facilities for a nominal fee, which could go towards upkeep.

The softer, less-appreciated benefit of more Indians participating in sports is that it will teach valuable soft skills such as team work, leadership and empathy to millions of young children in a manner in which only sports is capable of.

This will also be a great way for sports coaches to earn a living, now that a new infrastructure would exist.

Bharat Meets Desi Meets India

The final part of this puzzle isn't so much a solution to a real problem as much as it is the leveraging of a new opportunity. This is about irrigating one's roots or a backward integration of sorts.

Imagine a software professional in the Bay Area who feels they want to give back to their village in, say, Andhra Pradesh. So why not create a system that can help them counsel, support and create a brighter understanding of the world and its opportunities for young kids back home. Let's say this man or woman in the Bay Area is in their 30s or 40s. They mentor a young, aspiring software student in Hyderabad. Then, in turn, these students in Hyderabad mentor two or three younger students in Andhra Pradesh's Guntur district, along with guidance from their mentors in the Bay Area.

The rural students will be studying at the middle- or high-school in the Office of Bharat. They may be interested in computers, mechanics, fashion, agriculture or automobiles. With some smart software, their interests can be matched with mentors in the cities, whose interests can be matched with the diaspora abroad. So now four people in the village, two in an Indian city and one in the US are all connected. They are going to support each other, thanks to their common roots and shared professional interests.

The mentorship doesn't even have to be structured. It may start out with something as simple as Diwali or New Year greetings. Then one day, during a conversation, one of the students indicates an interest in tigers. And the mentor sends him four books about the the animals. Slowly, a relationship develops where the mentor gradually becomes a career counsellor, helping the students decide what subjects to pick in Class X or what stream to pick in college. Perhaps they can even guide them on which colleges in the US or UK provide scholarships to Indian students.

This is an amazing opportunity to connect three very different worlds, all of which share the same roots. Right now this connectedness has disappeared even though modern technology permits it in unprecedented ways.

This interaction will improve soft skills such as speaking and writing – after all, this interaction will take place over the internet and communicating with someone with better skills will only sharpen one's own.

So, we've not just created empathy, connection and support, we have also greatly boosted the self-confidence of a whole generation.

The government could also consider special screenings on the big screen of profiles of successful individuals from this district who made successful careers either in their villages or outside to inspire residents with the possibilities

Funding the Desi-Bharat Connect

The interesting question here is how do you support all of this? Who is going to facilitate it? Well, there are two possible solutions here. One option is to simply use existing networks such as Facebook or Google+ to create the connectedness.

The other option is to invite internet pioneers or entrepreneurs to create a customized version of such social networks. Perhaps the most attractive aspect would be the advertising revenues. After all, a potential long-term market of a billion people would be attractive to any advertiser or entrepreneur who intends to profit from such vast advertising.

Consider This

One of the positive side effects of the 'Office of Bharat' can be a revitalizing influence on a nearly-dead government service. With email now relegating letters and postcards to the dustbin of history, India's postal services have begun to die a slow death. Now imagine if the postal department was turned into a logistics partner for the 'Office of Bharat'. The postal department already reaches into every single village in the country. But what if it upgraded its reach by also providing logistical services to corporates at one end and farmers at the other?

Retailers would be able to deliver goods and services by simply piggybacking on the existing postal network. Farmers would be able to transport produce and processed foods to markets in the city at a low cost. The investment in buying new equipment and upgrading postal facilities for this transformation would easily be recouped by charging clients competitive rates for using the logistics service. The postal service would have found a new mandate and mission in not just connecting India, but revitalizing itself and the people!

This way we can ensure that the postal service itself as a whole won't go the way of the telegram.

The Way Forward

The first step towards creating an Office of Bharat would be for the central and state governments to jointly create an Office of Bharat Development Corporation or OOBDC. This entity would run on a profit-and-loss account basis.

The OOBDC would be the entity that awards contracts to concessionaires to build and operate Offices of Bharat in every block of every district in India. As per the contract, the concessionaires would build, own, operate and sub-lease all economic functions of each Office of Bharat, while maintaining the facilities for government offices and services.

Concessionaires shall bid to win contracts to kick-start work. The contract would award winning concessionaires 50 acres of land upon which they would build the Office of Bharat, as well as an additional 50 acres of land, which they can utilise to build efficient, rural, real estate developments. This would serve as an added economic incentive to participate in the bidding.

The concessionaires would also be required to incorporate a local flavour in the design of the OOBs so that it appeals to local sensibilities without seeming alien. Since public participation should be encouraged, the designs can be put to a public vote, with a couple of them making it to the 'build' stage. The OOBs can be built using a cookie-cutter approach – by simply copying the prototype structure – across all locations. The structures can be pre-fabricated to save on money, building materials and, crucially, construction time.

Effectively, the government develops brand-new rural infrastructure without spending a penny, and earns thousands of crores of rupees in additional revenue from the winning bids.

The Way Forward

CENTRAL AND STATE GOVERNMENT

OFFICE OF BHARAT DEVELOPMENT CORPORATION

An entity that runs on profit-and-loss account basis

OOBC awards contracts to concessionaires

Concessionaire bids to win contract

On winning contract concessionnaire builds, owns, operates & sub-leases all economic functions of each Office of Bharat

Also be required to incorporate local flavour in the design of the OOB

Revenue Model

Cost-Benefit

So why would the concessionaires participate in this? Two words: market opportunity. Imagine a hub located in a block of ten villages, each with roughly 20,000 people. A single shop owner or retailer would have a captive customer base of at least 200,000 people! Even though the goods sold here would have low margins, owing to the lower-income clientele, the volumes opportunity would be hard to pass up for any business, especially since we are talking of anywhere from 50 to 100 such block-level hubs in each state. Granted, not all blocks would have 200,000 residents, but companies can be given incentives to also work in low-density blocks by awarding them a certain number of high-density blocks.

Now, India has 672 districts. If we assume an average of 5 blocks to a district, that would give us 3,360 blocks where we will build a hub.

If each pre-fabricated hub costs Rs 50 crore, this would mean a total one-time construction budget of just Rs 2,00,000 crore. What's more, this cost would be borne entirely by corporate concessionaires. In addition, MGNREGS workers would have been engaged in verifiable work with tangible outcomes. Using pre-fabricated methods, the hubs could be built in less than a year with proper planning and execution. We would have created world-class rural infrastructure that could transform rural India for the better.

If executed correctly, most of the money invested in the project can actually go straight to the state and villages. Construction materials and labour will be sourced directly from the village. Cement and steel plants from that state will supply raw materials. And it will also give an opportunity for every state to do some genuine state-centric architecture; not that architecture is a necessity – but it will be a good spin off.

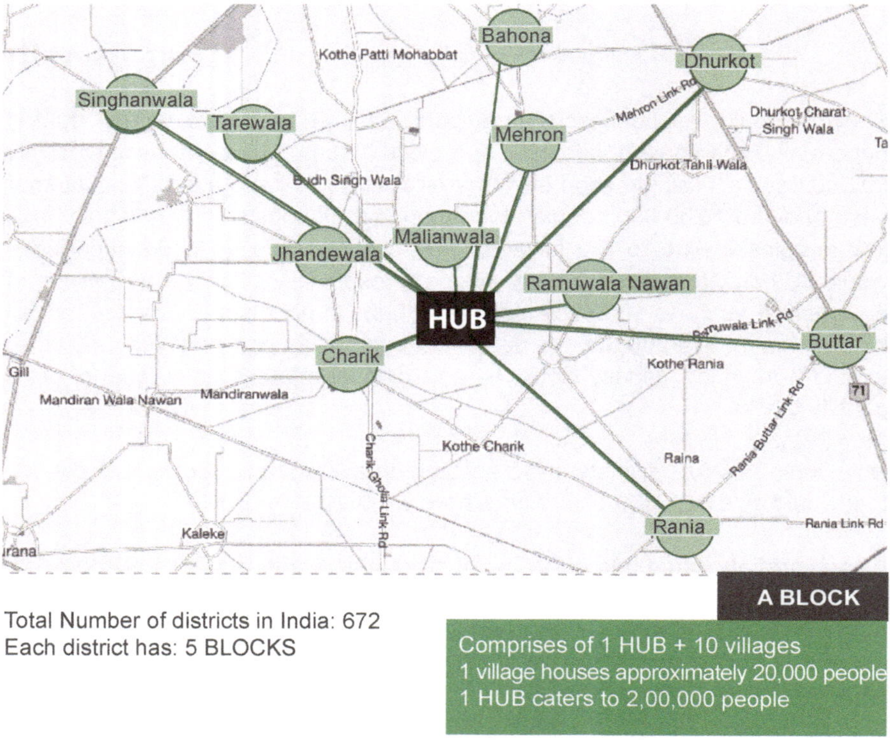

A BLOCK

Comprises of 1 HUB + 10 villages
1 village houses approximately 20,000 people
1 HUB caters to 2,00,000 people

Total Number of districts in India: 672
Each district has: 5 BLOCKS

672 DISTRICTS = 3,360 BLOCKS (~4,000 Blocks)

Cost of Pre-Fabricated HUB = Rs 50 crore
4,000 HUBS will cost = Rs 2,00,000 crore

REVENUE MODEL

India's GDP
Rs 114 lakh crore

Agricultural GDP
Rs 16 lakh crore

Average Agricultural GDP

$$\frac{\text{Rs 16 lakh crore}}{\text{4,000 Blocks}} = \text{Rs 400 crore}$$

Assuming 672 Districts = ~4000 Blocks

Revenue from Commercial Developments in Office of Bharat (OoB)

OFFICE OF BHARAT
Total saleable area = 15,000 sq. ft of retail

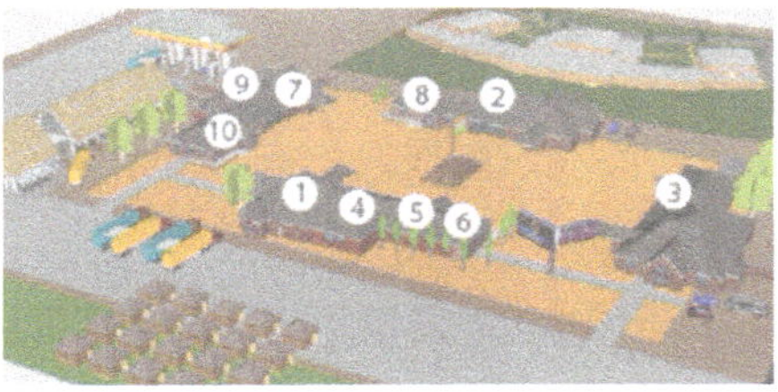

GDP of every Hub= Rs 400 crore.

1) Banks:
2x500 sq ft @Rs 35 lakh
= Rs 70 lakh

2) Pharmacy:
2x500 sq ft @Rs 15 lakh
= Rs 30 lakh

---

3) Shops/ Offices:
10 @Rs 25 lakh
= Rs 2.5 crore

4) Groceries:
2x200 sq ft @Rs 15 lakh
= Rs 30 lakh

5) Annual income from leased subzi mandi @ 0.5% of average agri GDP = Rs 2 crore

6) Auto-mobiles, bikes, tractors:
5x5000 sq ft @ Rs 2 crore
= Rs 10 crore

7) Apparel Stores:
10x1000 sq ft @Rs 50 lakh
= Rs 5 crore

8) Jewellers, Electronics, miscellaneous shops:
10x1000 sq ft @Rs 50 lakh = Rs 5 crore

9) Food outlets, Sweet shops, Offices, Rural Inn:
= Rs 5 crore

10) Total estimated income for developer:
= Rs 30 crore outright+ Rs 2 crore annual rent of subzi mandi space

---

Given these figures(and not including the un-estimated rents),
Consessions have a huge income potential for a modest initial investment of just Rs 20 crore to Rs 50 crore in the development of Office of Bharat campus.

Government shall provide 50-odd acres of land plus external infrastructure like roads, power supply.

New ecosystem

EXISTING ECOSYSTEM

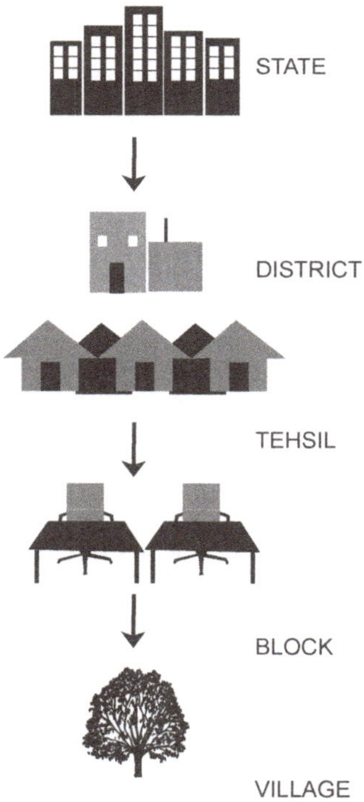

PROPOSED ECOSYSTEM

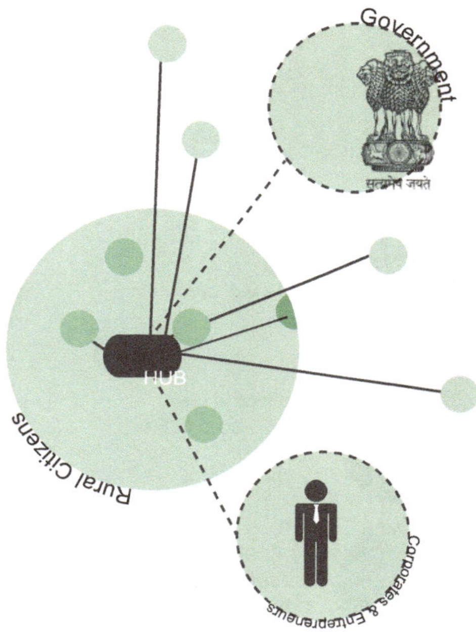

PROBLEMS (in current ecosystem)

- Unstructured
- No Homogeneity
- Decrepit State of Being
- Multiple Fiefdoms
- Working in Isolation & Anonymity

ADVANTAGES (of new ecosystem)

- Rural citizens have direct access to essential government services
- Government has platform to implement rural programs more efficiently & with maximum effect
- Corporates & entrepreneurs have direct access to rural markets
- Rural entreprenurial spirit unleashed
- The rural habitat with new jobs & modern amenities such as education, health, shopping, etc become the new destination for preferred living

The Stakeholders

Current Ecosystem

Rural citizens – currently have no connection to the government or urban life. They face grave economic hardships and find little social justice.

Government officials – currently scattered and divergent. There are no incentives or penalties for performing their work, or even showing up. Lack of infrastructure makes execution nearly impossible.

Corporates – have no way to access rural markets due to the great distances and poor infrastructure.

New Ecosystem

Rural citizens – are now assured of access to essential government services, and now have a one-stop shop for greater economic and social engagement with the rest of India, which improves their standards of living and quality of life.

Government – has a platform to implement rural programs more efficiently and with maximum effect. Also has a means of interacting and engaging with rural citizens in a manner that was not previously possible. In addition, the government will be able to create brand-new infrastructure with zero investment of public money.

Corporates and entrepreneurs – now have direct access to rural markets. They do not have to worry about poor infrastructure that hinders market access. They can also buy raw materials and farm produce wholesale, directly from the farmer. Many other market opportunities exist such as opening a rural sports academy, opening rural schools and for-profit polytechnic colleges, retail spaces, grocery and household goods stores, banks, food processing units, warehousing, transportation, and so on. The sky is the limit!

The Office of Bharat

By the Numbers

India's GDP: Rs 200 lakh crore
Agriculture is 14.1% of GDP: Rs 28 lakh crore
Average agricultural GDP per block (assuming 4,000 blocks): Rs 700 crore

Total number of Offices of Bharat (one per block): 4,000
Cost of each Office of Bharat: Rs 50 crore
Total cost of OOBs: Rs 2,00,000 crore

Total saleable areas in OOBs (commercial developments): 15,000 sq. ft of retail

Banks: 2 × 500 sq ft	@ Rs 35 lakh = Rs 70 lakh
Pharmacy: 2 × 200 sq ft	@ Rs 15 lakh = Rs 30 lakh
Groceries: 2 × 200 sq ft	@ Rs 15 lakh = Rs 30 lakh
Shops-cum-offices: 10	@ Rs 25 lakh = Rs 2.5 crore
Apparel stores: 10	@ Rs 50 lakh = Rs 5 crore
Jewellers, electronics & misc.:10	@ Rs 50 lakh = Rs 5 crore

Food outlets and sweets shops = Rs 5 crore
Automobiles, bikes, tractor showrooms = Rs 10 crore

Annual income from leased subzi mandi @ 0.5% of average agri GDP: Rs 3.5 crore

Total estimated income for developer: Rs 30 crore outright + Rs 2 crore annual rent of subzi mandi space.

Additional estimated income for developer:
Annual income from granary & Food-I.
Annual income from food processing units.
Annual income from sports academy.
Annual income from transport hub (petrol pump, repair shops, vehicle dealership)
Annual income from big screen and advertising hoardings
Annual income from rental of telecom towers
Annual income from low-cost hotel plot

Income from real estate development of additional Rs 50 crore

Given these figures (and not including the unestimated rents), developers have a huge income potential for an initial investment of just Rs 30 crore. The opportunity is immense. There is no reason any private real-estate or infrastructure developer would not be interested.

Current Growth Ratio:
Unevenly distributed

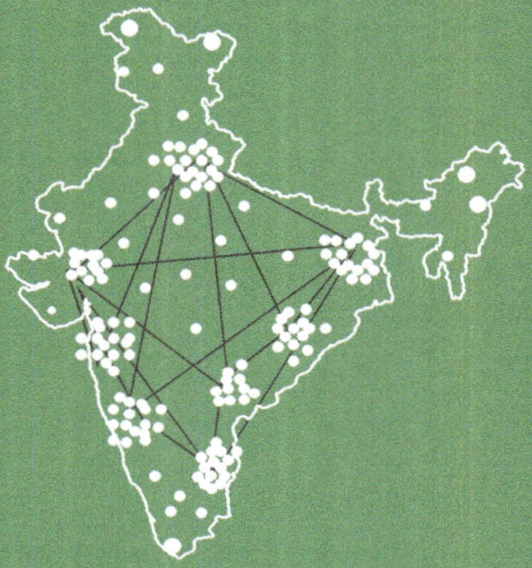

Proposed Growth Ratio:
Evenly distributed

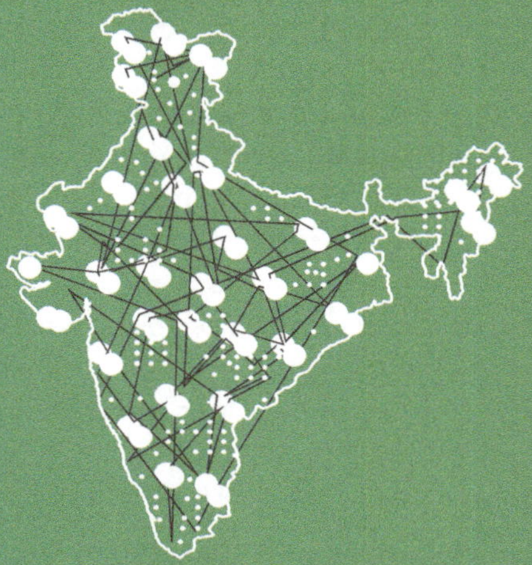

Current Ecosystem

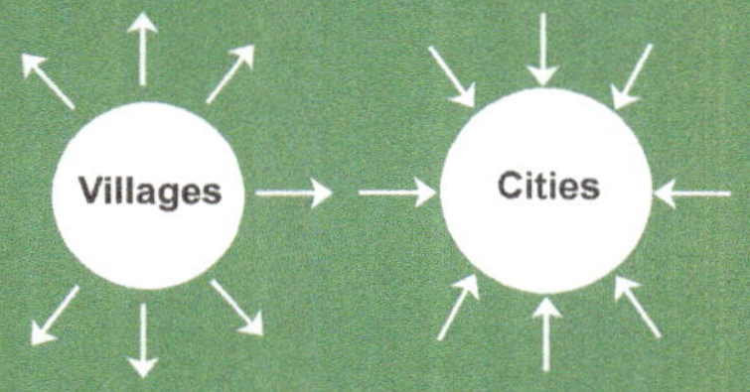

Villages PUSH Cities PULL

Proposed Ecosystem

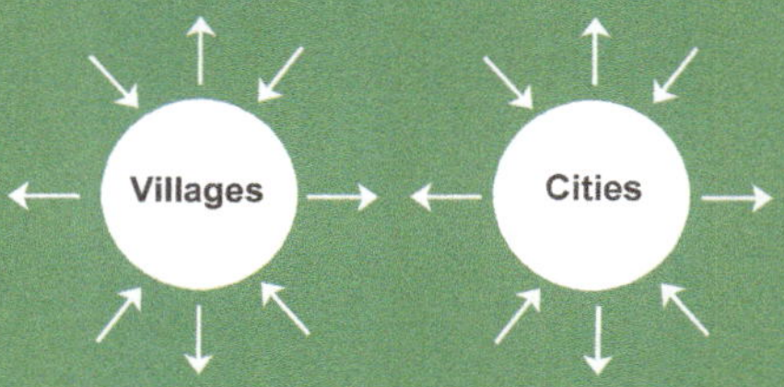

Villages PULL PUSH Cities PUSH PULL

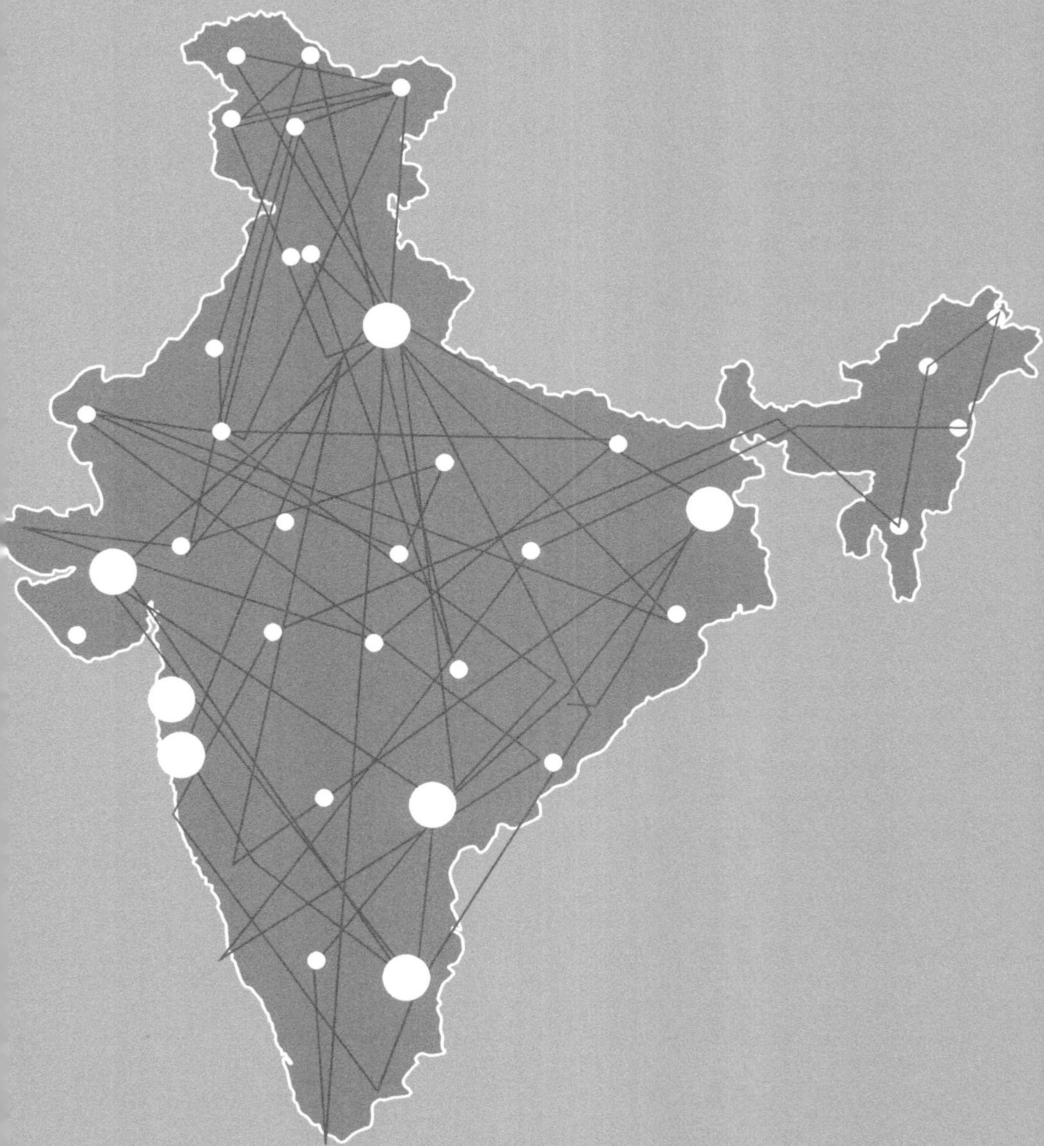

Index

Index

Index

Notes

1. http://timesofindia.indiatimes.com/articleshow/5755914.cms?utmsource=contentofinterest&utmmedium=text&utm_campaign=cpps
2. Ibid.
3. http://www.bbc.co.uk/worldservice/learningenglish/newsenglish/witn/2008/04/080407_mumbai_no_honking.shtml
4. https://www.earthsaviours.in/do-not-honk
5. http://www.missionpeaceblr.blogspot.in
6. http://www.ndtv.com/india-news/mumbai-blasts-cops-scouring-46-cctv-cameras-for-clues-461639
7. http://archive.financialexpress.com/news/no-footage-of-suicide-as-three-cctvs-on-sea-link-not-working/983055
8. https://economictimes.indiatimes.com/news/politics-and-nation/delhismove-good-but-public-transport-must-improve-beijingers/articleshow/50065095.cms?from=mdr
9. https://slate.com/technology/2008/11/honk-if-you-know-why-you-re-honking.html
10. https://economictimes.indiatimes.com/news/politics-and-nation/delhis-move-good-but-public-transport-must-improve-beijingers/articleshow/50065095.cms?from=mdr
11. Currently, these services are provided on phones and in cars by apps such as Google Maps. The Smart Citizen Card Model will, however, facilitate the provision of the same services in a far more customized manner.
12. http://www.statista.com/topics/1444/mcdonalds/

    http://overhowmanybillionserved.blogspot.in
13. https://timesofindia.indiatimes.com/city/delhi/after-cleanest-nov-day-in-years-delhi-sees-worst-pollution-of-the-season/articleshow/66519626.cms
14. http://epi.yale.edu/epi/issue-ranking/air-quality
15. http://www.financialexpress.com/news/india-ranks-155-on-environmental-performance-index/1221101

16. http://www.nytimes.com/2014/02/10/opinion/indias-particulate-problem.html?_r=0
17. http://india.blogs.nytimes.com/2012/02/01/indias-air-the-worlds-unhealthiest-study-says/
18. Vehicles account for 70% of CO (carbon monoxide), 50% of HC, 30-40% of NOx, 30% of SPM and 10% of SO2 of the total air pollution in these cities, of which two-thirds is contributed by three-wheelers alone.

    http://www.ipcbee.com/vol33/009-ICEEB2012-B023.pdf
19. http://india.blogs.nytimes.com/2012/02/01/indias-air-the-worlds-unhealthiest-study-says/
20. The Pollution Under Control (PUC) certificate is issued based on conformity to idle emission test for petrol vehicles and free acceleration smoke test for diesel vehicles.
21. http://cpcbenvis.nic.in/newsletter/inspection/ch60503.htm

    http://www.theigc.org/project/distributional-effects-of-air-quality-legislation-in-india/
22. A study by the Central Road Research Institute has found that overloading a truck by 30% leads to emissions of 119.2 gm of NOx against 3.17 gm/km under standard loading, while PM emission also goes up from 104.13 gm/km to 611.75 gm/km;

    http://timesofindia.indiatimes.com/city/delhi/10-yrs-on-CNG-advantage-lost/articleshow/10660532.cms
23. http://www.mnkjournals.com/ijlrst_files/download/Vol%201%20Issue%202/38-Ranbir%20Singh.pdf (D-232 / D-233 / D-234)
24. http://www.krishisanskriti.org/vol_image/02Jul201503070013.pdf (p.49)
25. http://www.theicct.org/sites/default/files/publications/ICCT_Briefing_IndiaPolicy Summary_20130703.pdf
26. The vehicular population in the national capital registered a 135.59 per cent jump between 1999-2000 and 2011-12 to touch 74.53 lakh;

    http://www.business-standard.com/article/pti-stories/74-53-lakh-vehicles-in-delhi-survey-113031900581_1.html
27. Even when compliance rates improve and stabilize (at about 90%) in

subsequent years, we would still make as a nation about Rs 20,900 crores across the 10 major cities in India, which would be more than sufficient to provide for the maintenance and upkeep of any established infrastructure.

28. Based on the argument made in the instance of the Honk Model.
29. The Global Status Report on Road Safety 2013 estimates that more than 2,31,000 people are killed in road traffic crashes in India every year. Approximately half of all deaths on the country's roads are among vulnerable road users – motor cyclists, pedestrians and cyclists;

    http://www.who.int/violence_injury_prevention/road_traffic/countrywork/ind/en/
30. http://timesofindia.indiatimes.com/city/indore/Traffic-violations-dropped-by-60-in-past-one-month/articleshow/16733364.cms

    http://timesofindia.indiatimes.com/city/noida/Traffic-cops-aim-for-road-safety/articleshow/29329993.cms
31. http://timesofindia.indiatimes.com/city/delhi/Pay-challan-get-a-driving-lesson/articleshow/14917656.cms?referral=PM
32. Motor Vehicles Act, 1988
33. http://timesofindia.indiatimes.com/city/delhi/Hike-in-traffic-fines-to-add-muscle-to cops/articleshow/12105824.cms
34. http://timesofindia.indiatimes.com/city/pune/CCTVs-lose-connectivity-trip-Punes-intelligent-traffic-system/articleshow/16415856.cms
35. http://www.indiantrafficnews.com/2007/04/11/146-mn-violations-daily-only-11000-booked/
36. Number of monthly active Facebook users worldwide as of 4th quarter of 2014 (in millions);

    http://www.statista.com/statistics/264810/number-of-monthly-active-facebook-users-worldwide/
37. What does it take to work at one of the world's best companies? http://www.octoberrecruitment.com/what-does-it-take-to-work-at-one-of-the-worlds-best-companies/#sthash.a1iO1PXL.dpuf
38. http://www.hindustantimes.com/newdelhi/delhi-has-more-mobile-

connections-than-people/article1-615633.aspx

39. http://timesofindia.indiatimes.com/city/delhi/1322-traffic-rule-breaches-in-25-secs-at-Dhaula-Kuan/articleshow/17070803.cms
40. For an introduction to the Smart Citizen Card Model, see Chapter 1, 'Towards a Honk Free India'.
41. http://rierc.org/social/paper114.pdf
42. http://bharatkalyan97.blogspot.in/2012/05/reducing-corruption-using-technology-r.html
43. This premise is introduced and discussed in greater detail in Chapter 1, 'Towards a Honk Free India'.
44. For an introduction and discussion of this concept, see Chapter 1, 'Towards a Honk Free India'.
45. http://timesofindia.indiatimes.com/city/nagpur/Traffic-violation-cases-on-the-rise-and-so-is-the-fine-collection/articleshow/6198945.cms
46. 46. http://www.indianexpress.com/news/half-the-cctvs-at-traffic-junctions-nonfunctional-traffic-dept-report/999101
47. For a similar economic model around the CCTV camera, see 'The Civic Cop';

    https://www.indiegogo.com/projects/saving-road-accident-victims-in-india
48. In emergency medicine, the Golden Hour refers to the first 60 minutes after the occurrence of a major multi-system trauma. It is widely believed that the victim's chances of survival are the greatest if he or she receives definitive care within the first hour of a severe injury. http://www.urgentcare.co.in/the-golden-hour/
49. For a more detailed discussion on how this is possible, please see the sections on 'Aligning Traffic Infrastructure', and the 'Pedestrian Commission of India', pp. 83-88.
50. http://www.bloomberg.com/bw/magazine/content/10_51/b4208012561750.htm
51. In conjunction with Civic Cop, p. 10.

52. http://timesofindia.indiatimes.com/city/delhi/Fast-track-new-Rao-Tula-Ram-flyover/articleshow/30813636.cms

    http://timesofindia.indiatimes.com/city/delhi/Parallel-Rao-Tula-Ram-flyover-to-take-2-years/articleshow/34393463.cms
53. http://geospatialworld.net/Paper/Application/ArticleView.aspx?aid=30276
54. http://www.extremetech.com/extreme/178777-facebooks-facial-recognition-software-is-now-as-accurate-as-the-human-brain-but-what-now
55. This concept of a 'cop licensing apparatus' is introduced and discussed in the context of 'Regulating the Informal Sector' in Chapter 6, 'Safer Cities'.
56. For more on the Emergency Button, please see Chapter 6, 'Safer Cities'.
57. *Kumau puttar* is Punjabi colloquial slang for a child who becomes an earning member of the family.
58. For a discussion on this concept see 'Paving the Way for a Safer City.
59. This premise is discussed in detail in Chapter 4, Safer Cities.
60. http://indianexpress.com/article/cities/delhi/hit-by-an-e-rickshaw-child-slips-out-of-mothers-arms-into-pan-of-boiling-oil/
61. http://www.bbc.com/news/world-asia-india-20765320
62. http://www.bbc.com/news/world- asia-india-20860569
63. http://in.reuters.com/article/2013/01/29/delhi-gang-rape-justice-verma-committee-idINDEE90S03W20130129
64. http://www.telegraphindia.com/1131029/jsp/calcutta/story_17504610.jsp#VOjIgSkxGfQ
65. http://www.newskarnataka.com/exclusive/Two-years-after-Nirbhaya-the-rod-is-still-a-weapon-of-choice/
66. http://timesofindia.indiatimes.com/india/No-fast-track-courts-for-rape-cases-in-UP-Bihar-and Gujarat/articleshow/39974350.cms
67. http://timesofindia.indiatimes.com/city/delhi/Fast-track-courts-slow-down-justice/articleshow/22774295.cms
68. http://www.sascv.org/ijcjs/pdfs/mishrapatelijcjs2013istissue.pdf
69. http://www.downtoearth.org.in/content/cse-road-safety-audit-delhi-tops-

road-accident-deaths-city-most-unsafe-cyclists-pedestrians

70. http://www.downtoearth.org.in/content/cse-road-safety-audit-delhi-tops-road-accident-deaths-city-most-unsafe-cyclists-pedestrians
71. http://online.wsj.com/articles/SB121615191024755599
72. http://www.marketresearchindia.in/Real_Estate_&_Construction_Market_Research_in_India.pdf
73. http://dgfasli.nic.in/working_group/chap_1.htm

    http://www.wsj.com/articles/SB121615191024755599
74. http://www.theguardian.com/world/2013/mar/31/india-tourist-visits-down-delhi-gang-rape
75. http://thecityfix.com/blog/where-are-footpaths-case-protecting-pedestrian-rights-india-himadri-das-sahana-goswami/
76. http://india.blogs.nytimes.com/2013/01/16/india-has-one-of-the-lowest-police-population-ratios-in-the-world/?_r=0
77. http://www.contracostatimes.com/ci_22792978/parents-volunteers-help-kids-get-safely-school-after
78. http://timesofindia.indiatimes.com/india/Beas-river-tragedy-7-keypoints/articleshow/36357851.cms
79. Lux is a metric unit of measurement for luminance. Luminance is defined as the intensity of light falling on a surface.
80. http://infochangeindia.org/women/analysis/a-brief-history-of-the-battle-against-sexual-harassment-at-the-workplace.html, http://www.mondaq.com/india/x/348338/employment+litigation+tribunals/Overview+Of+The+Sexual+Harassment+Of+Women+At+Workplace

    http://www.mondaq.com/india/x/238076/Discrimination+Disability+Sexual+Harassment/Indias+New+Labour+Law+Prevention+Of+Sexual+Harassment+At+The+Workplace
81. http://timesofindia.indiatimes.com/city/delhi/High-court-for-50-women-cops-in-Delhi-Police/articleshow/23476333.cms
82. Although most police stations have a 'Women's Desk' or a female constable especially assigned to women complainants, these constables are often

absent or not available due to other police work or duties. What is needed, therefore, is a person who is dedicated to resolving women's issues and is trained to understand them.

83. See introduction to A.P.J. Abdul Kalam's book Wings of Fire: An Autobiography.
84. This idea was first shared by the author, Goonmeet Chauhan, at a conference organized by ORF on 'Safer Cities' in February 2014, convened by Ms Nishta Gautam and has since been implemented by the Delhi Police with some appropriate changes in the form of the Himmat App. For more on the Himmat App, see Mobile App 'Himmat' for Women's Safety Launched in Delhi, January 2, 2015. *http://www.ndtv.com/delhi-news/mobile-app-himmat-for-womens-safety-launched-in-delhi-721221*
85. http://www.endvawnow.org/uploads/browser/files/understanding_womens_safety.pdf
86. See Chapter 5.
87. For a more comprehensive discussion on the PCI, the Civic Cop and the issue of pedestrian safety, see Chapter 3.
88. For a detailed discussion on the non-punitive model of the Civic Cop, see Chapter 3.
89. http://www.livemint.com/Opinion/rEm1CHLyACL8mtbr0IU3xI/Indias-street-vendors-come-out-of-the-shadows.html
90. http://www.telegraph.co.uk/news/worldnews/asia/india/10574342/Danish-woman-gang-raped-in-the-heart-of-Delhis-tourist-area.html
91. http://www.documents.dgs.ca.gov/dgs/pio/facts/LA%20workshop/climate.pdf
92. http://in.usgbc.org/leed
93. http://www.usgbc.org/Docs/Archive/General/Docs4045.pdf
94. Nearly 60,000 Global LEED Green Building Projects Span 10.6 Billion Square Feet: New Report from USGBC with Introduction from Boston Mayor Menino, November 7, 2013.
95. http://www.usgbc.org/articles/leed-spans-833-million-square-feet-green-building-space-india http://in.usgbc.org/articles/nearly-60000-global-leed-green-building-projects-span-106-billion-square-feet-new-report-us

96. USGBC's Green Building Certification Institute (GBCI) offers various accreditations to people who demonstrate knowledge of the LEED rating system, including LEED Accredited Professional (LEED AP), LEED Green Associate, and since 2011, LEED Fellows, the highest designation for LEED professionals.
97. http://www.saveenergy.co.in/energy-labeling.php
98. http://www.theteamwork.com/articles/2016-1503-categories-residential-colonies-properties-delhi.html
99. Magic Bricks.com is India's largest real estate portal
100. While a potential increase in property prices might serve to influence only those residents who are interested in selling their properties, the concession on municipal taxes envisaged by the system will seek to incentivize all residents within a colony to improve safety and security and therefore ratings.
101. http://techcrunch.com/2012/02/08/tripadvisor-q4-revenue-up-30-percent-to-137-8m-net-income-up-19-percent-in-first-quarter-as-a-public-company/
102. https://investor.google.com/financial/tables.html
103. https://www.forbes.com/2008/02/24/pollution-baku-oil-biz-logistics-cx_tl_0226dirtycities_slide.html#2fb9bcf31ef2; https://www.forbes.com/2008/02/26/pollution-baku-oil-biz-logistics-cx_tl_0226dirtycities.html#2f07ea01ffe7
104. http://articles.timesofindia.indiatimes.com/2009-11-21/india/28086994_1_filth-nobel-prize-safe-drinking-water
105. http://articles.timesofindia.indiatimes.com/2011-04-12/delhi/29409713_1_landfill-site-solid-waste-garbage
106. http://www.hindustantimes.com/India-news/Mumbai/Garbage-in-Mumbai-is-BMC-s-mess/Article1-1028016.aspx
107. http://www.hindustantimes.com/News-Feed/htfordelhi/Delhi-may-drown-in-its-own-waste/Article1-1052381.aspx
108. http://india.ashoka.org/fellow/shantharam-umanath-shenai
109. http://newindianexpress.com/cities/bangalore/Garbage-woes-will-pile-up-in-festival- season/2013/08/11/article1729007.ece
110. http://www.thehindu.com/news/cities/Delhi/ten-new-prospective-landfill-sites-identified-for-delhi/article4765297.ece

111. http://www.indianexpress.com/news/-waste--not/576844/
112. http://www.waste-management-world.com/articles/print/volume-9/issue-4/features/waste-sorting-a-look-at-the-separation-and-sorting-techniques-in-todayrsquos-european-market.html
113. http://www.troymedia.com/2012/05/31/robot-arm-intelligently-sorts-waste/
114. http://www.titech.com/assets/x/50534
115. http://news.bbc.co.uk/2/hi/europe/4620041.stm
116. http://www.waste-management-world.com/articles/2011/08/12-mw-waste-to-energy-facility-planned-in-surat-india.html
117. http://articles.timesofindia.indiatimes.com/2012-06-02/delhi/319829661power-demand-power-supply-previous-highest-demand
118. http://www.source.irc.nl/page/70647
119. http://www.firstpost.com/india/toilets-in-india-the-statistics-stink-744025.html?utm_source=ref_article
120. http://indianexpress.com/article/explained/one-year-of-swachh-bharat-and-its-been-no-clean-sweep/
121. http://www.thehindu.com/opinion/editorial/public-toilets-for-our-cities/article4256374.ece
122. http://www.newindianexpress.com/cities/bangalore/The-big-fat-truth-about-public-toilets/2013/10/21/article1846059.ece
123. http://kb.keepbritaintidy.org/toilets/publications/role.pdf
124. http://www.thehindu.com/opinion/editorial/public-toilets-for-our-cities/article4256374.ece
125. http://infochangeindia.org/urban-india/cityscapes/why-public-toilets-get-clogged.html
126. Hindi colloquial slang for godfather.
127. Dubai Mega Mall – Total area 1.21 crore sq ft; leasable area 37,70,000 sq ft.
128. Thulla is Hindi colloquial slang for policeman.
129. http://www.historydiscussion.net/history-of-india/religious-and-social-reform-of-india-the-indian-renaissance/1637 http://www.ncert.nic.in/

announcements/memo_lect_series/pdf_files/appndx%202/Second%20 RabindranathTagore%20Memorial%20Lecture/FINAL%20COVER%20 OF%20RABINDRANATHA%2007-01-09.pdf

130. https://indianexpress.com/article/india/india-ranks-131-in-hdi-index-where-do-we-stand-on-gender-inequality-maternal-mortality-schooling-4579963/
131. www.olympic.it/english/medal
132. https://rosethomson.wordpress.com/tag/super-goats/
133. http://indiabudget.nic.in/es2012-13/echap-08.pdf
134. http://www.businessworld.in/article/India-Wastes-As-Much-Food-As-United-Kingdom-Consumes-Study/27-08-2017-124858

    https://timesofindia.indiatimes.com/india/Food-worth-Rs-50-thousand-crore-goes-waste-in-India-every-year/articleshow/17980873.cms
135. http://apeda.in/agriexchange/Market%20Profile/one/ONION.aspx
136. http://timesofindia.indiatimes.com/home/education/news/Indian-students-rank-2nd-last-in-global-test/articleshow/11492508.cms
137. http://www.unicef.org/india/education.html
138. https://en.wikipedia.org/wiki/Literacy_in_India
139. http://delhi.gov.in/wps/wcm/connect/doit_labour/Labour/Home/Minimum+Wages/

Architectural Projects of the Author

DESIGN FORUM
INTERNATIONAL

SELECT CITYWALK, New Delhi

CHINTELS ACROPOLIS, Gurgaon

CHINTELS CORPORATE PARK, Gurgaon

ITO SKYWALK, New Delhi

SOLAR TOWER, Jaipur

NEW COURTS BLOCK DELHI HIGH COURT, New Delhi

VANIJYA BHAWAN, New Delhi

HELIX TOWER, Dubai

BESTECH PARKVIEW SPA, Gurgaon

CYBERWALK, Manesar

About the Team

Aditi Anand (Co-author)

Aditi Anand is a writer and trained lawyer. Her professional interest is in contributing to the genres of both historical biography and narrative non-fiction as part of a cultural retelling and mediation of significant historical and contemporary events. She is currently researching a legal biography based on the life of an eminent jurist.

Pierre Fitter (Co-author)

Pierre's career has ranged from NGOs to magazine journalism, TV news anchoring and, most recently, digital marketing. When not making a living off an increasingly #DigitalIndia, he dreams of owning a cabin in the woods – a haven he hopes to retire to, sooner rather than later.

Paramvir Virdee (Graphics)

Paramvir Virdee is an architect, digital artist and entrepreneur. He runs a boutique animation studio in New Delhi, where he explores the amalgamation of art, design and technology. He is also involved in academia with leading international architectural universities.

Jaskeerat Bedi (Graphics)

Jaskeerat Bedi is a design tinkerer who loves to observe people, cultures, movements and designs products with the hope of simplifying lives! She has worked across multi-design disciplines from space/furniture/product/ food design to service/digital design..

Mariyam (Curation)

Mariyam is an architect whose primary interest lies in the intersection of architecture and journalism. Having a concurrent interest in brand positioning and design communications, she gravitates towards architecture that is socially inclusive and ecologically sensitive.

About the Author

Goonmeet Singh Chauhan
Founder Partner,
Design Forum International

Goonmeet Singh Chauhan is a futurist, an urbanist and a practising architect. He studied architecture at the Indian Institute of Technology, Kharagpur, and thereafter started a practice, Design Forum International (DFI), with his course-mates Anand Sharma and Anoj Tevatia. Some of his notable projects include Select CityWalk, a marquee retail centre in the heart of Delhi, the New Courts at Delhi High Court adjacent to Jaipur House on the India Gate hexagon, ITO Skywalk, Vanijya Bhawan, Office of the Ministry of Commerce and numerous other developments across India for developers like Jaypee, Emmar, Tata Housing, NBCC, Bestech, Ansals, Aarone, Puravankara, Chintels, BPTP, etc. He is passionate about transforming the lives of the people of India and truly believes that our shared destiny can be altered at a fairly rapid pace. All we need to do is to put forth a unified dream and then use technology and ecosystem-based models to deliver rapid transformation. To deliver the dream of a great India.